# The Duality of Vision

# The Duality of Vision

## Genius and Versatility in the Arts

### WALTER SORELL

with 23 colour plates
126 in monochrome
and 22 line drawings

Thames and Hudson · London

*To Tamara Leslie*
*and Deborah Karen*
*and their belief in beauty*

© WALTER SORELL 1970

*Text photoset in Great Britain by BAS Printers, Over Wallop, Hampshire*
*Monochrome illustrations processed in Germany by Klischeewerkstatten*
*der Industriedienst GmbH und Co, Wiesbaden*
*Colour illustrations processed in Great Britain by Colour Workshop, Hertford*
*Printed by litho in Germany by Herder Druck GmbH, Freiburg i. Br.*
*Bound in Holland by Van Rijmenam N.V., The Hague*

500 49002 3

# CONTENTS

# Acknowledgements

I wish to acknowledge my indebtedness to the many librarians and curators of museums all over the world who have shown their interest in this book and have assisted with their counsel; my thanks go particularly to Miss Dominique Brugère of the Cultural Counsellor to the French Embassy and to Miss Marna Feldt of the Swedish Information Service.

Many private collectors gave permission to have photos taken of some of their treasures and to have them reproduced in the book, among them Charles B. Benenson, Erich Cohn, Victor W. Ganz, and Alexander Lewyt and Nita Seidler. My special thanks go to them and to those who assisted me in the collection of the pictorial material, above all, Artine Artinian, Peter M. Grosz, Heiner Hesse, Saki Karavas, Otto Kallir, Arnold Rood, Serge Sabarsky, Ruth Schneidman and Helen Wolff. I am also indebted to Felix Klee for his permission to include five poems by Paul Klee in my translation. My thanks likewise go to Josef Albers, who permitted the inclusion of two of his poems, published in *Poems and Drawings* by George Wittenborn Inc., New York, 1961.

I must express my gratitude to many of my friends who stood by me with advice and criticism while I wrote this book. Their encouragement, help and interest have been greatly appreciated, and I wish to mention their names alphabetically: Shareen Blair, Alessandra Comini, Theodore Front, Lea Kisselgoff, Gina Lalli, Marcia B. Siegel, and Penny West. I am also grateful for the help given by Barbara Abbey, Jacqueline Bernard, and Cathy Linda Roberg in my research.

This book would not have come into being in its present shape had it not been for the initial enthusiasm of my editors at Thames and Hudson, London, and Robert M. Amussen at Bobbs-Merrill, New York.

Most of the art work – not coming from museums and public institutions – was photographed by Susan Richter, whose untiring assistance has greatly helped to give this book its visual aspect. And last but not least I thank my wife for her patience and eagerness to do the tasks of a picture researcher, secretary, and errand boy.

# By Way of Introduction

The most awe-inspiring but also puzzling phenomenon is the genius or a major talent, a man who enriches the world with his works and deeds. Creativity in all its phases, forms, and stages is man's greatest marvel. It is a spark filched from the Creator, bestowing upon this man powers denied the many and instilling him with the consciousness of being apart. But to describe the genius as strong and strange, as being aloof while deeply rooted in his time, is to point at him without characterizing him. How can one define otherness, how can one analyze reasons and motivations for its manifestations?

Indefatigably, scholars and artists have tried in vain to define the precious talent of man to have talent, let alone genius. No doubt, talent is basic to genius, talent may come close to genius without ever reaching it. Any creatively gifted person possesses talent, but the genius is possessed by talent. Even great creative minds repeat, embellish, and extend what has been dealt with before them. The genius creates, he goes new ways, he often dares without being afraid of finding himself alone. He is, not necessarily, but more often than not, prolific.

Edward Robert Bulwer-Lytton, one of the prolific poets of the Victorian period, was termed 'third among living poets'. Yet posterity remembers him but vaguely as a facile rhymester, who judges this elusive quality in the lines of *Last Words*: '. . . Genius is master of man. Genius does what it must, and talent does what it can'. Probably an equally good definition was given to us by Henri-Frédéric Amiel when he wrote in his *Journal*: 'Doing easily what others find difficult is talent; doing what is impossible for talent is genius'.

But what is genius? The definitions vary from such extremes as William Hogarth's saying that 'genius is nothing but labour and diligence' to Anatole France's dictum that 'mediocrities sweat blood to produce rubbish, geniuses create wonders without an effort'. The truth is far from both descriptions. It is tempting to shoot epigrams at such a beguiling target which, at best, behaves like a phantom towards those who take aim at it. Books were written, sayings were said which all have tried to embrace the genius, to be able to listen to his heartbeat. Cesare Lombroso in *The Man of Genius* recognized the unmistakeable fanaticism which accompanies the genius, but he translated it into the Victorian concept that 'good sense travels on the well-worn paths, genius never; and that is why the crowd, not altogether without reason, is so ready to treat great men as lunatics'.

They are, no doubt, lunatics who show mankind the light of tomorrow, who help it build bridges from reality to illusion's realities across time. There is a need in the genius to do what has to be done and an urgency about doing it. Sometimes the need and urgency spill over into artistic activities which lie beyond the boundaries of his metier, of the discipline he chose or which chose him.

We are usually surprised when faced with such multiplicity of creativity. There is the writer who paints, the painter who writes, the architect who composes, and the composer who writes and paints, and a variety of variations in which talents mingle with equal power or with varied artistic degree. Our surprise is ill founded. Should we not rather expect a genius to be a genius in whatever he chooses to do and should we not rather wonder why all of them do not do everything and do everything equally well? Of course, the relationship between the various art forms the talent chooses, discloses a great deal about the artist's psyche, and so does the way in which he performs. The reason and timing for proving himself in another arena is indicative of his personality and his era.

The major talent cannot help but unfold all his forces and energies, and in doing so he is never aware of dissipation as a danger. No one can have enough talent, but, on a certain level, he can easily have too many. There are born dilettantes as there are born geniuses. A minor poet does not become less minor for being also a mediocre painter. And perhaps only extra-ordinary human beings have also the right to be dilettantes in another medium than the one in which they are masters. Sometimes to lack perfection of craftsmanship may add a certain charm or fascination to the totality of a genius, as Goethe proves. Also, greatness in one discipline does not necessarily guarantee sufficient self-criticism in another medium. The greatness of D. H. Lawrence as a writer did not keep him from believing he was an equally great painter.

There are highly creative men whose work in their very special field towers above anything that has been accomplished by others. One cannot very well imagine Bach or Beethoven,

12

Dante or Dostoievski devoting their time to creative attempts in any other field. Their creations are of such monumental totality that they seem to express everything that can be expressed. Also, their particular environments did not tempt them to explore different media. On the other hand, there are artists whom we could not imagine as having stayed all their lives within the boundaries of their proven creative activity. Their personalities, their artistic temperament and the climate in which they lived – be it Michelangelo, Leonardo, or Goethe – would make us think that they ought to have proved the universality of their geniuses even if they had not done so.

In his later years Goethe admitted that he could also have written many stageworthy plays if he had only wanted to. But essentially Goethe had always seen all his work and effort symbolically, and it mattered little to him how he expressed himself. This may be one, but only one, of the many keys leading to a better understanding of the universal talent. Goethe wanted to make clear that his artistic creativity was a means to shape life, to sharpen his awareness, to mature. With this in mind, the question arises what real reasons prompt a creative person to be creative.

Very few have ever consciously felt posterity looking with them at their typewriters or canvases. No real artist has ever created because he wanted to be pointed out when walking on the streets or sitting in a theatre, even granting the thousand and one vanities which have a hold on him – justifiably so, for where would mankind be today without man's vanities? No, the creative person gives *Gestalt* to the visions of his mind and imagination because he cannot help doing it and because of the conviction that whatever he does is worth doing for the moment that is, for the very day he can create. He rises from his daily work as man rises from his daily bath, cleansed, freed, relieved. He recognizes eternity as the whimsical woman who likes to play and have her fun with great men.

In an age of specialization like ours it is vital to think of those protean spirits who have been masters in many fields because they are absolute masters of themselves, or who would have felt deprived of their freedom without being able to toy with other thoughts, to escape into an alien landscape, to express themselves here and there now and then.

Furthermore, it must be said that, according to my experience, there is creativeness in many people as there is, to some degree, in almost all children. I do not doubt that there are a number of people who have certain artistic potentialities without ever testing them, without ever accepting the challenge of whether their abilities would not grow with growing experience. The reasons for not utilizing basic or dormant talents may be an insufficient urge for self-expression, perhaps fear of competing with others in the wide arena of the arts, or, after a few initial attempts, the disillusionment with their own abilities as much as with the immediate reaction of their environment. Such persons shying away from tapping their own potentialities may often have greater creative minds – however they try to suppress them – than many minor artists whose lack of inhibition and self-criticism propels them into the foreground. The hack has always had the loudest trumpet and, for the fleeting day and in his small ways which often include a good living, has known how to triumph in spite of himself. It is among these people that we find the greatest vacillation from art to art. They show an astounding facility to be mediocre in more than one way.

This book is not about them. It is about the geniuses with more than one talent, about the great talents not limited to one form of artistic expression. In naming some of them, well or lesser known, in telling the story of their struggles, aims and accomplishments, in relating and equating their multiple artistic realizations, I hope for a final mosaic showing the many faces of the mysterious image of creativity.

When the German poet Friedrich Gottlieb Klopstock was asked about the meaning of a passage in one of his poems, he replied: 'God and I both knew what it meant once; now God alone knows'. When asking ourselves what makes a man creative in more than one medium, we may, in the final analysis, come to a similar conclusion: the artist may have known while doing it why he had to do it. Now, when still alive, he no longer remembers, and, belonging to history, it is history which has made no notation of it. But it is there. One more marvel of man to be marvelled about . . .

Friedrich Dürrenmatt
Illustration to *Herkules und der Stall des Augias*

# PART ONE: TALENT, GENIUS, AND MULTIPLE CREATIVITY

# The Secret of Creativity

A PORTRAIT OF THE ARTIST AS HIMSELF

Man has always been proud, and rightly so, of geniuses of the past, even though he may feel inclined to evaluate some of them differently from his fellow men, or even differently in various phases of his own life. But whatever epithets he may bestow upon them, he recognizes them as the giants they are. Man is also well aware of the fact that some of his contemporaries have written their names into history; but history will deal with them in its own unpredictable manner, will let their signatures pale, or magnify their imprint.

It is surprising how quickly a cultural climate may change and, with it, the significance of the intellectual and artistic heroes of the past; how the taste of time can by-pass or even have contempt for men of stature or ignore periods of the past. In the seesaw of historic events, of coming phases and passing fads, even incontestable geniuses sometimes suffer, they may be blacklisted by aesthetes and snobs; but in time they all pretty well weather the ironies of man's changing moods. Geniuses are the one constant in the inconstancies of life, even though 'some are born posthumously', as Nietzsche said.

On the other hand, it is mainly their deeds, their works which bring about changes, in the course of which they dethrone their predecessors. Their creations are the bricks with which the world is built. But from time to time these builders throw stones at the very buildings on which they work. This act may be viewed as compulsive, but wholesome and necessary to keep the world of the arts from chronic sterility and from the curse of the stereotype.

The complexities and perplexities of creativity appear impenetrable, defying any attempts to systematize the vastness of their manifestations, to explain the inexplicable. Our scientists are coming frighteningly close to unravelling the secret of Creation, and one day man will undoubtedly use his inventiveness, imagination, and scientific skill to play-act God and recreate a double of himself in his technological image.

17

Another aspect of the near future, and a far different world to come, is the power of the computer and the growing passivity of man in the dawning electronic age. No one can foretell what influence a thoroughly computerized world will have on the artist and his creative will, how independent the computer's mind can become from the mind that feeds it, and how it may affect the sensibilities of the artist's soul.

If we accept the premise that all human beings have untapped creative potentialities, then the new machine will be able to exploit and expand this potential for human creativity. This must of necessity lead to a widening and lowering of artistic standards. The computers, on the other hand, may relieve man from a multiplicity of routine tasks and thus may help to free the creative mind.

What the future computerized world may unwittingly achieve is an even greater realization of man's unique capacity for being creative. With the computer spitting out data and facts, which have been collected and stored, compared and analysed, and rattling off the first draft of a translation, the difficulties in understanding the miracle of man's creative urge and ability become only more obvious and tantalizing. How do genes and environmental forces interrelate, how do emotions and thoughts fuse, induce, and produce a creative act? What is the role played by knowledge and training, by an accidental impression and the artist's readiness to react, to absorb, and to let his visions and dreams become reality? How about the multiple urge to create in more than one field? Will the various talents coexist peacefully, fructify each other, or cause conflicts of interest and emotion?

So many able minds have pondered over the marvels of man's creativity, have written epigrams and volumes about it. I can do little more than write my own thoughts on the margin of their thoughts and, to serve the purpose of this book, relate my annotations to the problem of versatility.

It will come as no surprise that the few universal geniuses, such as Leonardo or Goethe, have a stunning intellectual capacity which, by its nature, creates a curiosity about all the phenomena of life which is never satisfied. But the relationship between intellect and creativity is rather complicated, since neither intellect nor creativity can be weighed or measured. Moreover, there are various elements of intelligence, and the examples of verbal and spatial intelligence, for instance, circumscribe the creative preference of the artist in which they occur.

It is essential for him to have the capacity to record and to retain impressions, experiences, and facts, but also the ability to have them available at a creative moment's notice. What distinguishes the intellectual person – who is endowed with the same above-mentioned qualities – from the creative artist, is the latter's ability to form fluently new combinations of all these elements and to formulate them in a new, unusual way, or to channel them into artistic visualizations.

One of the most striking characteristics of the creative person is his readiness for and openness to unlimited experiences. He may be interested in the most insignificant manifestations, but when you see him speak to his shoemaker he will observe and absorb impressions different from those of the average person. We cannot say that he is usually garrulous and gregarious – there are probably such cases too – nor that he is uncommunicative. His interest will concentrate on aspects and values which have a special meaning to him. Basically interested not only in truth but also in beauty, his aesthetic sensibilities are particularly marked.

The quality and degree of intelligence and intuition play a tricky game. As there are visual and aural types, there are also artists whose intuitive feelings may outweigh their intelligence. In other words, they work at their craft with different stimulations, tools, and means. It is likely that the more intuitive artist will be rather inclined to withdraw and work in solitude, and the greater the artist's genius, the more august will be his solitude. The pioneering spirit knows no bounds and will have a predilection for being creative in more than one field.

The talented can progress, but the genius is progress. The talent has the ability to utilize what he absorbs and assimilates, he seeks to expand that which he possesses. The genius transcends his own limitations. Both may be versatile on their level with the distinction that the talent may become versatile at any time of his life, while the genius is born versatile. But chance, circumstance, his own will shaped and bent by his genes may decide for him to devote his energies to one art only. An awareness of our destiny may create a feeling of time consciousness, and an artist's heightened sensibilities are often attuned to the clock that times our being. Most geniuses lived to reach old age. Mozart, who died at the age of thirty-five, had no time left to be versatile, he had to fulfil quickly the destiny of his genius.

The appearance of a genius is so rare and his accomplishments so unique that we can hardly imagine him having taken any other road. As a matter of fact, we identify his upbringing, working habits, and interests so much with his achievements that we could not place him in another environment.

The artistic value of a secondary expression of creativity as determined by the artist's contemporaries or by posterity is of little importance in comparison to the meaning this deviation or escape from the artist's major performance may have for him and the development of his work. Most often the secondary art is one of those stimulations without which the artist cannot function in the field he completely masters. Our mind so often gathers momentum for one particular thing while it is purposely diverted or unconsciously occupied with something else. And no one can argue about where and how an artist should replenish his creative strength.

Without putting a specific evaluation upon an artist's work, we know that to be a work of art it has to be produced by an inner need, it must be the result of the totality of the artist, be it in his main or minor field of activity. If a writer feels compelled to paint, he may – not being sure of the craft – deceive himself by saying he only wishes to play with the idea of painting. Craft, the purely technical skill, may let him down, but, more often than not, the artist he is will be revealed in whatever he does.

The writer may not be a great painter. But standing in front of his easel, that very minute, he cannot help feeling what Cézanne must have felt when he said, 'The thing is to paint as if no other painter had ever existed'.

THE PSYCHOLOGICAL ANGLE

Freudian psychology, by its founder's own admission, 'can do nothing toward elucidation of the nature of the artistic gift, nor can it explain the means by which the artist works'. Probably the least impressive of Freud's observations was that desire for fame, power, and the love of woman lay behind the creative will of the artist.

No doubt, our wish images play their part in the process of creativity, as all the achievements of civilization seem to come from the taming of the *id*, the reservoir of man's instinctual drives. Freud also spoke of philosophers, writers, and artists as 'the few to whom it is vouchsafed . . . with hardly any effort to salvage from the whirlpool of their emotions the deepest truth to which we others have to force our way, ceaselessly groping among torturing uncertainties'. The artist's *id* communicates to the ego, and then the same intrapsychic processes are submitted to others. What is important is the ability and power with which the artist can control neuroticism. He shapes his fantasies and gives them social reference.

The image of the hungry artist in a garret, or the notion that the artist must suffer in order to be able to create, belong to the over-romanticized ideas prevalent in the nineteenth century. As a matter of fact, the artist will only suffer if creativity is hindered and hampered by environmental or developmental factors. It has been proved that art and neuroses are not necessarily synonymous, even though the artist's personal conflicts are intimately interwoven in his creations and determine the direction of his artistic development as much as they colour each work. There is an old saying that the artist doesn't see things as they are, but as he is. And Cesare Pavese circumscribes this idea: 'To be a genius is to achieve complete possession of one's own experience, body, rhythm, and memories.'

Sir Francis Galton addressed himself to the problems of heredity and eugenics in his book, *Hereditary Genius*. Galton strongly believed that no genius can remain hidden and must of necessity assert himself. Although it is difficult to prove the contrary, it is obvious that certain defects in our mental make-up, inertia for one thing, dissipation for another, may easily prevent talent from developing. There is always more than a grain of truth in well-worn sayings, and one of them is that character defeats genius. Moreover, the very same genes which carry with them the blueprint of any creative potentiality, may also carry failure and defeat.

Galton thought that 'the compelling drive of creativeness, sometimes contrary to the conscious wishes of its possessor, may give the creative activity the semblance of a special kind of addiction for which there is no cure'. The unusual is often frightening to the ordinary eye. There is an intense but disciplined exuberance of spirit and flesh in the genius that appears completely undisciplined to the person unblessed with such madness. It is difficult to say what is normal if we don't mean dull, but it is certain that the highly gifted and creative person is a man inspired. And inspiration was defined by Plato as 'the divine release from the ordinary ways of man' and as a state of 'creative madness'. Seneca echoed Plato in his *De Tranquilitate Animi* when he said, 'There is no great genius without a touch of madness'.

In antiquity genius carried the connotation of a guardian spirit of an individual, or of being possessed by a powerful demon, the latter best known to us is the demon whom Socrates implicitly obeyed. But more and more genius came to mean the visitation of the God-power itself, while talent, as defined by the Oxford Dictionary, is only the power or ability of mind or body viewed as something divinely entrusted to a person for use and improvement.

The saying that the genius lives only one flight underneath the madman explains visually the height that separates him from the down-to-earth creatures. The extraordinary height where he exists inspires his views, gives him the capacity for the unusual, for discovery and creative imagination. Many geniuses are endowed with an almost seismographic sensibility, their inventiveness has a touch of clairvoyance.

That some of the geniuses have ventured that one more flight up makes us believe that many more masterpieces than we dare think were probably created in a state of benighted unawareness. The Muse kissing the artist is an antiquated, though surrealistic, image of the automatic, unconscious release and expression of the imagination free of conscious control. A delusion of grandeur with the exalted feeling of an important mission to be accomplished is, in smaller doses, an occupational disease of many artists. Much of twentieth-century literature and visual art shows many symptoms of delightful paranoia.

Phyllis Greenacre, whose studies have contributed a great deal to the better understanding of giftedness, pointed out in *The Childhood of the Artist* that 'the creatively talented person sees three dots at once, not as three separate points, but as constituting different line and triangle forms'. This is based on a greater sense of the *Gestalt*, an unusual capacity for awareness of relations between various stimuli; form and rhythm are quickly reacted to; essentially there is a greater sense of actual and potential organization.

To the choice of form of creativity, the expression of more than one talent, she is most impressed 'with the probability that a potential genius has polymorphous possibilities, some of which may be inhibited by special circumstances of early development'; but she sees the most conspicuous sign in the fact 'that direction of development of geniuses or talent is largely determined by identification'.

To be able to be oneself to the largest degree, regardless of how one may be judged, uninfluenced by one's environmental pressures, the artist can fully realize his potentialities and move in whatever creative direction he feels driven. The degree of creativity depends on his freedom from the repressive mechanism controlling impulse, imagery, and the access to his own depths.

An interesting phenomenon is the masculinity-femininity relationship within the creative person, the male giving strong signs of and tendencies toward the feminine side of his nature, identifying readily with images and traits of great sensitivity, with a higher awareness of emotional response and interest in values, generally considered characteristic of femininity. These creative artists, however, do not necessarily belong to the effeminate types and have no homosexual leanings, although I found among the homosexuals a very high percentage of artistic potentialities. In borrowing C. G. Jung's terminology we could say that the male artist strongly identifies with the feminine traits of the *anima* at the expense of his masculine *persona* role, while the female artist tends toward the masculine traits of the *animus*.

In the last analysis, the miracle of the creative act, and the urge of multiple artistic expression, can be traced, investigated, researched, and interpreted, but the findings are like sand running through one's fingers. Only if we discover the psychological key to man's creative power, shall we ever learn its secret. But perhaps Walter Mehring was right when he said that to explain the artistic process psychologically is a contradiction in itself: 'For the spirit rises out of the *Gestalt;* it is the measure of all being'.

APPEARANCE AND ESSENCE

The layman likes to equate the man and the artist, but even though they seem to be one and the same, they are never quite the same. Abraham Lincoln was only partly right in saying that every man over forty has the face he deserves. But neither physiognomy nor behaviour patterns are guaranteed criteria for the recognition of talent or genius.

When I met Thomas Mann I could not help being reminded of my principal at the *Gymnasium* where I made my baccalaureate. Mann's face had nothing of the depth and mystery that lie in magic mountains and that could lead to death in Venice. And even when his erudition was voiced, his professorial tone belied his humour and hid the secret of the poetry in his thoughts. However, I once met a third-rate violinist who played in the coffee-house of a summer resort. He impressed the audience with his Beethoven-like head and a few studied gestures that had an air of importance. André Malraux tells in *The Voices of Silence* of Sainte-Beuve's error in equating Monsieur Beyle with Stendhal. M. Beyle was human in a way quite different from Stendhal's humanity. It happens only too often that an artist makes us

23

wonder how such a person could ever have written a master-piece. M. Beyle was the enthusiastic man characteristic of the early nineteenth century, a professional romantic in his amours, in his passion for Italy, music, and the theatre. Stendhal, on the other hand, had a coldly analytical approach to his characters and their situations. When he sat down to write, the process of his thinking was, with very few exceptions, unromantic.

Creative persons rarely present common stereotypes and, coming back to the example of Thomas Mann, I admit that after listening to him for some time I felt engulfed by his presence and could not help but become aware of his compelling personality. And if Sainte-Beuve had taken the trouble to peel off the outer layers of M. Beyle's appearance he might have found Stendhal underneath.

But the truth is that we often encounter a dichotomy between the man and the artist, with the appearance of the man proving to be different from the essence of the artist. This is only partly the fault of the onlooker, who approaches the highly gifted with a ready-made image of otherness which borders on the caricature of a stereotype of the non-stereotype. Also, trying to deduce the reality of the man from the artist's work leads to disappointments because the creative genius often hides in the habit of a man unconsciously denying its shape.

Generally speaking, creative persons are, by the nature of their nature, nonconformists, even though they may be quite conventional in appearance. They seem to accept the life surrounding their area of creativity as something unavoidable. Quite strong is their expression of independence where their interests are involved and where they feel motivated to assert themselves.

The highly creative man usually assumes a gesture and pose in life in contradiction to his work. This could easily have its roots in the artist's attempt to protect himself, the untouchable part of his creative being, against a crude outside world; it may arise from weakness and insecurity, it may be sheer playfulness, or result from a thousand and one reasons to disguise his real self. The choice of a pseudonym is a part of this pose or the artist's desire to separate clearly the man from the artist in the man. Some creative people prove an astounding ability to play-act, a very basic versatility in separating appearance from essence.

John Ruskin erred when he thought that 'Great art is produced by men who feel acutely and nobly'. Acutely, very likely, but not necessarily nobly, at least not as nobility, the expression of a noble spirit, was understood by him. It seems to me to be a *contradictio in adjecto* to assume a pleasant, nice, or congenial personality make-up in a genius. If nobility is equated with great art then I am rather inclined to Albert Camus' definition of 'real nobility' which, as he said in his *Notebooks*, is 'based on scorn, courage, and profound indifference'. I also feel that the creative person, who does so much for the spiritual enlightenment and the aesthetic pleasures of mankind, is mostly and, in a way, understandably, contemptuous of the very mankind which profits from his genius. He simply cannot help standing outside the ordinary scheme of things, on the periphery of our systematized existence.

The great artist may accept the role of the exorcist of the evil spirits of man. Then his temperament is that of a fighter, and the role he plays as liberator and healer is predicted by his psyche. It does not mean that he loves men. He may love mankind which to him has the faceless face of all. (Peter Altenberg, one of the last Viennese romanticists, found that he would have loved to be in love with democracy, if only the masses would not smell so badly.)

The genius or great talent lives in a constant state of armistice with the man he is. In reality, he can only function as a creator when he exists in a state of unreality. Whenever he comes out of his splendid solitude, he may only want to see whether man has already reached Mars or the Moon. Then his creative spirit compels him to return to himself in order to write, paint, sculpt, or compose about his inner vision of life, or what he thinks is or ought to be happening around the corner. T. S. Eliot said in *Tradition and Individual Talent:* 'The more perfect the artist, the more completely separate in him will be the man who suffers and the mind which creates; the more perfectly will the mind digest and transmute the passions which are its material'.

The image of the man in the artist suffering while in the process of creating is generally accepted and associated with the cliché-simile of 'giving birth'. The non-artist particularly visualizes the act of creation as one of being in labour, of suffering a thousand anguishes caused by the artist's inner vision which cries out for its own independent *Gestalt*. However often such a painful process may occur, we find in many cases of creation that there is, on the contrary, a surprising ease and almost unconscious or inevitable shedding of an idea, a feeling or a vision taking artistic shape spontaneously.

25

Self-involvement, being an inherent part of the creative act, brings about an experience of relief, preceded by moments best described as the pain of joy. Without it the artist could not feel a sense of liberation. It is his privilege to be able to reach a state of heightened awareness. Out of such total spiritual and physical experience, he gives life to something that existed in him, but of which he himself was only vaguely aware, or, as the case may be, with which he was 'pregnant' for many years.

The birth-giving act usually brings about physical relief as much as a feeling of fulfilment, perhaps of elated tiredness. It has its therapeutic side-effects. If the creative act has therapeutic value, then the creative process in any secondary or minor field of activity would, through its auxiliary nature, be charged with a definite task in bringing relief, restoring balance, creating a sense of freedom. Even as an act, pretended as being playful, the secondary art expression has a salutary effect, as we will find proven in many a case.

The non-artist also has erroneous ideas about inspiration and how it affects the creative process. The painter who sees a sunset does not paint the setting sun but the idea, a personalized image of the sun setting. The dilettante may experience an ecstatic feeling when embracing and kissing the girl he loves. However, upon leaving her he may write a poem with eyes of love that do not see to see, but only see to verbalize the cliché of a kiss. On the other hand, the poet's dream of a kiss trespassing reality can become the poetic visualization of a kiss. Bertolt Brecht remembered in his most lyric poem, *In Memory of Marie A.*, only the fact that he once kissed Marie A. Though he no longer knew her face, he recalled the kiss because he remembered a cloud he had seen that very moment. ('And then the kiss I should have long forgotten/Had it not been for that one cloud that was/Which I recall and which is always with me/It was quite white and came from there somewhere.')

The creative mind has all the freedom it can think of and must impose upon itself all limitations. The freedom of the versatile artist has the widest possible scope, but to enjoy fully what he is doing he must edit his own nature. That so many artists, in their secondary choices of creation, enjoy the smallest sparks, even if they do not always ignite into shining flames, is their privilege; and it is our pleasure to come closer to their very private way of being. Though such a work of art may be far from perfect, it is a sign of their genius.

## THE INTERRELATION OF THE ARTS

It is surely one of the greatest mysteries in the arts that the very same words which we so often use to say the necessary or unnecessary can be turned into poetry; that the secret of a beautiful image sleeps within a piece of wood, stone, or marble; that the same few tones and colours can be used over and over again in different rhythms, in ever-new colour schemes and forms. To put something into being where nothing was before, to give new life to shape and image – in whatever medium it may be – which, in turn, evokes a whole new world of sensations, is the act of creation.

Each art is a world in itself and, as such, works with its own tools and means. It may attack different senses, appeal to a variety of feelings, provoke thought reactions, but all art serves the same purpose: to heighten our feeling of existence, to challenge and to disturb, to give life meaning beyond the obvious, to make sense out of senselessness, to build bridges. The closer his heart is to his head, the better will the artist be able to see with the inner eye of a poet.

The poetic image is at the root of all art; it lies in the discovery of the wonder we are; it is the beauty deep within you; it is the purpose you find in the useless; it needs no explanation because it *is* if you can grasp it with your senses. It is not necessarily poetry which reveals the poetic image at its best. It is everywhere in life: in a human gesture of kindness and in the sparkling dust of stars circling above us in the infinite All; in the questioning eyes of a child as much as in the petal of a rose; or in the symbols of a mathematical formula. The essence of all life is poetry as much as it is the essence of all art.

The poetic image lies on the periphery of each art form, it is an essential part of its connecting tissues, and it is anchored at its core. Any artificial attempt at heightening our sense experiences, stimulated, for instance, by mescaline, has demonstrated how our senses overlap: we can see sounds, hear colours, touch tones, taste smells. The interrelation of all sensations is much closer than we realize.

Since we may assume that the great creative mind would be creative in whatever art it chooses to express itself, the interrelation of the arts gains in significance. Samuel Butler once said that, in essence, the art of music, painting, and writing are the same. This interrelationship, so important for man's versatility, begins with the most utilitarian form of expression: architecture. Whenever architecture reaches beyond the ordinary, it appears as lived-in sculpture which, in turn, is

27

arrested movement. Havelock Ellis maintained that the two basic artistic forms of early man were architecture and dancing. Both are close to each other in spite of their static and mobile contrasts for both have in common the basic need for a geometric pattern and a clearly defined design. The very first choreographer, Balthasar de Beaujoyeulx said in 1581 that ballet meant to him 'a geometric combination of several persons dancing together'.

Sculpture is the plastic fulfilment of one great moment out of many, of that one chosen moment which the sculptor keeps imprisoned in stone. Sculpture is closest to dance, or actually dance is sculpture in movement. Both dancer and sculptor attempt to create the illusion of movement rather than movement itself; the essence of an idea; a mood, a feeling, a thought within limited but well arranged forms and designs. Both try to catch the inexpressible (Wallace Stevens said that poetry 'is a search for the inexplicable'); a fleeting impression of life in a gesture, a pose, and in the rhythm of motion.

Dance is rhythm, and rhythm is an intricate part of music. Primitive man accompanied his dance with hand-clapping and singing until he built drums and bone-flutes with simple means. Music, as the most abstract of all arts, has become a most comprehensive art, notated and supported by an elaborate fabric of theories over the centuries. In its logic and abstraction its close relationship to mathematics is cliché by now. ('Music has many resemblances to algebra', Novalis said.)

Frank Lloyd Wright's father subjected his seven-year-old son to Bach, which he played on the organ for hours, and would force him to practise the piano. Wright wrote in his *An Autobiography:*

Music and architecture blossom on the same stem – sublimated mathematics. Mathematics as presented by geometry. Instead of the musician's systematic staff and intervals, the architect has a modular system as the framework of design. My father, a preacher and music-teacher, taught me to see – to listen – to a symphony as an edifice of sound. All my lifetime I have listened to Beethoven – especially – as the master-architect of all time; the most profound student of Nature known – one whose inspired imaginative resource is beyond comparison. I am grateful to music and to him for genuine refreshment in architecture – my field of creative endeavour. Dissonance will take care of itself. I wish more life to more creative music revealing the cosmic rhythms of great Nature, Nature spelled with a capital N as we spell God with a capital G. Why? Because Nature is all the body of God we mortals will ever see.

Gerhart Hauptmann (1862–1946), one of Germany's great dramatists, thought of himself as a sculptor when he was young and even called himself Gherardo Hauptmann, scultore. 'Through my toiling with wet clay I became more conscious of the joy in *seeing*, and through this awareness I gained perception, feeling and enthusiasm for form.' Throughout his career as a dramatist he often directed his and other dramatists' plays and also appeared on the stage as an actor. At the very end of his life, he put the question to himself for which he had no answer: 'Why have I not become a musician since, above all, I am a musician?'

But Ernst Barlach had the answer. He recognized the great affinity between the dramatist and sculptor when he said that 'the sculptor with his gift for sharp observation and his feelings for palpable reality veers toward the writing of drama'.

If Hauptmann's primary source of inspiration had come from music, he would never have sculpted or painted, but might have become another Richard Wagner, writing poetic plays for his compositions. The musician has rarely taken to sculpture or painting as another artistic outlet. Painters have more often shown understanding and emotional closeness to music. The most outstanding example is Wassily Kandinsky, whose affinity to music can be seen in many of his works; but music seen from the painter's viewpoint also occupied his theoretical thinking.

Herbert Read pointed out that it must have occurred to painters many times in the past that their 'colours might be composed like sounds in music, and many such harmonic elements exist even in classical painting'. One of Kandinsky's canvases of his Paris period has a structure very reminiscent of a score of music. This is an extreme case. But most of Kandinsky's compositions evoke the feeling of an orchestration of images translated into plastic symbols. 'The musical analogy is always in the background', Herbert Read says, 'and the concepts of time, rhythm, interval, and metre hitherto reserved to music are freely introduced into the aesthetics of painting. Kandinsky's aesthetics (a total aesthetics covering all the arts) stands or falls by the justness of this analogy, and from the early days of the *Blaue Reiter* it was based on discussion with composers like Arnold Schönberg.'

Aesthetic affinities and influences in constructive thinking or mere sense stimulation coming to the painter from music are a far cry from actually creative attempts in composition. The fact remains that very few composers have painted and very few painters have ever felt induced to compose. Of course, there exists a great deal of programme music, and from Bach to Berlioz, from Schubert and Wagner to Richard Strauss composers have painted with sounds and musically recreated impressions of the visible reality, of atmospheric images. The Germans have a very expressive term for it: *Tongemaelde* (tone painting). Sometimes the poetic and descriptive intensity which can 'speak' to us through music can accomplish more than painting. Claude Debussy told Jean Aubrey in a letter about Stéphane Mallarmé's reaction to his composition inspired by Mallarmé's poem, *The Afternoon of a Faun:* 'This music extends the emotion of my poem and fixes the scene much more vividly than colour could have done.'

Composers are very close to the word. ('Music resembles poetry', said Alexander Pope.) The link is obvious in the *Lied* and opera, with the composer calling the tune in the truest sense of the phrase, using the poetic and dramatic word mainly as a point of musical departure. (Mozart: 'In opera the text must be the obedient daughter of the music.')

The painter's resistance to music as a secondary artistic outlet is compensated for by his intimate relationship with the word and literary image. Leonardo da Vinci alluded to this affinity when he wrote in his *Notebooks:* 'Painting is a form of poetry made to be seen'.

In essence, however, all the arts are intimately tied together and, as will have to be exemplified, one art exerts its complementary or fructifying effect on the other. Such a versatile artist as Robert Schumann recognized this when he wrote:

The educated musician will be able to study a Raphael Madonna with great advantage to him as much as the painter will when studying a Mozart symphony. Moreover, a sculptor sees every actor as a statue, who, in turn, perceives the sculptor's works as a living figure; for the painter a poem turns into a picture, the musician transposes the painting into sounds.

The interrelation of the arts becomes more relevant and pronounced in periods of great socio-cultural changes. Then the arts do not move closer to one another; but the artists feel closer to them as a unified form of expression because of their tendency to see in abstractions, to strip every artistic articulation to its fundamentals, to the bareness of its inmost being.

## THE WRITER–PAINTER RELATIONSHIP

This book deals essentially with versatility and artistic pheno-mena as we find them in the creative urge of Western man. Only little can be said about Indian, Chinese, or Japanese artists. Their being is very different from the action-driven Western artist, who believes that, basically, progress means the destruction of tradition, and who idealizes personality and his own aggressively inventive genius.

The Oriental, on the other hand, relies strongly on a life defined by symbols rather than the concrete which, to him, has as temporary an expression as life itself. If one can believe in one's present being as a momentary manifestation of an unmanifested Reality, then one can feel the temporary as the expression of eternal harmony. A. E. Coomaraswamy pictured the heart and essence of the Indian experience as one 'to be found in a constant intuition of the unity of all life, and the instinctive and ineradicable conviction that the recognition of this unity is the highest good and the uttermost freedom'.

A world of difference lies in such feeling of unity. It is exemplified by Indian dance and drama, which has always remained one art form. Philosophically, we can see in the Indian dance the expression of the whole being, which is not body alone but the embodied soul's attempt to express itself, its nature and visions, through its mind, senses and body acting in unison.

The man most responsible for the rebirth of the traditional Indian arts was Sir Rabindranath Tagore (1861–1941), poet, painter, prose writer, composer, and politician. He descended from a wealthy Bengali family and became the voice of India. In his youth he wrote propaganda poems and songs and, although he always remained interested in politics, he trans-cended nationalistic bounds. His work had universal appeal, his speculative, deeply felt religious thoughts intrigued the intellectuals, the simple flow of his colourful images of nature's and love's beauty as well as the rich fabric of his stories touched the peasants and workers. His was a prolific genius, producing about fifty plays, a hundred books of verse, many of which he set to music, and forty volumes of novels, stories, and essays. Out of accidental sketches grew calligraphically-styled images. Later, in colours, he painted portraits with sweeping strokes which had a strange poetic tonality.

From D. T. Suzuki's interpretation of Zen we learn that Nature is spontaneous and creative, and that man, being a part of Nature, acts best when he acts in freedom from constraining patterns, i.e. as spontaneously and naturally as

Nature. Rinzai (Lin-Chu), a prominent master during the T'ang dynasty (618–905) in China and high priest of the Zen movement, stresses in his *Sayings* that only faith in your Self leads to true understanding. When faith is lacking you find yourself hurried by others and unable to be your master. To be one's own master, whether walking or standing still, is all that matters. ('Even when you are not trying to achieve something extra-ordinary, it will come to you all by itself.') What does it mean to be master of oneself? God created the world out of his free will, it says. He was his own master, and each of us has something of this in him, 'the same in essence as the divine will'.

Translated into terms of artistry and creativity, the artist, having mastered true understanding, would theoretically be able to create with an almost divine will in the most diverse disciplines but in a spirit of harmony. The state of enlightenment sought by Zen is a kind of mystical revelation, a sudden breakthrough, as a flash of intuition; experiences of withinness not unlike those of Christian mystics. Zen never neglects to stress that 'not to think of anything', being the gist of Zen Buddhist teaching, means to transcend thinking and to reach 'the source of thinking where all things come out, including art and religion and life itself'. Zen recognizes the reality of man's earthboundness and teaches the believer to regard every act in life, mean or noble – from pouring tea to selling his produce to writing poems – as a potential road to enlightenment. His earthbound existence may be brought closer to enlightenment even through a jolting joke or a blow on the head.

Zen brought forth some very refined ink, paper and brush works. Calligraphy was practiced by the Zen artist until, as D. T. Suzuki informs us, all the mechanics of it were forgotten and the artist achieved the state of *Wabi* or simplicity. ('Draw bamboos for ten years. Become a bamboo. Then forget all about bamboos when you draw.') One of the Zen artists, whose ink drawings are most illustrative of the Zen spirit, was Sengai (1751–1837), a priest of the Seifukuji Temple in *Plate 2* Chikuzen. The secret of creation for the Zen artist lies in giving expression to 'the cosmic spirit in its rhythmic movement', according to Hsieh Ho, a Chinese art critic, who lived in the sixth century. 'The intellectual bridle', D. T. Suzuki explains, 'is meant to make us carry the load of utilitarianism, but when we come to the realm of art and religion, we are to let down everything we have learned, to put on ourselves and go out into experience in the nakedness of primary being'.

1 Ch'en Shun RIVER LANDSCAPE

2 Sengai 'THE FIST THAT STRIKES THE TEACHER'

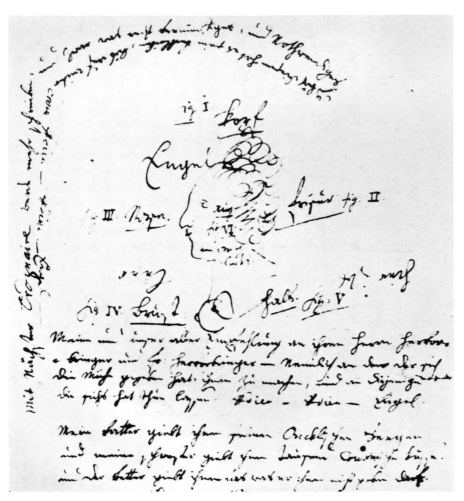

3   Wolfgang Amadeus Mozart
PAGE OF A LETTER TO MARIA ANNA
THEKLA MOZART

4   Felix Mendelssohn–Bartholdy
MENDELSSOHN AT THE ORGAN OF THE
CHURCH IN HEIDELBERG

The creative genius of Chinese art has never been restricted to painting or poetry. The Chinese introduced the term 'painter-poet'. Some of these were the most versatile artists of Leonardo-esque proportions. They were usually men of means, gentlemen scholars, poets, calligraphers, musicians, and painters. The famed Wang Wei (699–759), who lived in the culturally brilliant T'ang period, gave Chinese monochrome landscape painting its most fluid expression, a new style of profound emotional statements equal to those evoked by his calligraphy and by some of his poetry:

> *I sit alone deep in the bamboo grove.*
> *I strum my lute whistling a melody.*
> *Nobody knows I am in the bamboo grove*
> *But the bright moon looking down at me.*

Su Tung-po (1036–1101) was another of those rare geniuses of multiple creativity. He was an outstanding painter-poet, calligrapher, musician, and scholar. But he also was a well-known politician, farmer, and excellent chess player. Most of his poetry was music to the ear and feeling to the mind, like his *The Tamed Bird:*

> *I have a tamed bird. Try to caress him with your gentle hand*
> *And he, in fear of so much love, believes this is his end.*
> *And try to let him fly free into any tree.*
> *His little wings*
> *Will bring him back into his cage –*
> *Where then he sings and sings*
> *Your praise.*

Lin Yutang, who had great admiration for this multiple genius wrote in his biography of Su Tung-po:

The scholars were poets, calligraphers, and painters at the same time. At the outset it must be made clear that in China calligraphy and painting are one and the same art, the same in technique, in medium, and in spirit and principles of criticism. One cannot understand the origin of the southern school of Chinese painting without understanding the aesthetic principles involved in Chinese calligraphy. For the founders of this school, of which Su Tung-po was one, were men nurtured in the spirit of Chinese poetry, and trained in the mastery of the brush and in all the principles of rhythm and composition in Chinese calligraphy itself. Calligraphy provides the technique and aesthetic principles for Chinese painting, while poetry provides the spirit, the emphasis on tone and atmosphere, and the pantheistic delight in all the smells and colours and sounds of nature.

A contemporary of Su Tung-po was Mi Fei (1051–1107), a gifted writer of poetry and prose, scholar and musician, the idol of the Sung period. He interests us most because of the particular fame he enjoyed as a master calligrapher, a work he did with the same brush and ink he used for his paintings. Brush-writing, long considered by the Chinese as a sister art to painting, was elevated to a most expressive art at that time.

From then on, and especially during the Yüan period (1280–1368), painting became more and more linked to calligraphy. There was a constantly growing interest in brushwork, and the delightful display of strokes creating the image of a beautiful line, were equally applied to the art of painting and writing. The Yüan painter-poets were accomplished in all the arts; they have become the most exemplary specimens of the gentleman amateur in art history. This movement of the 'literary man's' painting, called *wen-jen-hua*, reached its climax during the reign of the Ming Dynasty (1369–1644).

These calligraphies are the highest development of that picture-writing with which man originally began to express symbolically his thought-feelings. Ancient man, drawing and sketching crude images of animals and objects on the walls of his cave, did it for ritualistic practices or magic purposes, most probably not as yet to communicate ideas. His gradually awakening sense of beauty was still rudimentary.

*Plate 1*

But ever since those early days drawing and painting were intimately bound to writing. The highly developed art of Chinese calligraphy had its counterpart in the illuminated pages written in the monasteries and cloisters of medieval Europe. Also, the Russians, speaking of their Byzantine icons, say that they were written – the word for it is *iconopis*, as if in their semantic consciousness their painters had been scribes.

## Environment as Creative Stimulus

It can be said that every century has its Napoleon, but not every Napoleon his century. Even if we strongly believe that a genius or great talent cannot be suppressed, it has often happened that a particular gift could not fully unfold because the time into which this genius was born was not ready to receive it, or that it came a decade or two too late. Those who follow the path of the pioneers are easily recognized and embraced by their contemporaries, since the overwhelming majority of people always limp behind the time, although history usually treats these talents ingloriously as imitators or epigones. The unrecognized genius has a rough time among his contemporaries, although he is rewarded by history with such enviable epithets as trail blazer or pioneer for new concepts, for opening new vistas. It has also frequently happened that the genius is recognized during his own lifetime, that he is sufficiently employed, read, and listened to. But even then his real merits can only fully be established at a later time. Whatever the case may be, public approval plays a great part in the life of any artist since, seen from a psychological viewpoint, it restores the very balance which creativeness may have disturbed.

The socio-cultural climate of a period or a region has far more to do with creativity, with the quantitative and qualitative end of it, than is generally known or admitted. Also what at a given time may be considered creative or a work of art, is often more relevant to the culture itself than to the personality of the artist who produces the work. The pressures of a period can be crucial for productivity.

Since their emancipation the Jewish people have proved to be creative in all fields of the arts and in science at a higher ratio than any other. Is it possible that they were an uncreative people before the eighteenth century, or was their environment inimical to the unfolding of their talents? Herded together in the ghettos their only outlet was to study the Talmud, to fiddle, to sing and to dance. Those who dared escape the ghetto in the fourteenth and fifteenth centuries to join the wandering entertainers at fairs, sometimes settled down, mainly in Northern Italy, as dancing masters, a profession which was in great demand during the Renaissance. Almost all of them became converts to Christianity. The most outstanding dancing master of the time was Guglielmo Ebreo of Pesaro, who at that time laid down the ground rules for the later theatrical dance. And that so many of the famous violinists are Jews may not be a mere coincidence but may have its roots in those ghetto days when their forefathers fiddled in the *Tanzhaus*.

The age of enlightenment – Lessing's play *Nathan the Wise*, written in 1779, symbolizes the decisive turning point – and the assimilation process which followed it in the nineteenth century generated the creative contribution of the Jewish people to the culture in which they lived and to mankind in general. Although the Yiddish language was spoken after the fifteenth century, it was only after the general emancipation, after the middle of the nineteenth century, that a Yiddish literature came into being.

It is also very unlikely that the flowering of the artistic and humanistic activities in the Renaissance is the result of sudden genetic changes toward creativity. It seems rather that the cultural climate played a great role in interest and recognition, in appreciation and encouragement of all kinds of productive activities. Among the great changes that took place at the end of the Middle Ages and the beginning of the Renaissance many occurred on a spiritual level; but those happening on the social and economic level were closely interrelated with them. Painters and sculptors were no longer dependent on the guilds, and their rise from the level of the artisan to that of the scholar and poet created a different status for them in the feudalistic society. Their ascent, which also guaranteed them better and ever-rising fees, has been attributed to their alliance with the humanists. The interest of the humanists in the work of the visual artists has been seen in the fact that classical antiquity held the poet and artist in equal regard. On the other hand, painters and sculptors looked up to the humanists, to scholars and poets, who, to a great extent, set norms and standards, dictated fashion and fads. And when, as discussed in a later chapter, Michelangelo felt the need to express himself through forms of poetry then fashionable, we can see social pressures or environmental influences at work.

Painting, sculpture and architecture began to be differently assessed during the Renaissance: the medieval workmanlike point of view no longer then had any validity. This brought about a new self-consciousness of the visual artist. Medieval anonymity faded, the Renaissance was proud of its artist personalities. One no longer worked ten years on an altar in order to serve the community and to honour God, putting little importance to one's own credit. The Middle Ages knew of no intellectual or spiritual need to seek and recognize individual and independent values in originality and spontaneity. This was the discovery of the Renaissance, which began to create a personality cult. A fundamentally new element was introduced with the discovery of the genius, of a strongly profiled personality, who was permitted to do away with tradition and rules. The person was often more in the foreground than the work. These were new concepts which created the competitive, individualistic foundation of modern man's race with himself. It must be stressed that the universal personality itself was not new in the fourteenth century. The medieval architect of churches, for instance, served as sculptor, painter of the window panes, muralist and carver of the altar. But in the Renaissance he became a recognized genius, all-embracing in his will to conquer the unknown, to beautify the known.

The Middle Ages took a long time in waning for the common man who lived out a past era while a handful of men created a new world. If Ezra Pound's saying that culture is made by twelve people has any relevance, it certainly had in those days when modern man was born. An atmosphere of rebirth was conjured up by an elite of intellectuals, artists and ruthless men. The power and purposefulness of the individual and all his talents were more decisive than any laws and customs. The Renaissance was a transition period and yet, at the same time, the first climactic and most brilliant moment in a long historic chain of daring developments. Then, the men of this elite felt as if a divine power had given them the strength to rediscover the past as well as their own being through mind and body, and they leaped into a life of joy and passion marked by greatness. The cultural climate was ready to stimulate, to further and embrace wholeheartedly the genius. In rebuilding the world and giving the future a solid basis, challenges coming from all sides had to be met with great skill and resourcefulness. For the great ones it was unthinkable not to strike out in as many directions as possible.

After the Renaissance the arts became gradually specialized and compartmentalized. The groundwork for this trend was laid in the seventeenth century, which was mainly distinguished by a rational and factual approach to knowledge and the arts. Under the impulse of scientific advances reason and order governed intellectual life. Except in the various fields of the sciences, genius was not necessarily equated with originality. The strong belief in the universality of reason no longer stressed the interest in the artist as a magnificent phenomenon and in his private experiences with their creative reflections. It was a golden age for science with Galileo, Newton, and Leibnitz at work; it was unique in the greatness of its philosophers, Descartes, Pascal, Hobbes, Spinoza and Locke; and it produced a great many artistic geniuses, particularly in the visual arts. But the triple attack of science, philosophy, and criticism created an atmosphere which was not conducive to the flourishing of a multiple talent. There were of course exceptions: Milton, Molière, and Lully.

The eighteenth century, the century of enlightenment, carried the rational approach to its ultimate implications. But it also started the great movement of Romanticism with the result that an ambivalent mentality came into existence which turned the age of reason into one of faith in reason. It was an age of upheavals in which the final vestiges of medievalism were destroyed, in which man asserted his will for freedom through revolutions; historically, through the French Revolution, the American War of Independence, the emergence of enlightened despots; intellectually, through the work of the encyclopedists, through Voltaire and Rousseau. It was the age of social reforms, the rise of the bourgeoisie to prominence, the age of letter-writing, pamphleteering, and the beginning of the novel.

The existing sciences made great progress in the eighteenth century. The systematization of knowledge in the sciences of life, botany and biology, was notably advanced by the Swede Carolus Linnaeus. Benjamin Franklin was a rare phenomenon in his time, embracing science, literature and politics, proving his talents as philosopher, editor, organizer, and orator. With the world of feudalism collapsed, with an uncertain feeling of freedom acquired but not fulfilled, with the constant progress of science toward departmentalization, man pursued his interests in channels of ever-narrowing limitations. We do find, however, a few individuals who engaged in varied artistic endeavours. Voltaire left his mark on this century, which some scholars have called 'the age of Voltaire'; Rousseau's influence was also felt strongly in many fields, and one usually neglects to stress that he was a fine musicologist and a composer of some stature; Johann Wolfgang Goethe is often referred to as the last polyhistorian, and is considered the last universal genius with far-reaching interests and the ability to be creative in the most diverse fields. But these few giants mark the end of what could be called the Renaissance genius.

'Every man must learn how to draw, maintained my father', Goethe wrote. This is quoted to introduce the nineteenth century, often referred to as the age of the waltz, which helped people to gyrate in a state of oblivion; it was the era in which Napoleon's dream of world domination came to an end; when Metternich erected a net of police states against which the populace stood twice on the barricades. It was the period in which the Industrial Revolution triumphed, and Romanticism tried to escape from it in an often weird and always exalted manner that resulted in such extremes as the extolment of the noble savage and the idolization of woman as the dream image, the unattainable for which the male was ready to sacrifice his life.

It could be said that Romanticism actually began with Goethe's *The Sorrows of Young Werther* (1774), whose hero's glorified suicide projects romantic sentimentality, melancholy and utter disgust of life into the nineteenth century. Werther is the forerunner of the Byronic hero, the melancholy young man, brooding in a melodramatic manner upon something mysterious and evil in his background which is never explained or revealed. These are the first instances of man's isolation from the realities of life, from his self. The first realization of life's futility set in, and it is in no way surprising that mid-twentieth-century existentialism returned for substantiation and impetus to such nineteenth-century philosophers as Kierkegaard. The phenomena of our own time are the consequence of the last century, either as its logical continuation or as violent reaction to it.

Tastes changed with the socio-cultural shift at that time. The bourgeois finally dethroned the aristocratic tastemakers. Under its dominance the figure of the virtuoso, the artistic image of technical bravura, and the dandy, the social image of elegant perfection, came into being. Both prototypes show the symbolic and growing schizophrenic split in society which gloated over the downfall of such an aesthete and dandy as Oscar Wilde and which laid the foundation for the great artistic revolutions in our age by running perfection of technique into a state of sterility and the stereotype. However, Paganini and Taglioni are not the only virtuosi, but also the men who conquered Mount Everest for no other purpose than to conquer, and by so doing, to prove themselves and to bridge the ever-widening abyss between the demands of society and the individual being. The fourth archetype created by the bourgeoisie is the most natural antidote to itself, the bohemian, the nineteenth-century ancestor of the beatnik and hippie. From Théophile Gautier, who wore a red waistcoat to spite the smug bourgeois, to Jean Cocteau, who sought spiritual resurrection through opium, the bohemian has demonstrated his indifference to, and loathing of, middle-class standards and life, order and routine.

If Goethe's father insisted on his son taking lessons in drawing, the same can be said about singing and, above all, playing the piano. The piano came into being in the late eighteenth century, and was immediately associated with Romanticism and even more so with the bourgeois home. The piano was an essential piece of furniture in any bourgeois house, as the phonograph or television is in a twentieth-century home. Every daughter of a middle-class family took piano lessons, much as many proletarian daughters went to ballet. To be concerned with the arts became a status symbol of the bourgeoisie. Art, in all forms and manners, moved into the homes of the higher and lower middle-class.

All this created a ready-made condition for the understanding and appreciation of the artist, for a great deal of exaggerated adoration of the creative personality. On the other hand, bourgeois conquest of the arts brought about a levelling-down process which was unavoidable. This condition not only opened the door to multiplicity of creativity, as manifested in such geniuses as William Blake, Dante Gabriel Rossetti, and E. T. A. Hoffmann, it also tempted artists, accomplished in one discipline, to dabble in another field and, moreover, it turned into a seedbed of dilettantism. In the nineteenth century, art became a currency more in use than at any other period, enjoyed *and* practised by the many. It was the contradiction of the time that the value of this currency, although more appreciated, became depreciated.

The twentieth century is characterized by the radical changes in the approach to and concepts of the arts, a revolution which has its roots in the last century and has not yet come to a stop. Experiments follow one another with ever-growing acceleration. There can be no doubt that we are about to destroy the heritage which Renaissance man dreamt of and created, we are about to liberate ourselves from four hundred years of Renaissance domination. The masses have taken over the role of the bourgeois and have conquered the artistic media.

It is difficult to find one's bearings in a time in which scatological words are scribbled over eschatological questions facing man, in a world in which life, as mirrored by the artist, is denuded to the ugliness and banality of its reality. The only values left are those of shock, alienation, and non-communicativeness. But the impact of shock has a way of wearing off, one feels alienated and after a while cannot help but ask oneself whether the awareness to which we are aroused is not too high a price to pay for the loss of identification and affection. Non-communicativeness, in an age that has perfected communication, an age that has penetrated into the cosmos as much as into the mechanics of mental behaviour, seems like the game of a child who wants to spite and punish himself for having discovered that life is not a child's game, but one that adults play as if they had remained children.

The anti-cliché has become the cliché of our time. The rebels against establishment have created their own establishments which, in turn, have generated their own rebels. We have muddled through a period, a transition, full of upheavals and changes to be changed, we have waded through jungles of -isms and crept through tunnels whose goals have often revealed themselves as their very points of departure. The public has been able to observe the artist arriving at destinations without having made a journey.

Man in this period of continuous flux has shown the same feverish intensity to rebuild his world as a handful of people did in the early days of the Renaissance. In spite of growing specialization, a surprising amount of versatility, though not always creative, has made itself felt. The latter half of the century strongly advanced the idea of the multi-media, in which artists of similar minds but of different crafts have worked together towards the idea of a total theatre, a *Gesamtkunstwerk*. Time and again the ultra-modern artist has attacked polished perfection, seeing in it the way back to cliché and to the face of a stereotyped past. Thus, casualness and improvisation, being the aim of these artists, have been behind many experiments in painting and sculpture, and they have become motivating forces in the theatre arts. To mention only two of many symptoms of the period's malaise, pop art and utter surrender to the notion of audience participation, show a self-effacing and self-destructive trend in the arts. And the realization that the novel as an art form may have run its course altogether or, at least, needs to go through a rejuvenating process, only adds to the fact that the arts in general reflect the crisis of the time. The scientifically-inclined and technologically-oriented period is hungry for information. This is why the non-fiction book dominates the market. A new type of writer has been born, the recorder of great events, the digester of the miraculous, the non-creative recreator of creations. To him, versatility is easy. Also, with the looser approach to technical perfection, many more people than in any previous period pride themselves on being minor artists. Since there are so many of them, they do not mind this stigma and feel free to express themselves through various media simultaneously.

It was different in the very beginning of this century when lonely pioneers went into a wilderness to claim new land for themselves and the generations to come; the cultural climate was just right for the creative will to exert itself in more than one area. There was an atmosphere of nervous haste to search and to find and to be different. The creative will was propelled into many directions. Not that all the results were artistically valid. But the search in a changing world which the findings were destined to help change was at least an honest expression of man's determination. These daring beginnings were greatly exploited after the mid-century.

It was the turn of the century which was so conducive to the creation of the new, and the preparatory work for twentieth-century revolutions in all fields of human activity was accomplished within a ten-year period. The years from about 1895 to 1905 shook the foundation of the past. They saw some of the most decisive changes clearing the way for the realization of man's dreams: the advent of mechanistic science, with the great discoveries of the Curies and Roentgen, with Freud's probing of man's psyche, with Edison developing the kineto-scope and Marconi sending long-wave signals over a distance of more than a mile. Horseless cars started to rattle along the roads and poison the air to the puzzlement of the people, and the Wright Brothers made Leonardo da Vinci's Renaissance dream come true in 1906. Einstein repudiated Newton and began to rebuild the world of Galileo and Copernicus, greatly aided by Niels Bohr. The first cubic houses without ornament were built and turned the tide toward the great monolithic block, the huge single concrete, steel or glass cube, which suggests the Aztecs rather than the Renaissance idea of Apollonian fulfilment of form. Schönberg went to the early Greeks for the atonal mode of musical expression and opened the gates for later experimentation. Picasso learned to paint cubistically from Congo masks. Isadora Duncan threw off the yoke of the artificiality of the nineteenth-century dance. Adolphe Appia and Gordon Craig rejected the concept of naturalism and preached the supreme law of suggestiveness in the theatre and the inviolability of an overall design. Stanislavsky's 'theatre of inner feeling' was destined to do away with the hollow pathos of the classical method of acting and its counterpart of superficial realism.

Many of the artists who grew up in that period set out on various roads to give their time its twentieth-century image. The environment was a creative stimulus for them to try their hands and minds at many things and in more than one area. If nothing else, it gave them a feeling of protean power, denying the past, refusing to continue on its timeworn path, trying to point the way into the future. This century started with a bang, not a whimper.

Now, the process of demolishing the past is far advanced. The blueprint for tomorrow's world is waiting to be realized. Understandably, a very decisive difficulty during such a long transition period is the unavoidable fact that the wrecking crews are the builders of the age to come.

## In the Name of Music

Many writers feel stimulated by the visual impact of a landscape, the monotony of the thundering sea or the mysterious silence of mountains. Virginia Woolf used to read a few pages of the Bible before starting her work in the morning. It was not the content that she needed as a stimulant, but the cadence of the language, its rhythm, the majesty of its melody.

Indeed, it is music more than anything else, that serves as the inspiration for many artists. Thomas Mann told me how much music meant to him and to his ability to create. Erich Maria Remarque could write with greater ease when his automatic record player was on. From Kierkegaard to Susanne K. Langer, philosophers have taken refuge in music to sweep clean their ganglia for the process of clear thinking.

Music is not only the brandy of the damned, as George Bernard Shaw said, but it is also the ambrosia of the chosen. In its abstract existence, music can be neither confined nor easily described. With its emotional power it can soothe, elate, and create a feeling of ecstasy. We may find names, terms, definitions, and descriptions for what music does to us, but as one of the most abstract forms of expression it is the word's antipode as the prime agent of all literalization. That verbal language is also sound tends to separate it from music rather than unite it. The learned Dr Johnson called the opera an exotic and irrational art. The composer uses words with the love for something he can completely dominate. The more he penetrates language, the less it can be disengaged from its music. This makes the translation of operas more difficult than even the translation of poetry. Also, the failure or success of the sung word is rarely attributed to the text but to the music.

*Plate 7*

And yet most composers take to writing, or to writing rather than painting, which, intrinsically, would be so much closer to their medium. I know of only one outstanding composer who could also artistically express himself with pen and brush: Arnold Schönberg. True, there have been a few composers who, due to genetic or environmental reasons, have also shown inclination to drawing and painting. But they are surprisingly few compared to the writer or performing artist with similar leanings.

45

Ermanno Wolf-Ferrari (1876–1948), the son of a German painter and an Italian mother, was an excellent draughtsman and intended to paint before becoming a composer. Ferruccio Busoni (1866–1924), a child prodigy as a pianist, composer of neoclassic music, conductor, and teacher of repute, wrote poetry as well as the text to his compositions. He designed sets and costumes. His desire was to fulfil himself 'from all sides in the arts' as the human being he was, seeking entity within and without.

*Plate 6*

Once, he thought he would become an architect, and he sketched the ideal house he wanted to build for himself and visualized the city of the future. His caricatures show eloquently his wonderful sense of humour. There seems to be an interesting hereditary sequence in Busoni's family since Ferruccio's parents were both musicians, although not composers; his two sons, however, became painters.

Felix Mendelssohn-Bartholdy (1809—1847) had a distinct talent for drawing and painting. Undoubtedly, he was encouraged by the nineteenth-century trend among the well-to-do middle-class which saw to it that the drawing talent of the children was recognized and furthered. Mendelssohn, who travelled a great deal, liked to illustrate his letters with landscape drawings (another fashionable tendency of the romantic era). In his watercolours and drawings we are aware of a diligently learned craft, executed in a clean, academic style. In contrast to his music we find no originality in Mendelssohn the painter, but a slavish belief in copying nature, as one of his letters to his nephew, a would-be-painter, indicates:

*Plate 4*

Thank you very much for the drawing which . . . I like very much. If, however, you intend to adopt painting as a profession, you cannot become accustomed soon enough to regarding the substance of a work of art as more serious and important than its form – in other words, that means . . . to contemplate nature lovingly, closely, intimately and inwardly, and to study all your life long. Study thoroughly how the outer contours and the inward structure of a tree, or a mountain, or a house always must look, and how it can look, if it is to be beautiful – and then reproduce the impression . . . it will be good in any medium if only it testifies to your love of substance . . .

The claim that Mozart (1756–1791) was a writer with any particular gift would be difficult to defend, even though the total impression of his collected letters can easily serve as the equivalent to an autobiography. He spoke very freely of his feelings and thoughts in these letters, most of which were written in German. A few letters in French and Italian prove

*Plate 3*

that he could express himself well in languages not native to him. In his mother tongue he was particularly conscious of how he wrote. Preciousness, the fad of his time, is often noticeable. In one of his letters to his father from Paris he interrupts himself, saying: '– a nice style, isn't it? – Have patience – I am not in the mood today to write more elegantly (zierlicher) –'.

Probably the strongest characteristics emerging from his letters are humanity, warmth, and simplicity without servility. This may be considered an achievement in an aristocratic society that counted its artists among its servants. Sometimes Mozart could be crude in his letters, but what is strongly conveyed above all other things is a great sense of humour. Whenever he wanted to be particularly humorous he was inclined to write in rhymes. It may be too generous to call his rhymes verses. But on occasion they have a Benjamin-Franklin-humour, wrapped in a homily, as the following letter, written to his sister Nannerl on the day of her wedding in 1784, shows:

. . . This is why I want you to accept a little advice from my poetic brains; now listen:

> In marriage you will have to learn a bit
> of what before was only half a riddle;
> experience will teach you soon
> why at the time Eve acted as she did
> and then gave birth to Cain.
> But, sister, all the duties in your married life
> I'm sure you'll do with pleasure as a wife.
> Believe, they aren't heavy, hard nor quite in vain.
> And yet there are two sides to every coin:
> However many joys your married life will gain
> it's grief that all your joys will join.
> And, if your husband in a gloomy mood
> is angry with you and is rude,
> which seems to you not fair nor right,
> then think: another whim of men, and say:
> O Lord, Your will be done by day
> – and mine will then be done by night.

## THE WRITER-COMPOSER
### Friedrich Nietzsche

Friedrich Nietzsche (1844–1900) danced with the pen. His Zarathustra said, 'I should only believe in a God that would know how to dance'. To Nietzsche dance symbolized rhythmic freedom. But his dance-mindedness had little to do with

47

the dance as an art form. When he spoke of his own style as a dance and could say, 'Every day I count wasted in which there has been no dance', he thought of a life free from weakness and ordinariness. His thoughts danced and defied gravity when defying the traditional morality of the weak.

His verses and prose reveal the master stylist. Thomas Mann, in his *Speech About Nietzsche*, said that 'his very language is music and manifests a sensibility of the inner ear, a mastery of cadence, tempo, rhythm . . .' Mann spoke of Nietzsche's passion for music and projected his own love for it into his interpretation of Nietzsche's dependence on music 'to which were tied the ultimate decisions of his conscience'.

I am alluding to the fructifying effect of music on writers and creative men in the beginning of this chapter. Music as stimulation and relaxation for any person of higher sensibilities does not have to be stressed. But there are very few examples of writers who are drawn to the creative process of composing music. I will speak of E. T. A. Hoffmann, the romantic genius, in another context. In general, however, it can be said that the composing poet is a very romantic figure, even though he may have lived at a time as far removed from nineteenth-century Romanticism as the troubadour or Minnesinger. The few great examples of poet-composers are historically placed at the very beginning of Romanticism with its founder, Jean Jacques Rousseau, at its climactic point with E. T. A. Hoffmann, and at the end of the era with the most romantic of all poet-philosophers, Friedrich Nietzsche.

'Life without music is sheer error, strain, exile', said Nietzsche, whose love-hate relationship with Richard Wagner accompanied the philosopher through his life. Nietzsche possessed such a great gift for improvisation at the piano that Wagner, who had once listened, remarked that for a philosopher he fantasied well enough. At the age of sixteen Nietzsche began to compose Lieder and when he was twenty-one he said about himself that 'had it not been for the absence of some fortuitous events I might have had the courage to become a composer'. It was at that time that the first draft of his Lied, *A Maiden Fishing*, was put on paper, a Lied of which *Plate 12* he later said that it was 'most magnificently composed in some future style with a scream all its own and other similar ingredients of quiet lunacy. It is based on a poem which I wrote as a junior high school student'.

Nietzsche is probably a prime example of the frustrated composer whose musicianship and compulsive feeling for music found its sublimated expression in his writing. He never gave up trying his hand at composing Lieder, piano music, marches. Hans von Bülow thought that Nietzsche's *Manfred-Meditation*, composed for the piano at the age of twenty-eight, was 'the most unpleasant and amusical work' he had ever heard. The influences of Schumann and Brahms hit the listener of Nietzsche's Lieder in all their obviousness. When Nietzsche was forty-three years old and had written such masterpieces as *Thus Spake Zarathustra*, *Human, All Too Human*, and *Beyond Good and Evil*, *A Hymn on Life* was published in Leipzig: melody by Friedrich Nietzsche, orchestrated for chorus by Peter Gast.

Thomas Mann rightly said that 'he loved music as no one else' and that no other art was closer to his heart. That he never could find the creatively liberating impulse was another matter and probably a great gain for the world of letters. Did he himself not say that 'One's own self is well hidden from one's own self' and that 'Great men's errors are to be venerated as more fruitful than little men's truths'?

## Jean Jacques Rousseau

At the age of eighteen Jean Jacques Rousseau (1712–1778) had a scant knowledge of music, although he was deeply and genuinely interested in it. His flair for music may have been inherited. His father, a reckless but learned man, who failed in his trade as a watchmaker, had been a dancing master in his youth and was undoubtedly musical.

When Jean Jacques came to Lausanne on one of his walking tours – the restless mind of the young Rousseau developed a fury for journeys – he called himself a Paris musician. He composed a small piece which he played with little success in the house of one of the first citizens of the town. Like many other good teachers he soon learned more and more by teaching. On another of his walking tours through France his little knowledge of music saved him from starvation.

In Chambéry in the province of Savoy where he stayed for ten years with his patroness Louise de Warrens (who also elevated him to her lover), he was considered a fine music teacher. At that time he became very excited about the then new *Treatise of Harmony* by Jean-Philippe Rameau and plunged deeper into the adventure which music seemed to hold out for him. When he was twenty-five a piece of lyric, undoubtedly written by himself, was set to music by him and published in the *Mercure de France*. His probing mind became more and more interested in the history of music.

Five years later Rousseau, still thinking of himself as a talented musician, left Chambéry for Paris where he hoped to make a fortune with his new system of musical notation. His 'revolutionary' idea was to substitute numeral signs, ordinary arithmetical numbers, for the conventional symbols representing musical notes. He invented these new musical figures because he had difficulties in reading the accepted music notes, and he found his own invention a simplified and attractive version.

When he arrived in Paris, he not only felt like the proud inventor of a new system of notation, but he also brought great hopes and a musical comedy, *Narcisse*, with words and music by himself. But the members of the Academy of Inscriptions eyed his invention with academic suspicion and buried his hopes with reference to a monk who previously had a similar idea of equal impracticality. Rousseau's *Dissertation on Music* which contained his notation system remained unnoticed. And nothing came of *Narcisse*. But *Les Muses Galantes*, another opera in three acts, was presented with Rousseau as conductor. Rameau found faults with many sections and did not believe that the good parts in this opera could have been Rousseau's original work. 'And it is true', Rousseau said in the *Confessions*, 'that my work, unequal and unregulated, was sometimes sublime and sometimes very flat, as is bound to happen with a composer who forms himself only by some bursts of genius and who does not base himself on scientific training.' But this work was given a trial performance in Paris and was later also heard in Versailles.

Voltaire ('I did it very quickly and very badly') had collaborated with Rameau on *La Princesse de Navarre*. Rousseau was asked to improve on text and music. He altered as little as possible, but was neither credited as its third author nor was he paid for it. A year after he won the prize for *Essay on the Origin of Human Knowledge*, which determined his career as one of the most influential philosophical writers of the eighteenth century, he once more tempted Euterpe with another composition. Within six weeks he wrote the opera buffa, *Le devin du village*, fashioned after Pergolesi's style. *Plate 5* After its production he could rightly say: 'Soon there was nobody more sought after in Paris than I'. Forced to take sides in the ensuing 'Guerre des Bouffons', fought between the adherents of the French and Italian type of opera, Rousseau upheld the Italians and was hanged in effigy by the artists of the Opéra.

5 Jean-Jacques Rousseau
FRONTISPIECE FOR 'LE DEVIN DU VILLAGE'

6 Ferruccio Busoni THE LESSON

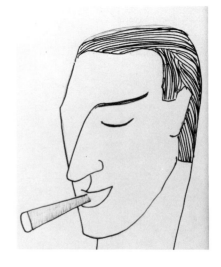

7 Arnold Schönberg PORTRAIT OF ALBAN BERG

8 Igor Stravinsky SKETCH OF SERGE DIAGHILEV

9 Igor Stravinsky DRAWING OF C. F. RAMUZ

10 George Gershwin SELF-CARICATURE

He contributed articles on music for Diderot's Encyclopédie and wrote his popular *Dictionnaire de musique* in 1768. Together with Giambattista Cimador he set his own play *Pygmalion* to music with little success. But theatre seemed to have been an obsession with him. He persuaded the Théâtre Français to perform a comedy he had written while in Venice. He was so bored by his own play that he left before the final curtain and went to the Café de Procope where he told his friends how little he thought of it.

*Le devin du village* is hardly ever performed nowadays. I saw one of its rare productions in the baroque garden of a Swiss millionaire in Meilen. These two rustic acts breathe the atmosphere of a Watteau painting. Already the young Mozart made light of it in his parody, *Bastien et Bastienne*.

Today, when Rousseau's name is mentioned, one does not think of him as a musicologist (which he undoubtedly was), let alone as a composer (as which he tried to make his mark and failed). After all, he had set aflame more than a whole century with the music of his thoughts.

### RICHARD WAGNER'S VERSATILITY

We are used to the idea of an actor becoming a stage director, a dancer turning into a choreographer, and we can easily imagine the harpsichordist of the Baroque and later the first violinist or concert master calling the tune and swinging the baton.

Far more complex is the case of the composer as a conductor, with the exception of the virtuoso, who obviously plays his own music as well as the composition of others. Paganini may serve as a prime example. But in the same way as a playwright staging his own play more often than not fails to do justice to his own imagination, a composer may not necessarily be the best interpreter of his own work. Some people maintain that Bruno Walter gave a better reading of Mahler's works than Mahler himself. Richard Strauss was considered a wonderful conductor, but of the works of other composers. It seems that the originator's closeness to his own material makes him lose the needed aesthetic distance, and his interpretation of his own music falls short of great inspiration.

Like the stage director the 'star' conductor as a prominent figure in the field of the performing arts is relatively new, dating back to the second half of the last century. Richard Wagner was the first one to interpret Beethoven freely, no longer depending on the score of the first violin. His treatise *Über das Dirigieren* (On Conducting) is the turning point in the art of conducting and coincides with the first star conductor, Hans von Bülow, whose greatest accomplishments fall into the 1880s.

It was Bülow who best characterized the duality of Wagner as a human being with the remark that he had the full face of Faust and the profile of Mephistopheles. Although there is no doubt that the psyche of an artist has a decisive part in his creative process, I will not dwell on Wagner's socio-political thinking, on Wagner, the apostle of Teutonic folklore, or on his militant anti-semitism and his egomaniacal attacks on his patrons. He was compulsive in whatever he did, but in his stupendous versatility he left his mark on the world of music and gave the theatre a new concept of totality, of the *Gesamtkunstwerk*.

He was the first great propagandist in Germany and what he promoted was a Wagnerian World which, however detestable it may be, is fascinating nevertheless and has mesmerized such diverse personalities as Nietzsche and Hitler. He idealized a mysterious abstraction which he visualized as 'The Folk, the sum of all those who feel a common need'. There can be no objection to Wagner's idea of 'folk' being 'always the fructifying source of all art'. What matters is the manner in which the creative artist uses the folkloric elements as poetic essence for his work. In his theatricalizations Wagner glorified and mystified what he perceived as a super-human music-drama. At the end, the shining knight-errant Siegfried turned into the high priest Parsifal. Wagner spoke of 'the highest human *Kunstwerk*, the *complete* drama', and the result was a magnificent attempt at a compromise between music and drama. He visualized the *Gesamtkunstwerk* as 'the united lyric work of art' of which the perfect form is the drama.

The great united work of art, that must embrace all the *genres* of art and in some degree absorb each of them in order to use it as a means to an end, to annul it in order to attain the common aim of *all*, namely the unconditioned, immediate representation of perfected human nature, – this great united work of art cannot be recognized as the arbitrary need of the individual, but only as the inevitable associated work of the humanity of the future.

What Wagner thought of the other arts outside music, poetry, and drama showed his fanatic determination to squeeze every artistic expression into the Wagnerian formula. He condemned poetry that did not serve his *Gesamtkunstwerk* ideal, he thought little of sculpture and architecture if they did not serve the purposes of state and church. Sculpture and

54

painting were acceptable to him when they bowed to the dictates of his total theatre image.

The musician in Wagner dominated the poet, and only through his facility of musical expression could he achieve his poetic expression. He, however, saw himself primarily as a poet and said in *Eine Mittheilung an meine Freunde* (A Communication to all My Friends): '. . . with regard to all my dramatic works I was in the first instance *Poet*, and only in completing the process of my work on the poem did I become once more Musician. Only I was a poet who was conscious in advance of the power of musical expression for the working out of his poems'.

But had he not perceived his impressive work for the theatre with all the power of music that was in him, the result would have been disastrous. His dramaturgic sense failed him. As a dramatist he had great visions, as his tetralogy of the *Nibelungen Ring* proves, but his point of attack in each of the four operas was wrong and thus caused endless repetitions. Some of his arias are not badly written, however; essentially he was not a poet but a versifier who wrote rhymed lines for music. Most of the time his verses are bombastic, hollow, and trite. Two examples, from *Tristan* and *Parsifal*, with literal translations will suffice:

| | |
|---|---|
| *Tristan:* *Heller schallend* | More brightly sounding |
| *mich umwallend,* | growing around me, |
| *sind es Wellen* | are they waves |
| *sanfter Lüfte?* | of gentle air? |
| | |
| *Sind es Wogen* | Are they billows |
| *wonniger Düfte?* | of blissful scents? |
| *Wie sie schwellen,* | How they swell |
| *mich umrauschen,* | and rush around me, |
| *soll ich atmen,* | shall I breathe, |
| *soll ich lauschen?* | shall I listen? |

*Parsifal:*  *Des eig'nen sündigen Blutes Gewell'*
  *in wahnsinniger Flucht*
  *muss mir zurueck dann fliessen,*
  *in die Welt der Sündensucht*
  *mit wilder Scheu sich ergiessen:*
  *von neuem sprengt es das Tor,*
  *daraus es nun strömt hervor*

(twelve more lines to follow, forming one sentence)

55

> The waves of my own sinful blood
> > in maddening flight
> > must flow back to me then
> > into the world of sinful rage
> > streaming with wild shyness:
> > again it forces the door,
> > in torrents it pours forth . . .

One could also easily prove that his prose was faulty and never succeeded in expressing any thought with profound clarity. But writing as much as he did was a necessity for him. As his biographer Ernst Newman explained, Wagner benefited greatly by his versatility: '. . . no one can doubt that his music is all the richer for the stimuli his nature received from so many quarters'. That he was a compulsive writer kept him of course from composing more operas. On the other hand, in wanting to prepare and educate the public for his Ring cycle by writing *Opera and Drama*, one of his many prose books, he 'also felt an imperative need of coming to an understanding with himself' Apparently he had to purge his intellect in order to free his emotions so that they could function fully.

Wagner's influence on the development of the opera was undeniably of the greatest consequence. His visualization of a total theatre went far beyond the opera and included the influential ideas of the stage designers Adolphe Appia and Gordon Craig as much as the rejuvenating ballet concepts of Serge Diaghilev. Twentieth-century theatre would have been the poorer had Richard Wagner not lived up to his destiny.

ARNOLD SCHÖNBERG

Arnold Schönberg (1871–1951) could not help being original in whatever he did. He was the prototype of the pioneering artist.

*Plate 7*

The influence of Wagner and Debussy was inescapable for any composer toward the end of the last century, and Schönberg was no exception, as his *Gurrelieder* and *Verklärte Nacht* unmistakably prove. But the restlessness of his spirit soon made him break through the confinements of traditional composition. Also, having become mature in the artistically explosive and contagious atmosphere of his native Vienna at the turn of the century, he felt the need for the realization of new forms. Schönberg became more and more obsessed by the notion of his Messianic mission. There was a rare and raw intensity in this creative mind which found its materialization in the development of the twelve-tone technique, in his painting, writing and teaching.

However unusual and revolutionary Schönberg's atonality may have sounded in the very beginning, it was only a logical step from or rebellion against the chromaticism that Wagner and Debussy practised and that led to atonality. As so often happens with innovators, the past places them in front of the door leading into new realms of experience. What matters is to recognize the door and to have the strength, courage, and urge to step out alone, facing the hazards of the unknown. This is what Schönberg did.

It was Wagner who started to give the libretto a new seriousness. He was followed in this by Verdi and Debussy as well as by most twentieth-century composers. Their leaning toward literature can be seen in the choice of the highly literary libretti, as in Alban Berg's *Wozzeck* and *Lulu*, in Stravinsky's *The Rake's Progress*, or in Hugo Weisgall's *Six Characters in Search of an Author*. Schönberg struggled with the writing of an oratorio and turned to the poet Richard Dehmel, some of whose poems he had put to music previously:

. . . your poems have had a decisive influence on my development as a composer . . . For a long time I have been wanting to write an oratorio on the following subject: modern man, having passed through materialism, socialism, and anarchy and, despite having been an atheist . . . wrestles with God . . . and finally succeeds in finding God . . . And above all: the mode of speech, the mode of thought, the mode of expression, should be that of modern man; the problems treated should be those that harass us . . . Originally I intended to write the words myself. But I no longer think myself equal to it . . .

He finally wrote his own libretto, *Jacob's Ladder*, which, however, he never set to music. The idea of making a musical statement of religious thought accompanied him his whole life. His final opus was *Modern Psalms*, which he was working on before he died. The last words set to music were: 'And yet I pray as all that lives prays'. The idea of man's identity, of man's dialogue with the silence of God finally found expression in his work *Moses and Aaron*, in which word and music are closely interlinked, in which he achieves – though through other means than Wagner's – a total dramatic integration of orchestral music, voice, and bodily movement. Schönberg the librettist, worked most intimately with Schönberg the composer, who, however, retained the upper hand. Schönberg explained this: 'It is only while I'm composing that the text becomes definite, sometimes even after composition'.

As an artist he was very much of his time. His language has the tormented tone of German expressionism. He felt that whatever he wrote had a certain inner likeness to himself – witness his Moses, who in his loneliness fashioned a great vision and brought freedom and law to his people.

'An apostle without incandescent fire preaches a false doctrine', he once said. He was no such apostle. Alban Berg, the most prominent of his pupils, wrote of him as a teacher:

From the very beginning genius has the impact of a teacher. His speech is teaching, his action is exemplary, his works are revelations. In him hides the teacher, prophet, and messiah . . . Inseparable from his artistry and his great humanity, his unique way of teaching is furthered by his strong artistic will to bring forth the highest accomplishment – no matter whether he turns to his own creativity, to conducting, writing critiques, or finally to teaching.

Schönberg spoke about himself as a teacher in the opening statements of his *Theory of Harmony:*

'This book is about what I have learned from my students . . . Had I told them only what I know, then they would only know this and not more. Perhaps they may even know less. But they know the essential: to search! I hope my students will search! Because they will have learned that you only seek in order to seek. To find may be the aim, but it can easily become the end of all striving.'

He thought that it didn't take much doing to let mediocre talents evolve smoothly. But when the teacher is up against problems, he must recognize them in order to cope with them successfully. That is the mark of the teacher.

There was only one Schönberg whatever he did: compose, teach, write, or paint. As a painter he put on loud colours with large strokes, but brought to the achieved clashes of conflicts an astounding clarity. The soothing half-tones, transitions, harmonious in themselves, are missing, but Schönberg knew no compromise. He exhibited with the group of *Der Blaue Reiter* – a title coined by Franz Marc – in 1911. During the year preceding this exhibition, a period in which he needed money badly, he wrote to his publisher in Vienna:

. . . You know that I paint . . . And I am to have an exhibition next year. What I have in mind is that you might be able to get one or the other well-known patron to buy some of my pictures or have his portrait done by me . . . Only you must not tell people that they *will* like my pictures. You must make them realize that they cannot but like my pictures, because they have been praised by authorities on painting: and above all that it is much more interesting to have one's portrait done by or to own a picture by a musician of my reputation than to be painted by some mere practitioner of painting whose name will be forgotten in 20 years, whereas even now my name belongs to the history of music. For a lifesize portrait I want from 2 to 6 sittings and 200 to 400 kronen. That is really cheap, considering that in 20 years people will pay ten times as much and in 40 years a hundred times as much for these paintings. I am sure you quite realize this . . . there is just one thing: I cannot consider letting the purchase of a portrait depend on whether the sitter likes it or not. The sitter knows who is painting him: he must also realize that he understands nothing about such things, but that the portrait has artistic value, or, to say the least of it, historical value.

Schönberg painted many self-portraits, about twenty-one altogether, yellow, green, blue, with such titles as *The Red Look* or *The Blue Look*. He painted many of the people who were close to him, and a series of visions, one of them *Vision of Christ*. But he became very conscious of being a Jew and formally returned to Judaism in 1933, in the shadow of Nazi terror. Ten years previously, when the first signs of flagrant anti-semitism were felt in Germany, he was supposed to have taught at the *Bauhaus*. Already at that time even the *Bauhaus* was infected by Nazism, and Schönberg wrote to Kandinsky:

. . . And you join in that sort of thing and 'reject me as a Jew' . . . How can a Kandinsky approve of my being insulted: how can he associate himself with politics that aim at bringing about the possibility of excluding me from my natural sphere of action; how can he refrain from combating a view of the world whose aim is St Bartholomew's nights in the darkness of which no one will be able to read the little placard saying that I'm exempt!

There was humanity in Arnold Schönberg, a genius of versatility. He was an apostle living, acting, creating with incandescent fire.

### THE COMPOSER AS CRITIC

The artist-turned-critic is a phenomenon with which the art world is blessed or cursed, depending on how one looks at it. That most critics are frustrated artists goes mostly unrecognized. But is it not logical to choose an area of activity in which we are vitally interested? Is not familiarity bred by love and enthusiasm before it breeds, besides its proverbial contempt, criticism and boredom?

A case can easily be made of the fact that he who knows how the body moves or how a brush and chisel is handled, or he who plays an instrument or possesses the facility to articulate his thoughts well without being able to achieve an artistically valid and creative level will be a better critic of a specific discipline than the one who is unfamiliar with its technique. We expect the critic to possess knowledge and background of the art he is called upon to judge and we accept his psychological fitness, his personal likes and dislikes as a matter of fact.

The creative artist, the genius, as a critic is naturally a much rarer phenomenon than the frustrated artist. The creative artist–turned–critic could theoretically be rather charitable and generous in his attitude toward his fellow artists if it were not for his 'ungovernable passion for Art which is the cause of all my trouble, all my real suffering', as Berlioz once said. We are inclined to forgive and overlook a great deal when facing a genius, and his prejudices may appear to us like passionate battle cries for a new credo. Also, in retrospect such a critic's weaknesses can be better justified and fit into the totality of the artist's work, than when he is our contemporary.

A composer may become a critic for as many reasons as any other critic. He may feel temperamentally drawn to criticism, or he may be forced to become a critic by circumstances beyond his control, mostly of a financial nature, or he may feel like a compulsive teacher who realizes that he can widen his sphere of influence through print.

### Robert Schumann

To Robert Schumann (1810–1856) writing was second nature, and the critic became the alter ego of the composer Schumann. He was a writer long before he became a composer and concert pianist. His father was a well-known novelist. Robert inherited the urge to express himself in the best and most precise manner and to acquire an encyclopedic knowledge. In his youth Schumann wrote poetry, novels, and verse plays. His style became influenced by Jean Paul, one of the most revered writers among the German romantics.

We find in Schumann's diary an entry made early in his youth: 'I am not quite certain about what I really am'. And some time later: 'It is strange that I must cease being a poet when my emotions begin to speak most strongly'. That he should have felt forced to compose when carried on the wings of emotions, only proves that he was not really a poet, let alone a romantic poet. Basically, he was an essayist with a flair for criticism. Environmental influences turned him into a composer, although he undoubtedly brought to music a most innate readiness, an emotional need, as he admitted.

Schumann often visited the house of a certain Doctor Carus whose wife played the piano and had a very good voice. Being exposed to good *Hausmusik*, to Lieder and chamber music almost daily, and coming under the influence of Clara Wieck, the daughter of his piano teacher and his future wife, he one day 'became determined to devote himself exclusively to music'. These were Schumann's words.

However, he never gave up writing, to which two volumes testify. He became one of the most important music critics, writing mainly for the periodical *Neue Zeitschrift für Musik* which he had founded at the age of twenty-four. Even though he tried to uphold the classic ideals he turned into a champion of such new masters as Chopin, Berlioz, and Brahms. Perhaps the most outstanding feature in his critical writing was, besides his well-phrased language, a surprising objectivity towards his colleagues. (Or is it true, as someone maintained, that a genius can be understood only by another genius?)

Schumann's music has made him immortal, while, as a writer, he is not as well known as he deserves. Some of his observations are penetrating and enlightening and have the epigrammatic impact that lies in brevity:

Nothing worse can happen to you than to be praised by a scoundrel.

He who is afraid of preserving his originality is in the process of losing it.

Whenever you play an instrument be not concerned with who listens to you. Play always as if a master were listening.

Frederick Chopin

Take off your hats, gentlemen, a genius!

I thumbed thoughtlessly through the score (Variations on a Don-Juan-theme, opus 2).

There is something magic about the hidden enjoyment of music without sound. Moreover, it seems to me that every composer has his own peculiar way of writing notes seen from a purely visual viewpoint: Beethoven looks different on paper from Mozart in the way Jean Paul's handwriting differs from that of Goethe. But here I felt as if only strange eyes would look at me in a wonderful way, eyes of flowers, basilisk eyes, eyes of a peacock, eyes of a girl.

In Schumann's *Maxims and Reflections* we also find this aphorism:

One composes out of many reasons: because of the desire for immortality or because you just happen to find the grand piano opened; because you want to become a millionaire, sometimes also because friends praise you, or because you looked into beautiful eyes, or out of no reason at all.

The writer Robert Schumann began to compose because he found the piano standing open. But instead of chance it was exposure that awakened a dormant gift in this versatile talent, whose poetic emotions found refuge in the sanctuary of music.


### Hector Berlioz

Schumann once wrote: 'Is Berlioz to be regarded as a genius (that is musical genius) or a musical adventurer?' He probably was both. Louis Hector Berlioz (1803–1869) was a romantic realist whose ideas of orchestral colouring stood next to Wagner's and were of great influence. He was consumed by his passions, and his greatest passion was music. He gave up medical study for music. In spite of his native genius and strong ambitions he never reached the fame which he felt was justifiably his. Perhaps he was a greater artist than musician and therefore less popular and appreciated. Perhaps he did have ill-luck, which made him write: 'The luck of having talent is not enough, one must also have a talent for luck'.

He had a great talent for verbalizing his thoughts. He loved to write letters and was a fine lyricist which he proved with a few libretti. He was a passionate talker and inimitable raconteur. His *Mémoires* were posthumously published in 1870. As early as 1844 his *Treatise on Instrumentation* was highly acclaimed. But his flair for writing found its best expression in his criticism. He could verbalize and define a musical experience with great wit. His observations are as sharp as his ability to describe them is enlightening. He admired Gluck, Beethoven, and Mendelssohn, but Mozart's operas only with reservations. He disliked most of the Italian composers. He little appreciated Bach ('I do not think they meant to annoy me', he said after Russian artists had performed a Bach concerto), but he was enthusiastic about Glinka's compositions.

Berlioz made his living as a daily reviewer for nearly thirty years. In 1835 he wrote to a friend:

. . . I work like a black for the four papers which give me my daily bread. These are the *Rénovateur*, which pays badly, the *Monde Dramatique* and the *Gazette Musicale*, which pay little, and the *Débats* which pays well. With all this I have to fight the nightmare of my musical position: I cannot find the time to compose . . .

As a critic he could be bitter and sarcastic when he faced the unforgivably bad. But realizing the weaknesses of the great, he said in a letter in 1862:

I write to you in the middle of one of those abominable reviews of the kind which it is impossible to do right. I am trying to support our unhappy Gounod, who has had a fiasco worse than any yet seen. There is nothing in his score, nothing at all. How can I support what has neither bone nor sinew? Still I have got to find something to praise . . . And it's his third fiasco at the Opéra. Well, he'll have a fourth one. No one can write dozens of operas, not great operas. Paisiello wrote 170, but of what sort? And where are they now? . . .

An artist as passionate and articulate as Berlioz could not help being a passionate critic. He also knew his own weaknesses well and tried to cope with them. When he was asked by a professor at the Conservatoire who took great interest in a young composer named Georges Bizet for his private opinion about *The Pearl Fishers*, Berlioz wrote candidly:

The critic may easily be dense and the work good. I entertain a vigorous hate against certain kinds of music which are none the less healthy, and I have had to reverse many a decision in which I proved a foolish judge. I hope for love of you that these three acts will please me. *But* don't go hanging yourself, nor let the author do the same, if they bore me . . .

*Claude Debussy*

Berlioz is 'a monster. He is not a musician at all. He creates the illusion of music by means borrowed from literature and painting. Besides, there is, as far as I can see, little that is French in him,' wrote Claude Debussy (1862–1918), another composer who wrote critiques because they helped him make ends meet.

Debussy's career as a critic began in 1901 when *La Revue Blanche*, a modern magazine with a limited circulation, offered him the post of a music critic. He began his first article:

Having been asked to speak about music in this review, may I be allowed to explain what I intend to do? On these pages will be found sincere and honestly found impressions rather than criticism; for this too often takes the form of brilliant variations on the theme of: 'You're wrong because you didn't do as I did'; or 'You're talented and I'm not; that can't go on'. I will try to discover the forces that have brought works of art into being, which I think is more worth while than taking them to pieces like an old watch.

He used the space in the papers – he continued to write reviews for the daily paper, *Gil Blas*, in 1903 – to promote his ideas for a simpler approach to the arts. The flag of symbolism was held up. Debussy's music was appreciated by the avant-garde, but the reactionary critics and the general public rejected him. Out of this isolated position of defence he was far more aggressive than Berlioz ever was in his most scintillating critiques. In order to fight Wagner's dominating influence Debussy took up a chauvinistic attitude and could be unpleasantly sarcastic. After having heard the *Ring* at Covent Garden, he spent an evening 'as a reward for good behaviour at a music-hall'. The *Ring's leitmotiv* suggested to him 'a harmless lunatic who, on presenting his visiting-card, would declaim his name in song'. But Debussy conceded that Wagner wouldn't ever quite die: 'Some splendid ruins will, however, remain, in whose shade our grandchildren will dream of the past greatness of a man who, had he been but a little more human, would have been great for all time'.

Debussy's likes and dislikes were ostentatiously displayed in his writings. His style was flowery and had a touch of the *art nouveau*, then in vogue. When reviewing the presentation of songs by Frederick Delius, he wrote:

They are very sweet and innocent songs, music to rock the convalescents of the rich neighbourhoods. There is always a note hanging over a chord like a water-lily in a lake, tired of being watched by the moon, or like a balloon blocked by the clouds.

Edward Lockspeiser, one of Debussy's biographers, has pointed out that Debussy must have liked this passage because he used the identical words for his critique about songs by Grieg of whom he said on another occasion that he is 'no more than a clever musician, more concerned with effects than with genuine art'.

Debussy could not refrain from personal attacks on his helpless victims. 'At last I saw Grieg. From in front he looks like a genial photographer; from behind his way of doing his hair makes him look like the plants called sunflowers, dear to parrots and the gardens that decorate small country stations'.

This is journalism at its lowest and in utter dissonance with the image we have of the composer Debussy, who gave us lyric works of subtle and gentle impressions, such as *La Mer, Claire de lune, L' Après-midi d'un faune*, let alone his opera *Pelléas et Mélisande*.

From the very beginning Debussy had created an imaginary figure for his critiques, a certain Monsieur Croche, a stand-in for the composer. This character had an 'intolerable smile . . . especially obvious when he talked of music'. Asked what his profession might be, he replied: 'Dilettante-hater', and speaking about music, Debussy lets his *alter ego* say: 'I try to forget music because it obscures my perception of what I do not know or shall only know tomorrow'.

This Monsieur Croche is modelled on Paul Valéry's imaginary Monsieur Teste who says: '. . . I can remember what I want. But the difficult thing is not that, but to remember what I shall want tomorrow'. The philosophy behind this suggests Igor Stravinsky's attitude when he maintains that the artist's task is to 'insult habit', to escape old formulae, ever to be ready to exchange today for tomorrow.

## IGOR STRAVINSKY

Igor Stravinsky (1882–) has not become a critic. He has always made a living by composing and conducting. Next to Picasso, he is the most unique creative artist of this century, casting an inimitable spell, initiating styles, influencing several generations of his contemporaries, composers as much as choreographers and painters. From his revolutionary *Le Sacre du Printemps* (1913) with its displaced accent and polytonal chord to his later formal-structural peculiarities as well as to his embracing of neo-classical and serial music, his work has remained a dominant force.

He once described himself to a gendarme as an 'inventor of music'. He feels that the very act of putting his work on paper, the purely physical effort, cannot be separated from the spiritual or psychological influences. Since in his eyes, and to his ears, 'Music creates a common order between man and time', he enjoys the idea of the arranging of materials, of working with the precision of an architect, creating blueprints without ornaments, forming simple but forceful structures. There is a strong inner relatedness in his structures which shows a clearly organized mind, always fascinating, often witty. His music creates the excitement of nowness, the sound of immediacy, surprising but always pure, denuded. He is never the same, but always recognizable.

The same clearly structured mind speaks out of his many books, from *An Autobiography* (1936) to his six lectures delivered at Harvard and collected as *Poetics of Music* (1942) to his *Conversations with Igor Stravinsky* (1959), *Memories and Commentaries* (1960), *Expositions and Developments* (1962), *Dialogues and a Diary* (1963), *Themes and Episodes* (1966), the latter ones written with the help of Robert Craft.

Stravinsky reveals himself in his writings as a serious observer of man and an inspired and painstaking craftsman. Reading his Harvard lectures, one cannot help feeling that Stravinsky's art of composing as well as his art of living turned him into a philosopher, into a teacher with a mission. He never holds forth, but tries to share the results of his analytical mind with his audience.

His *Lebensphilosophie* has been spread over many pages, but it is not only wisdom which flows from his lips and pen, it often is a bright humour and sarcastic wit, lacerating at times, which make his writings hilarious comments on opponents and situations, on life and art.

Most artists are sincere and most art is bad, and some insincere art (sincerely insincere) can be quite good.

The purchase of a Renoir at Sotheby's not long ago for $170,800 is to me an example of a flagrant lack of respect for money.

From time to time, and mainly in a doodling mood, Stravinsky drew. His portraits of Diaghilev, Picasso, Ramuz, and others show his ability to create with intense boldness, and with the same sparseness we remember from his music, the total image of a personality (*Plates 8, 9*).

What Stravinsky said about Diaghilev after his death, 'The truth of the matter is that everything that is original is irreplaceable', can be said about Igor Stravinsky too.

## ERIK SATIE

If there ever has been an artistic expression of highly polished sophistication in the guise of childlike and sometimes primitive naiveté, then it can be found in Erik Satie's work (1866–1925). If ever there was an example of an artist who was old in his youth and became young in his years of maturity, then Erik Satie is he.

As a musician and composer he lived through two distinct phases of his career, but in both of them he could express himself with equal facility verbally and visually. Satie had a strange sense of humour which, for instance, made him write

Erik Satie
Medieval drawing

his scores in red ink and without bar lines. The biting sarcasm in his humour must be related to his critical reaction to a culture in decay into which he was born ('I came into the world very young in a time which is very old') and whose bierbearer he later became. This was after 1910, after he had withdrawn from the artistic scene of Paris for about twelve years.

'I had an ordinary childhood and adolescence', Satie wrote in *Mémoires d'un amnésique*, 'no moments worth recounting in serious writing. So I shall pass them over'. With little interest in formal studies, he escaped a thorough conservatory training and arrived at Montmartre as second pianist of the Chat Noir. He was twenty-two years old when he became a Montmartre eccentric and a serious, though self-taught, composer.

The music which he then composed was religious in nature. In his mid-teens he discovered Bach and was drawn to mysticism and the Catholic Faith. His cabaret activities did not keep him from becoming the official composer of the Rosacrucian sect which he left to found his own denomination: the Metropolitan Church of the Art of Jesus the Conductor. Its official organ, *Le Cartulaire*, was written and its publication paid for by Satie who used it to excommunicate his enemies. Between 1892 and 1896 he presented himself as a candidate for election to the Académie three times. He responded to the rebuff he received with a pontifical letter addressed to Camille Saint-Saëns in *Le Cartulaire*:

I have acted not according to foolish presumptions but in response to a conscientious sense of duty . . . Your aberration can only arise from the feebleness of your ideas about this century and from your ignorance of God, the direct cause of aesthetic degradation. I pardon You in Jesus Christ and embrace You in God's grace.

His music had a Gothic character, and Debussy called Satie a 'gentle medieval musician who strayed into this century'. Satie's notebooks were filled with drawings of medieval inspiration, and both his music and drawings belonged to his pretentious pose. He undoubtedly believed in himself and in his destiny, but his scurrilous humour made him play the fool in God's name with a serious mien.

This phase was followed by a retreat into silence. When Satie awoke after his self-imposed hibernation of twelve years, he was a changed man, or at least the world saw in him a changed man. In between he had composed popular chansons

Erik Satie
Medieval drawing

to make a living and he had gone back to school, the Schola Cantorum, to study counterpoint. During this period, to be exact in 1903, he composed *Three Pieces in the Shape of a Pear*, a work which was published eight years later. When Cocteau heard him play this spoof of certain academic forms, he decided to work with him on a ballet. Their mutual effort was called *Parade*, it was a scandal and ushered in the uninhibited experimental tendency of our century. Satie's music included parts for typewriters, sirens, airplane propellors, telegraph tickers and lottery wheels. Satie was in his 'humouristic' period.

At that time he became a leader of the postwar demolition crew of everything traditional ('Show me something new; I'll begin all over again'). As a member of the famous *Les Six* he exploited the absurdities of existence and wedded the spirit of jazz and the music-hall to the poetry of banality. In 1920 he turned to Dada with his *furniture music* ('. . . we must bring about a music which is like furniture – a music which will be part of the noises of the environment . . . Furniture music creates a vibration; it has no other goal . . . Furniture music for law offices, banks, etc. No marriage ceremony complete without furniture music . . .'). At about the same time Satie's *Socrate, a drame symphonique*, was heard in Paris for the first time. It was described as 'variations on monotony'. Its rhythmic repetition conveys the feeling of white music and reminds one of Satie's reverie on a plate: 'How white it is! no painting ornaments it; it is all of a piece'.

A one-act lyric comedy, *Le Piége de Méduse* (The Ruse of Medusa), which Satie had written with incidental music nine years earlier, was published with engravings by Braque in 1922. When this play was performed at Pierre Bertin's Théâtre Bouffe, Darius Milhaud said about it:

The hit of the evening was without a doubt Satie's extraordinary play in which his wit sputtered in every line; the unbridled fantasy of the play bordered on the absurd. Bertin, in the part of Baron Medusa, made himself up to look like Satie; he seemed to incarnate the man. A stuffed monkey on a pedestal interrupted the action from time to time to do little dance numbers.

The absurdity in this burlesque is carried to great lengths when, for instance, the baron's future son-in-law is examined by him through a magnifying glass, or when the baron is involved in an adventure on the telephone and at the very end talks to a horse.

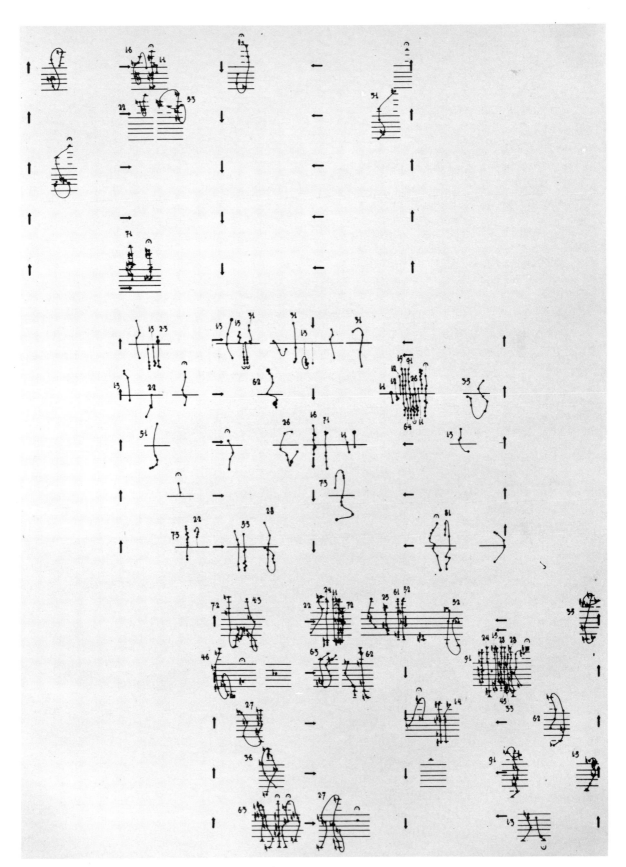

12 Friedrich Nietzsche SCORE OF 'DIE JUNGE FISCHERIN'

A year before his death, Erik Satie joined the Dada painter, Francis Picabia, and Jean Borlin of the Ballets Suédois in creating his final buffoonery with the ballet *Relache* (No Performance) which turned into a scandal similar to the one caused by *Parade*. For the first time in ballet history a film, René Clair's witty surrealist *Entr'acte*, was injected, 'the only entertaining moment', as the critic René Dumesnil wrote. 'The music . . . was affectedly, almost showily plain . . . It finished in indescribable tumult. However, the curtain came up for the usual bows. Driving a midget five-horse-power Citroën, Erik Satie popped out on stage . . . and ironically greeted the worthy audience whom he had just ridiculed magnificently . . .'

Satie once said that music was thrust upon him. It was only one means for him in which he probably could be bolder than through verbal or visual means. His notebooks are full of joyous non sequiturs and sophisticated nonsense ('The shadows of millennial trees indicate seventeen minutes after nine'). He could say about one of his scores, 'this work is absolutely incomprehensible, even to me'. He had the courage of playing fool to no king, of unmasking confusion by confusing, of writing dead-pan music, of creating boredom as creative stimulus. If music would not have been thrust upon him as a career, he could have easily become a James Thurber with Gallic esprit, as *A Musician's Day* from his *Mémoires d'un amnésique* illustrates:

An artist must regulate his life. Here is my precise daily schedule. I rise at 7:18; am inspired from 10:30 to 11:47. I lunch at 12:11 and leave the table at 12:14. A healthy horse-back ride on my property from 1:19 to 2:35. Another round of inspiration from 3:12 to 4:07. From 5:00 to 6:47 various occupations (fencing, reflection, immobility, visits, contemplation, dexterity, swimming, etc.).
Dinner is served at 7:16 and finished at 7:20. Afterwards from 8:09 to 9:59 symphonic readings out loud. I go to bed regularly at 10:37. Once a week I wake up at 3:14 A. M. (Tuesdays).

Being of serious demeanour, it is unintentional when I laugh. I always apologize very affably.
I sleep with only one eye closed; I sleep very hard. My bed is round with a hole in it for my head to go through. Every hour a servant takes my temperature and gives me another.

For a long time I have subscribed to a fashion magazine. I wear a white cap, white socks, and a white vest. My doctor has always told me to smoke. He even explains himself: 'Smoke, my friend. Otherwise, someone else will smoke in your place'.

GRAND
CINQ~MATS

Erik Satie
Drawing

The writing of diaries has become somewhat outdated in the mid-twentieth century. There is a touch of romantic exhibitionism to the writing of a diary with the forethought of having it published one day. Nowadays the artist veers more toward the psychoanalyst's couch to associate freely. There are exceptions among the contemporary diarists whose annotations written on the margin of their time sound convincing and inevitable. Nijinsky's diary records his dialogue with God. In Virginia Woolf's diary we find her mainly communing with herself about the arts and her own work. André Gide's *Journals* are of a more personal kind, and so are Jean Cocteau's. Moreover, their diaries were not published before their authors had reached a certain mature age, and their accomplishments give their self-revelations the necessary interest.

Only a high degree of brilliancy can justify the publication of a young man's diary such as that of Ned Rorem (1923–), who, as a composer of symphonic works, songs, and an opera, has made a name for himself, but still stands at the very beginning of his career. His writing is brilliant. His is a case of mental logghoria, conveniently helped along and supported by dazzling articulation. He writes in the form of a diary – and presumably will continue to do so – pretending that the very personal is actually impersonal. While doing his mental striptease ('I do love to see my name in print, even in the phone book'), he likes to undress his friends, most of whom are the great or near-great in the arts. ('At no time did I feel the hot, lazy, demoralizing magic which proved so fatal for Maurice Sachs during his friendship with Cocteau twenty years ago. Nor did I find him beautiful . . . From his social style – that of an actor – I have no reason to believe that the identical conversation was not repeated with the next admiring young American who came to call . . . Creating is like shitting: indeed this was the image he used'.) Rorem writes the glorified gossip column ('Marie Laure took my measurements – lying on my back, arms outstretched – and found them to be according to the classic golden law'), but with the ambition of turning out a literary book. ('Gide constructed musically, or so he thought – *Les Faux-Monnayeurs*, if anything, is fugal, and a fugue is formal, rather than rhetorical, only inasmuch as its trademark is contrast to tonalities – in any case he practised more than, say, Roger Martin du Gard, Aristotle's concept about tragical verisimilitude: "What is plausible and impossible is preferable to what is implausible and possible".')

In our age of nudity and a minimum of verbalization Ned

Rorem's books give the impression of an opus like Samuel Pepys' diaries and Rousseau's confessions rolled into one and translated into the intellectual lingo of the 1950s and '60s. The typewriter has taken the place of the analyst. I could very well imagine that Ned Rorem despises people who pay a lot of money to learn all about how to live with themselves and how to adjust to life, since he is out to leave the adjusting to the other people whom he expects to accept him as he is.

He began his diary in 1945 when he was an *enfant terrible*, and selections from it during the years 1951 and 1955 have become the famous *Paris Diary of Ned Rorem* which very often sounds as if written by an *adolescent terrible* ('If I – when we – remain jealously home at night, our loved ones out fornicating how much more aching is the dying man's gaze from the hospital window to one walking by and vanishing into a vital tomorrow!').

He moves in circles where a good-looking young man with a flair for flamboyance and the gift of an artist is more than welcome. He has an excessive capacity for drinking and loving, a particular skill for social climbing (Lully made his career with it) and acceptable eccentricities. His sharp-tongued wit makes its way into his writing which bristles with epigrammatic insults, well-phrased descriptions and aphorisms ('Composition is notation of distortion of what composers think they've heard before. Masterpieces are marvellous misquotations'). If the *Paris Diary of Ned Rorem* has a moral, then it probably says how easy it is to move in high society as long as you are aware of how low it can sink.

There are moments in which he reflects about life and death and the forces that blast him forward into action, often monotonous and useless, and he finds that 'my strength is still stronger than myself. I suppose this is why I keep a diary (or let myself be painted, fornicated, led into foreign countries). Fear of being forgotten is so compulsive I'd like to be remembered for each time I go to the bathroom, and I'd even prefer not to go alone'.

He seems to be very much aware of what he is doing and of his brilliance in doing it: 'Works of art must have a plan; beginnings and ends. A diary necessarily has no form beyond the accidental one of improvisation; hence, though it cannot be a work of art (improvisation precludes this), perhaps it *can* be a masterpiece'.

Ned Rorem, the composer, sitting down to write, is besides other things a compulsive case of magnificent articulation. *Le compositeur s'amuse.*

John Cage (1912–), composer, writer, lecturer, and raconteur, is a strange case of vociferous silence. He wrote a book of 276 pages which he called *Silence* and which contains his famous essay, *Lecture on Nothing*.

In 1937 he wrote: 'I believe that the use of noise to make music will continue and increase until we reach a music produced through the aid of electrical instruments which will make available for musical purposes any and all sounds that can be heard'. In 1952 he composed one of his most startling pieces, called *4′ 33″*, in which he pursued the other extreme, that of utter silence. Based on the concept that there is no absolute silence, the pianist sits silently for four minutes and thirty-three seconds, and then leaves the piano and stage. 'The music I prefer, even to my own and everything, is what we hear if we are just quiet.'

It is not indeterminacy on Cage's part that his music moves from the extreme of eardrum-puncturing sound effects to all the unintentional noises in silence. He is quite conscious of what he is doing and determined to find the proper equivalent for art in a non-art world, as he sees it. Art no longer interprets, shapes, dramatizes, narrates life. It *is* life. Theatre is seeing and hearing, is the now happening at the moment by chance. Non-intentional life divorces the creative act from the artist's conscious thought and unconscious desires, and for this non-creative process of untraditional creativity Cage accepted the term Indeterminacy. He was the first to have staged a 'happening' at Black Mountain College, North Carolina, in the summer of 1952.

You may call him a poseur or fool. But then the pose he strikes has influenced a whole generation of painters and dancers (not so much musicians) for whom he became a prophet in the shape of a Pied Piper. If he were a fool, which he isn't, he could not have written the non-essay, *How to Improve the World (You Will Only Make Matters Worse)* from which I quote at random since the writing is in a randomesque manner:

> We ought either to get
> rid of God or to find Another Who
> doesn't permit mention of trust in Him
> on pieces of money.        Or taxation could
> be augmented to the point where no one
>        has any money at all. In which case
> we could keep God.

His books are printed in a typographical rage, elevating typography to the handmaid of visual art. But if one can get beyond perhaps perplexing or irritating devices and his ambiguous boldness, there is reward in his coy wit, in the wisdom in parenthesis, in the meaningful anecdote lost at the bottom of a page with all the asterisks beginning to shine like bright stars, trying to penetrate the darkness of chance, adjusting life's indeterminacy.

John Cage believes that we should not try 'to bring order out of chaos nor suggest improvements in creation but simply to wake up to the very life we're living, which is so excellent once one gets one's mind and one's desires out of its way and lets it act of its own accord'. Tossing three coins six times and a clandestine look at the sacred book *I Ching* may decide for John Cage his compositional choices. Perhaps he is right, and life, in its systematically unintentional chaos, does the same for each of us.

History may have a second thought about John Cage's music. But as a versatile personality standing at the crossroads of our time and pointing with determined indeterminacy at nowhere, he may, after all, make us discover a liberating sense in all the nonsense which is ours and which he pursued with stubborn fanaticism to its ultimate conclusion.

## The Performing Artist

The most obvious concurrence and most intimate relationship of talents take place in the performing arts. This reaches far back into antiquity when the cultural climate was propitious for it. But we also see interesting aspects of it in the Middle Ages when there was no theatre in our sense, when the church had turned the space around the altar into a stage and the clergy acted in liturgical plays. When some time later the mystery and miracle plays gave way to the enactment of Biblical scenes by members of the various guilds we find anonymous writers among the actors, who made their living as craftsmen and artisans. Their involvement in the impersonation of Biblical characters occurred as a response to a community need. At a later stage of the Middle Ages, the troubadours and minnesingers took the spotlight. These bards were poets, composers and singers in one person and, while coaching the minstrels of their train in their very personal art, they acted as teachers and directors at the same time. Moreover, as masters of etiquette they held great power and were the virtual dictators of fashion and manners.

Ever since man's evolution in historic times, he could not help play-acting as a means of escape from self and a means of realizing the more important aspects of his ego in relation to his fellowmen and the universe. Great acting is characterized by the ability to experience and reshape another human being beyond one's own self for the experience of the spectators, regardless of the method used for achieving this end. What matters solely is the actor's metamorphosis. No one knows better the process of such magical changes than the actor himself. If he has more than his expected share of imagination he will be inclined to improvise, to change his lines to suit this process within him, to write or rewrite his lines.

ACTORS AS PAINTERS

It has frequently occurred that actors took up painting. In most cases it is a manner of escape, a playful dabbling in a medium which seems to offer a safe refuge as remote as possible from the actor's real métier. He apparently finds relief in doing something that takes him away from the cruel scrutiny of the public which he must face in the very act of acting. When painting he probably glides into other tensions, but here at least he is by himself. Errors can be erased and corrected, he is free from stage fright. The privacy in being with colours and a canvas is a relief, no matter whether he takes it seriously, or only plays with the idea of getting his mind off the excitement on stage.

There are a few examples worth mentioning. A cultural curiosity was Mozart's brother-in-law, Joseph Lange (1751–1831). He was an actor and director at the Viennese National-theater, but he also painted and composed. His opera, *Adelheid von Pouthien*, was produced in various opera houses at the time. He also wrote an autobiography in which he says, 'The urge to draw, to shape, to act began to develop when I could not yet walk'. He claimed that he approached the stage from the viewpoint of the painter, who visualizes on stage the unfolding of a series of tableaux. History has taken little notice of him. But Joseph Lange lived at a time and in an environment which boasted some of the greatest creative minds. Among them he was at best a superior mediocrity that needed several outlets to prove his small calibre.

The legendary Iffland ring, which to this very day is handed down from one great German actor to the greatest

*Plate 14*

actor of the next acting generation, goes back to August Wilhelm Iffland (1759–1814). From the day when he played the part of Franz Moor in Friedrich Schiller's drama *The Robbers* at the Mannheim premiere in 1782, Iffland was recognized as an acting genius. He also wrote plays; as a matter of fact, sixty-three of his plays are extant. Goethe, as stage Direktor in Weimar, produced Iffland's plays more often than Schiller's or his own. Goethe recognized the 'realist' in Iffland and refers to Iffland's *Die Hagestolzen* as his 'best play, the only one in which he reaches from the prosaic into the sphere of the ideal'. Today Iffland's plays have accumulated the dust of oblivion and, together with several of his drawings, mainly of contemporary artists, are only of interest to the theatre historian.

*Plate 20*    Sarah Bernhardt also tried her hand at painting and sculpting. She had a certain facility in these pursuits, and her biographer, Cornelia Otis Skinner, rightly remarks that 'they served as outlets for her boundless energy. Also she was finding in them a source of additional income; but she was honest to realize that her works sold chiefly because of her signature on the bottom of each'. Sarah Bernhardt's case is here presented to show that a little talent in one area can of course go a long way when carried on the wings of fame accumulated in another field of activity. It would be a different matter, from an artistic and psychological viewpoint, had she strongly believed in her talent as a painter and sculptress.

What Sarah Bernhardt and many other artists may achieve in finding a minor artistic outlet is a shift of the burden of tension weighted so heavily at one point, into another channel. The change itself creates relief. Also, the power of self criticism is understandably weaker in the painting actor than in the actor on stage, if for no other reason than that in this avocational pursuit only surplus energy is used up.

Josef Kainz, a Viennese-born actor (1858–1910), was seen on many European stages and in New York, too. Toward the end of his life he fell passionately in love with drawing and painting. 'I am drawing every minute, and I have already done a few paintings', he wrote in 1909. He often referred to the 'harlot nature' of the acting profession, a feeling which may have led him to test himself in other media. That a man of his restless character would turn to writing for the stage, over which he had supreme command as an actor, was almost inevitable. He took his writing attempts very seriously. But the great actor in him recognized the insufficient results of the dramatist Kainz when he wrote: 'An ambition which will never be satisfied, deprives me of more energy than necessary'. He also translated from the English and French, but soon realized that 'Byron's poems cannot be translated', though he tried very hard to give them the right German phrasing and feeling. He was more successful with his translations of Byron's *Sardanapal*, Beaumarchais' *The Marriage of Figaro* and *The Barber of Seville*. One of his triumphs was his appearance as Figaro in *The Marriage*, in his translation and under his own direction. In this multiple function, it was the actor in Kainz who shaped the play, verbally and visually, for himself. We can often observe that the actor-turned-dramatist visualizes the written word or the directed stage image from the view-point of the actor, who remains the focal point in such a creative process.

ACTORS AS DRAMATISTS

Many actors have been tempted to write roles for them-selves, and to do so they had to write new plays. Since it cannot be doubted that the question: who was first, the actor or the dramatist? must be answered in favour of the actor, many of them have always sought to find the right material for themselves and their colleagues. In ancient Greece, the leader of the chorus was the most logical person to direct the chorus and to prepare the text. Of course, not everyone can be Thespis. But Aeschylus, Sophocles and Euripides were actors blcsscd with the rare gift of creating thoughts in dramatic form and of manipulating words easily. They rightly per-performed the duties of the director-choreographer of their own plays in which they also appeared from time to time. We know of Aeschylus that the masks and costumes he designed for *The Furies* possessed such frightening intensity that during the first performance a number of Athenian women are said to have given birth prematurely. In his youth, Euripides was a painter, the cup-bearer to a guild of dancers, and an athlete.

Sophocles, who was particularly endowed with beauty, had many talents besides being one of the world's greatest dramatists. He was carefully trained in music by the famous musician Lampros; he proved his acrobatic dancing skill in his play *Nausicaa* in which he was seen in a ball-juggling act long remembered by his contemporaries; he was an accom-plished actor, but due to the thinness of his voice – his only shortcoming – he often chose feminine roles. This would be proof enough of the genius who can excel in whatever he touches and in whatever he tests himself. To round off his achievements, Sophocles was also an ordained priest and,

78

13 After Filippo Carporali SALVATORE VIGANÓ

14 Joseph Lange ALEXANDER AND CAMPASPE

15   Edward Gordon Craig ISADORA DUNCAN

16   Vaslav Nijinsky DRAWING MADE AT ST MORITZ

17   Anna Pavlova PORCELAIN STATUETTE

18   Anna Pavlova in 'The Butterfly'

antonin Artaud
17 decembre 1946

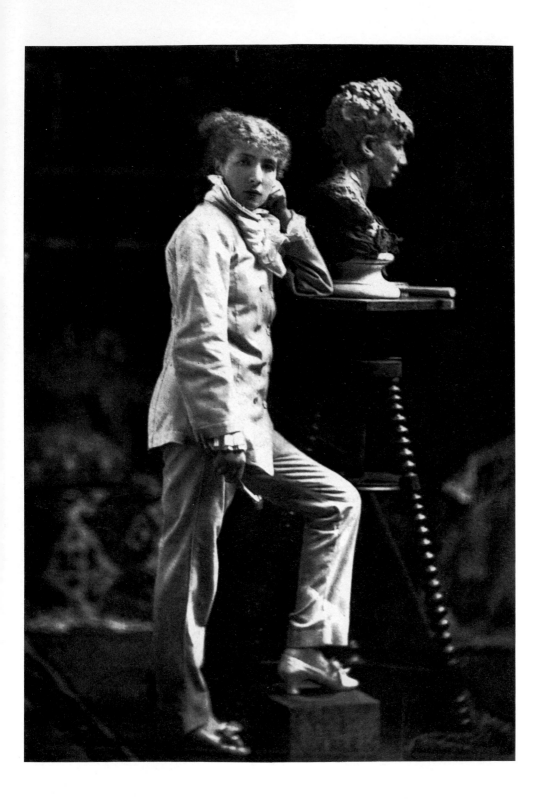

20  Portrait of Sarah Bernhardt with sculpture

without having any pronounced political convictions, he was twice elected to the Board of Generals who administered the civil and military affairs of Athens, and, moreover, he was a director of the Treasury Department which controlled the funds of the association of states known as the Delian Confederacy. He may rightly have been called 'happy in his long life, his fortunes, his talent', but his poetic genius knew about the horrors of life, about the anxieties and suffering of man. At the end of his career, which his contemporaries considered a total fulfilment of life, he could write: 'Not to be born is, past all prizing, best; but when a man has seen the light, this is next best by far that with all speed he should go from where he has come.' Such philosophic resignation at the end of his life makes his greatness more human and real.

Probably the best example of the multiple genius on stage can be found with the players of the *commedia dell'arte* which began to flourish in the fifteenth century and whose records show its popularity lasting well over two hundred years. This theatre of improvisation came into being as a badly needed antidote to the pastoral and rather stiff court dramas of the time. Each player was a certain character type which he remained throughout his career. Once the familiar figure of the Dottore, then the player remained always the Doctor of Bologna; the same held good for Arlecchino, Pantalone, Brighella, the Capitano, and the rest. They were stock characters with stock phrases and lines. Before the play went on they were told the bare outline of the happenings and had to create their own text spontaneously with the help of those inescapable lines which characterized their types. The results were improvised farces and crude comedies of manner. The acting, not the play, was the thing. It consisted not only of speaking and miming. These actor-playwrights had to be excellent dancers, acrobats, and fencers. The marvels of make-believe, of fun and laughter were their *raison d'être* on stage.

History records that Molière was a direct descendant of the *commedia dell'arte* players. And Molière, together with Shakespeare, open the *Reigen* of the many actors who turned dramatists. But it is the irony of history that few of those many actors-turned-playwrights after Shakespeare and Molière, down to Emlyn Williams and Noël Coward, established themselves as important writers of dramatic literature. Harold Pinter, who also began his career as an actor, may be the exception in our time.

Comedians have most often proved to have the best talent for converting what may originally be a gift for improvisation into playwriting. The most brilliant example is the Viennese comedian of the mid-nineteenth century, Johann Nestroy, whose genius in acting and writing was of equal calibre. In our own days, it is Peter Ustinov, whose parental lineage on both sides was blessed with many famous composers, writers, painters and actors and who himself climbed to impressive heights as an actor, playwright and director, who is highly musical and quite gifted as a draughtsman. It seems that in Peter Ustinov's case the intensity of talent, predestined by his chromosomes, could have gone in any direction into which the circumstances directed it. The brilliant conversationalist Ustinov makes us believe in a happy balance between the dramatist and actor as if almost the one would be less fulfilled without the other.

The shift from acting to writing has often occurred when the actor, obviously plagued by the theatre bug, recognizes his minor acting talent, which, however, is articulate and persuasive enough to find the verbal expression that he himself could never give a viable stage reality. His knowledge of the theatre, his familiarity with stage tricks tempt him to write for the theatre which, as one of the most immediate and ephemeral art forms, can take a great deal of punishment. In the 1960s, particularly in New York, the improvisational theatre, essentially devised and written by actors – sometimes with the assistance or in the presence of a notating writer – has celebrated a triumphant comeback. It may be a passing fad or of more momentous consequence. But, if nothing else, this so-called 'open theatre' is symptomatic of an age that sees little significance in and actually mistrusts the poetic and the printed word.

Or has this trend of the actor-turned-writer occurred in all ages because acting and playwriting are of all disciplines most intimately close to each other and, with the theatre being the impure art form it is, interdependent upon each other? Already in 1836 Heinrich Heine complained in his *The Romantic School*:

A great number of our actors are also dramatists and write plays for themselves. It is said that a careless utterance of Herr Ludwig Tieck brought about this misfortune. In one of his critiques he remarked that actors can always perform better in a bad play than in a good one. Based on such an axiom an endless number of comedians took to the pen, wrote plenty of tragedies, and sometimes it was made difficult to decide: did the vain actor write his play so badly with the purpose of being able to act well in it? Or did he act badly in his own concoction to make us believe the play was good? The actor and the poet whose relationship until now approximated one of colleagues (somewhat like the judge to the poor sinner), entered the phase of frank animosity. The actors tried to oust the poets from the theatre altogether under the pretence: they knew nothing of the demands of the stage, of the strong effects and theatre tricks. Only the actor has learned them while being on stage and he knows how to use them in his plays . . . This way the German actors have emancipated themselves from the poet and poetry itself . . .

I do not claim that a stage director must of necessity be an actor too, but, more often than not, the great stage directors started to work in the theatre as actors. The image of the stage director, who stamps his personality on a play, on a group of actors, or on an entirely new trend of his creation – as Constantin Stanislavsky or Erwin Piscator have done – is relatively new in the theatre world. It is a twentieth-century phenomenon anticipated by the many revolutionary new histrionic movements toward the end of the last century when the classical approach to stage presentations in general and to acting in particular had run their course. Before that time one only mentioned the work of a director when it was done by a famous actor.

There can be no doubt that directing a play is even more intimately related to acting than any attempt at playwriting. Apart from acting, directing is a special talent which, however, was often displayed by artists who showed a minor gift as actors. In many cases it may be arrived at through channels of frustration which frequently open up new channels of compensation. It is a way found from the rather recreative to more creative potentialities. The two most important image-makers, the above-mentioned Stanislavsky and Piscator, began their careers as actors. But so did Max Reinhardt, who started as a minor actor at Otto Brahm's *Freie Bühne*. André Antoine, the founder of the Théâtre Libre in 1887, the most significant new stage experiment of its time, was a clerk of a gas company and an amateur actor.

Bertolt Brecht was an interesting maverick, a born performer on stage and in life, who, from the very beginning, leaned toward writing and directing. He became known through his playwriting, and it was only later in life, when the East German government subsidized the Berliner Ensemble, that he returned to the tasks and problems of the director and actor, creating his theories and credos for the kind of epic theatre he visualized. How much the socio-cultural climate has to do with creativity and with the direction it takes in a specific discipline is proven by the creation of the epic theatre, Brecht or Piscator style, which came into existence as the most natural outgrowth of the confused era of the 1920s. And it could only have been born in defeated Germany while the fever of its moral and economic inflation was high.

In the case of Antonin Artaud (1895–1948), whose genius went beyond all concepts of theatrical realizations, the shift from the actor to director-playwright and revolutionary theorist was an isolated process although triggered by seeing the Balinese dancers. Without belittling such outside stimulation, it could be comfortably maintained that any other stimulus at that point of Artaud's life would probably have caused the change in him as well.

*Plate 19*

In order to help us find our own identity on stage, this philosophically inclined iconoclast returned to primitivism, as Picasso did before him and as the modern dancers did in Germany and America. Artaud rejected the Aristotelean as much as the epic theatre. On the one hand, his theory discarded the narrative style, the probing of man and his inner conflicts within given situations; on the other hand, it refuted the stress on social conditions, on painting a huge canvas of events bigger than man and on shocking the spectator into social awareness. Artaud wanted to go back to myth and magic in order to express on stage what is inexpressible through words, which he intended to eliminate as much as possible. He tried to expose the deepest layers of the human mind with the help of the physical language of gesture and movement supported by expressive shapes and light. He envisioned 'a theatre of cruel purgation', a theatre 'difficult and cruel for myself first of all' – hence his term, *Theatre of Cruelty*.

He gave the word cruelty a new connotation, seeing in it the life force, an implacable drive that makes things happen. The cruelty which he endured as a lifelong torture within himself, had aspects of a 'pure and detached feeling' that would reconcile us 'philosophically with Becoming'. Artaud's struggle was a struggle against our mechanized civilization and for finding the rhythm of our personal pulsebeat. To live and re-live life from the depths of existence was his aim, and he wrote: 'If I am a poet or an actor it isn't because I want to write or declaim poems but to live them.'

This is why this actor-dancer-poet tried to seize the spectator by the lapel of his despair. Artaud wanted to involve the spectator in an all-absorbing spectacle as if he were to witness a mass communal rite or a surgical excision. He was the first to visualize a theatre that would inundate the audience, capture the spectator's imagination by attacking his sensibility on all sides, a concept which became the motto of the avant-garde in the sixties.

There was a great deal of the compulsion of a madman in Artaud's approach to the theatre (and for many years he was confined in an asylum). But within the framework of the performing arts he is a prime example of a man whose creative concepts were all-embracing and who, though starting as an actor, broke through the confinement of all limitations, giving proof of a multiple vision par excellence.

DANCERS AS WRITERS, CHOREOGRAPHERS, AND PAINTERS

Artaud recognized movement as *the* primary artistic force and the magic of its potentialities as highly expressive and dramatic. The dance – so often referred to as the mother of the arts – has always had innumerable practitioners but has brought forth only a very limited number of creative talents, i.e. choreographers, who write the scenario and, so to speak, direct it. With the exception of the protean genius of Jean Cocteau, who also tried his hand at choreography, I know of no choreographer who would not have been a dancer first. The physical immediacy and the body as sole instrument of this art necessitate a thorough knowledge of what the body can do. In retrospect it seems that, similar to the actor-director relationship, many of the great choreographers have been minor talents as dancers, particularly in the ballet. However, I am inclined to think that, more often than not, these artists gave up dancing as soon as they discovered their choreographic gift.

Most dancer-choreographers of stature have been renowned teachers and a good many of them have been articulate in bringing to paper their thoughts and convictions on their art. In the letter-writing age of enlightenment, the choreographer Jean-Georges Noverre wrote his brilliant epistles against his contemporaries, his *Lettres sur la Danse et sur les* *Plate 13* *Ballets*. Salvatore Viganó, who crowned the work of Noverre in the early nineteenth century, is known as the creator of the choréodrame. He put Noverre's history-making innovations into the most dramatic stage realities.

Stendhal extolled Viganó as an unmatched genius and, with characteristic romantic exultation, thought that he could take his place next to Shakespeare. Viganó showed no special liking for the dance as a boy; in fact, he was more interested in literature, and critics of that period thought that he had the makings of a great poet. But his love of music, inherited from his mother, who was the sister of the well-known composer Boccherini, was even stronger in him. He began to compose at an early age, and an intermezzo of his was performed in Rome when he was only seventeen. Finally, however, he decided to make the dance his career. His is another case of genetic trends. His mother, father, and several uncles were dancers. In the light of this, it is understandable that Viganó as a boy first rejected following the career of his parents and close relatives. His non-dancing uncle Boccherini may have been a strong inspiration, or the open door of escape from having to be a dancer. After having proved himself in two other fields of activity, it was easier to accept the inevitable: a dancing career.

From 1790 to 1812 he toured the European capitals with his wife, Maria Medina. Theirs was a sensational success. When he became estranged from his wife, Viganó went to Milan where he choreographed at La Scala some of the most important ballets of the period. His poetic and musical abilities helped him in the creation of his ballets. Stendhal wrote about his working methods and reported from his observations of rehearsals that, if Viganó could not find a musical motif which expressed what he had in mind, he himself composed it.

Contrary to the trend of the period, the romantic dancers and choreographers in the nineteenth century apparently had no particular urge to express themselves in any other art form. The only rather restless and inquisitive mind belonged to Arthur Saint-Léon, who was famous as a dancer and violinist and who became an important choreographer: furthermore, he was one of those who tried to find a solution for the notation of the dance, about which he wrote in his work, *La Sténochorégraphie où l'art d'écrire promptement la danse.*

The rebellious artists around the turn of the century, and those who immediately followed them, showed great propensity for articulating their ecstatic feelings in more than one way. The dancers were no exception. In general, the modern dancer in his bare feet and with an open, expressive mind has been more easily articulate than the tradition-bound ballet dancer. Many of these dancers have discharged themselves well as speakers and writers, some of them have shown a natural talent for drawing and painting. Isadora Duncan, the first rebel in the days of the *fin de siècle*, possessed a thoroughly poetic nature with an innate feeling for music, movement,

*Plate 15*

88

and the word. She even was able to translate a certain lyricism of living into reality, to which her autobiography testifies. Isadora wrote with a catching rhythm and a contagious feeling of ecstasy. Some of it had the lilt of Walt Whitman's verses:

I see America dancing, and her dance will be clean!
I see America dancing, free, generous, compassionate, tender, brave, standing with one foot poised on the highest point of the Rockies, her two hands stretched out from the Atlantic to the Pacific, her fine head tossed to the sky, her forehead shining with a crown of a million stars.

That she did not write poetry was only due to the fact that so much of it went into her dances. Moreover, if anyone has ever succeeded in living poetry in its most flamboyant style and in ever-changing dramatic rhythm, it was Isadora Duncan.

For Isadora's compatriot and contemporary, Ruth St Denis, who fell in love with the mysticism of the Orient, dancing was a means to a much more important end. Feeling that our civilization was growing decadent because 'too many of us take from without instead of giving from within', she became a crusader for the sacred dance. She was an eloquent spokesman for her ideas and put some of them down as poems:

> *In terrible aloneness*
> *I have passed*
> *From dancer to the prophetess.*
> *The language of my prophecies*
> *Is still the dance,*
> *As in my former days,*
> *But now the words*
> *Are differently arranged . . .*
> *Not by earthly music*
> *Is my body moved and trembled,*
> *But by the Ever Presence.*

With the Bible in her head and a philosophy in her heart she was seen in many countries and on many continents with her Orientalized dances and her faith in the holiness of the unity of body and soul. Ruth St Denis was probably a better salesman for her ideas than a poetess, although many poems and pages of prose are proof of the easy flow of her pen. The word was a necessary extension to the limitations of her movements as a dancer. The genuine fervour of her religious quest forced her to brandish the word like a sword in front of a blind and deaf world.

How seriously the verbal expression was forced upon Ruth St Denis can be seen from the sheer quantity of her output as a writer. How playful – in contrast to it – was Anna Pavlova's creation of a few statuettes which she loved to shape. She knew not how to give them any facial expression, but they all were the narcissistic image of how this great ballerina saw herself moving. When she wanted advice and help to make her statuettes more perfect, she was told that 'they were so attractive just because they were made by an instinctive sensitiveness, and should not be corrected as they would then lose their charm', according to her husband, Victor Dandré, who went on to say: 'In my opinion it is these statuettes that give one the very idea of Pavlova; not by facial resemblance, for that she could not attain, but because she can be immediately recognized by the lightness of the figure and the grace of the movements.' Pavlova's desire to sculpt was a psychological need to visualize herself in plastic form.

*Plate 17*

The male dancer most often associated with her and as legendary a figure as she herself is Vaslav Nijinsky. He has gone into history as a symbol or myth, and he is also known to the man in the street as the dancer of that fantastic leap through the window in the ballet *The Spectre of the Rose*. But to know this alone is not to know Nijinsky, although it may characterize him as the most proficient dancer of all times. Only known to those more familiar with the art was Nijinsky's invaluable contribution as a choreographer. He was the first to use archaic, untraditional, angular, non-balletic movements and he anticipated the many experiments and changes in the *danse d'école* which were made in the decades following him. Nijinsky may have been the best dancer of his time, but he was a genius as a choreographer. Serge Diaghilev's instinctive sense of where a major talent lies was uncanny. He encouraged Nijinsky to choreograph *The Afternoon of a Faun* after having listened to the dancer's new and daring concept. Although Nijinsky excelled in what he was asked to dance by the famous choreographer Michel Fokine, he was in no way satisfied. He was possessed by an innate simplicity which rejected the idea of grace for grace's sake. His peasant-like mind told him to search for the expression of emotions by means of natural gestures and steps.

Nijinsky's case shows that in a man of genius multiple talents exist in a dormant state. Almost in unawareness, but certainly

22 Enrico Caruso CARICATURE OF CONDUCTOR GENNARO PAPI

23   Angna Enters APHRODISIAC – GREEN HOUR

24   Mary Wigman SKETCH OF 'TODESHAIN'

in a state of innocence, Nijinsky began to create a work of stunning difference from what he and his company, The Ballets Russes, were used to doing. A few years later, a schizophrenic condition benighted his mind. During moments of lucidity, he gave a wonderful account of his ability to draw and paint. It was in 1919 that Nijinsky felt that his nervous system was giving way from time to time. His condition prevented him from working on his art, from practising. He felt as if, having lost contact with himself, he longed more than ever to express himself. And in those weeks and months he channelled his visions into drawings and into the writings of his *Diary*.

*Plate 16*

His visualizations were of two different types: the delicate figure drawings in pencil, rhythmically graceful and moving in beautiful circles and curves; the other type were geometrically rhythmic, powerful, vivid colour abstractions, diametrically opposed to any graceful aspect. But both types leaned heavily on the circle, a fact readily interpreted by the psychoanalysts as an obvious sign of withdrawal. For Nijinsky the circle had had deep meaning as a choreographic symbol several years previously. With his sense for the archaic and primitive form he had employed the circle as often as he could and particularly in *The Rite of Spring*. Whatever he had done as a choreographer was the volcanic expression of a tortured soul haunted by strange images. Why should his drawings or paintings be different? Sir Herbert Read referred to them as works of art and not as proof of a pathological case when he wrote the preface to the catalogue for a Nijinsky exhibition in London in 1937. He saw in these works the automatic expression of the unconscious, so characteristic of surrealism which denies the principles of logic and reality and which has a psychic language, being the language of the artist's own inner or subjective reality:

. . . These drawings have a general characteristic which immediately suggests the fully conscious art of Nijinsky – his ballets. Their rhythm is a dancing rhythm. But far from assuming that the unconscious has retained traces of the discipline and knowledge acquired during the artist's conscious existence, I think we should rather conclude that the art which we admired in the dancer was all the time an expression of innate characteristics, of individual qualities within the unconscious itself. This is, after all, the only possible justification of the word 'genius'; for by 'genius' we mean precisely those qualities in an artist which cannot be taught or learnt, but are his from the hour of birth.

Nijinsky's *Diary* reads like a spiritual testament. It was written in hours of agony in which light and darkness fought within him. The book is distinguished by the prophetic language of a William Blake, it is the outcry of a tortured genius who escaped the mire of everyday life, the meanness of the commonplace, and who embraced mysticism wholeheartedly. 'A twinkling star is life – and a star that does not twinkle is death', Nijinsky wrote. 'I have noticed there are many human beings who do not twinkle.' In his writing as in most of his paintings we can see the uncontrolled flow of the unconscious mind, the surrealistic blueprint of a bleeding ego. 'Understand that I do not think when I write – I feel.'

There were many things which plagued Nijinsky's mind. He dreamt of ruining the Stock Exchange where the poor are deprived of their savings ('God wants me to win, and I am not afraid. He wants me to break the Stock Exchange . . .'); he dreamt of buying theatres so that he could give free performances for the people who could not afford to buy tickets; he dreamt of building a theatre in the round (an idea which goes back to primitive days); he saw serious danger in mechanical progress without man's soul keeping step with it; he spoke of love, and how God wants us to love; he spoke about the truth ('If I tell the truth, the whole truth, man will kill me'); he was continually afraid that people wanted to harm him, there was a Strindbergian *Inferno*-feeling about this persecution mania; and finally the Christlike suffering and the total embrace of God, with the last pages signed: 'God and Nijinsky' ('I want to write this book in order to explain what feeling is. Many will say that these are my opinions only, but I know that my point of view is the right one, because it comes from God. God is in me. I have made mistakes but I corrected them with my life. I suffered more than anyone else in the world'). Meister Eckhart, the German mystical theologian, said: 'God only expects one thing from you; that you go beyond yourself and allow God to be God inside you.' *The Diary of Vaslav Nijinsky* echoes this thought with great lucidity.

There have been many more dancers and choreographers in this century who have given us some volumes of interest. Ted Shawn, Serge Lifar, Pearl Primus, and Doris Humphrey wrote about dance and dancers with more than average skill. It is amazing that when dancers turn to writing, their most prosaic topics often show the touch of the poet, as if being a dancer presupposes innate lyricism. Mary Wigman wrote probably the most poetically valid book, *The Language of Dance*. In the first chapter she says:

*Plate 24*

94

The medium of creativity granted me was the dance, always and ever the dance. Therein I could invent and create. Therein I have found my poetry, have given shape and profile to my visions, have molded and built, toiled and worked on the human being, with the human being, and for the human being. It might very well be that I love the dance so immensely because I love life, because of its metamorphoses and elusiveness. Time and again I have felt enraptured by its 'die and arise'. To face life the way it approaches us, even to approve of it when it appears unbearable, to remain true to oneself and to obey 'the law that called us into being', to help accomplish the predestined changes of time, space, and form in ourselves – isn't all this the process of growing which we have to follow? To live life and to affirm it in the creative act, to elevate and glorify it? That is what I want to write about . . .

And about the artist's creativity she offers a few explanatory thoughts:

Creative ability belongs to the sphere of reality as much as to the realm of fantasy. And there are always two currents, two circles of tension, which magnetically attract one another, flash up and oscillate together until, completely attuned, they penetrate one another: on the one hand, the creative readiness which evokes the image; on the other hand, the will to act whipped up to a point of obsession, that will which takes possession of the image and transforms its yet fleeting matter into malleable working substance in order to give it its final form in the crucible of molding.

*Plate 23*

To catalogue Angna Enters' achievements would be to enumerate almost all the arts. She is a painter, mime, scene and costume designer, director, musician, and a writer of essays, plays, and novels. We can reduce all this to the three essential art forms which have occupied her 'in an unpremeditated progression and then all three simultaneously', as she says, to painting, writing, and miming.

Angna Enters feels that whatever she did, 'came about fortuitously. In my search by way of the written word to discover the classic line of life, and thus relate it to my images, I never thought one day I might try to be a writer. The writing happened accidentally, like the working in mime and painting – though now, looking back, I can see that all I did seemed to fall into logical progression consistent with my way of working – which is to plunge directly into whatever interests me'.

Geoffrey Holder, the West Indian dancer-painter, may be a good example of a man of many talents, partly nourished by natural instincts, partly channelled by learning and strict

Geoffrey Holder
Study

discipline. As a dancer he is stunning because of his improvisational and intense feeling for movement, and a very similar impulse is noticeable in his choreography. He has done some writing, composing, and acting as well as designing sets and costumes for ballet companies. At an early age he learned to paint. 'When my feet are not working, my hands are', he likes to say. While his feet move in an almost uncontrolled manner, his remarkable body moves with natural ease. In the performing arts, delivery, technique, and composition are never subjected to the same self-criticism and discipline as in Holder, the painter. When painting, he never permits his natural gifts to get the better of him. It is as if his alter ego were a disciplinarian, directing his hand and seeing to it that form and content preserve the intensity of his temperament and yet prevent his improvisational impulse from getting out of hand.

The list of creative artists who are basically dancers but feel the need to prove themselves in another art form at one point or another is endless. With most of them it is not so much a question of high artistic achievement as the realization of personal fulfilment.

In this age of specialization Alwin Nikolais is a rare artist who unified almost all forms of expression into one artistic image. He has used his multiple gifts with the purpose of creating the kind of total theatre he has envisioned. When we recall how much the cultural climate of the Renaissance cities contributed to the stimulation of the artistically gifted person, then the opposite extreme, the few stimuli available in the remote Connecticut town where he grew up, nevertheless nourished the dormant talents of Alwin Nikolais.

He was the youngest child of a large family and was left a great deal alone. The odd mixture of his Germanic and Russian parental background provided him with a Dionysian urge and an analytical mind. Music was the only art he was exposed to early in his life; it was respectable – a leftover from nineteenth-century bourgeois life – in his family and town to play the piano. But he also loved to play with a theatre box as a child, a favourite play object which instilled in him a three-dimensional vision. Looking back to the early years of his life, Alwin Nikolais thinks that even then – though not consciously –creativity *per se* was more important to him than the means. Together with his older brother he spent some months of the year in a university town in Massachusetts where he was exposed to the theatre. He was eleven or twelve years old when he felt that whatever went on on a stage was marvellous.

Some time later, an actor passing through his native town

made his take up acting while he began to paint and learnt to manipulate marionettes. And still in his formative years he took advantage of any opportunity to work with little theatre groups, a period in his life in which he learned a great deal about props, sets, and sound. To make a living after leaving school he became an accompanist for silent movies. This gave him a skill in musical improvisation.

In other words, Nikolais partly found and partly sought the opportunities and avenues open to him in order to find fulfilment for his needs to be creative in whatever medium. He practised each of them, he incessantly worked on himself. The circumstances of his life – the privilege most great talents have – helped him piece together organically what finally effortlessly turned into a multiple, unified creative effort. The theatre remained the focal point of his interest. His perception of the magic of the stage, his joy in the flexibility of illusions derived from it is still the same joy he felt as a young boy.

*Plates I, II*
His is a total theatre of motion, sound, light, colour, and shape. Therefore, besides acting as a choreographer, he also plays the part of a painter, sculptor and composer. One of his sayings is: 'I like to mix my magics'. He told me, 'Too much mystery has been taken away from us. Man recognizes a great blackness of the unknown facing him and he wants to be bombarded on all his senses. Only the reaction of the totality of our senses verifies a total experience'.

Alwin Nikolais
Doodle

# PART TWO: THE PAINTER WHO WRITES

# The Renaissance Genius

There were many tangible and intangible phenomena which crystallized into that many-faceted accomplishment of man known as the Renaissance. A new image of man was created by himself and reflected in his works and deeds. This rebirth took place as an awakening in the full blaze of light. 'Out of the thick Gothic night our eyes are opened to the glorious torch of the sun!' said François Rabelais (1490–1553), the archetype of the physician who, at heart, is a writer.

The ideal image of the new man was essentially derived from the Greek notion of man as the measure of all things, but with the power of *Moira*, the inevitability of the god's decisions, reduced to the inevitability of man's own nature, doing with him and for him whatever he chooses to do, whatever he wills. There was nothing he could not be or become, success or failure. 'Men are themselves the source of their own future and misfortune', wrote Leone Battista Alberti (1404–1472), one of the co-founders of the Italian Renaissance. His *De re aedificatoria* was the first printed book on architecture and, together with his buildings of pure classical style, was of great influence in spreading appreciation for antiquity. Alberti was one of the first universal geniuses peculiar to this period, an architect, painter, sculptor, musician, playwright, and humanist.

In the second year of the seventeenth century, Shakespeare was able to draw a vivid picture of Renaissance man in Hamlet, who addresses Rosencrantz and Guildenstern: 'What a piece of work is a man! how noble in reason! how infinite in faculty! in form and moving how express and admirable! in action how like an angel! in apprehension how like a god! the beauty of the world!' Such belief of man in himself had to lead him on to the path of self-fulfilment. Breaking the fetters of medievalism and trying to find the way back to the grandeur of antiquity, Renaissance man, however, never broke with his immediate past. In learning to believe in himself, he attempted to reconcile the contemplative man of the past with the man of action; he tried to divorce theology from politics, to search for a way to an intensified secular existence without denying God. Marsilio Ficino (1433–1499), priest, physician and scholar, the central figure of Neoplatonism, made of Plato's thoughts a philosophy of love and beauty.

Sensing the beauty of the world and discovering the godlike power in his hands, Renaissance man pushed open all gates for his own insatiable drives to prove himself, to best his fellow-men, and to glory in his own greatness. Leonardo expressed the irrepressible ambition ruling his age when he said: 'Wretched is the pupil who does not surpass his master'. The medieval introspection turned into a curiosity to learn, to find through logic and observation, to be instructed while being entertained. Experimentation laid the groundwork for the multiplicity of creativity.

This spirit created such men as Paolo dal Pozzo Toscanelli (1397–1482), who lived immersed in his studies as cosmographer, mathematician, and physician. It is assumed that his map of the world was used by Columbus on his voyage in 1492. That very year Pietro Aretino (1492–1556) was born, *Plate 27* son of a cobbler, a man whose life exemplified the Machiavellian daring that dominated the political and social life. Living by his uncanny instincts and on his merciless wit, Aretino wrote:

I am a free man. I do not need to copy Petrarch or Boccaccio. My own genius is enough. Let others worry themselves about style and so cease to be themselves. Without a master, without a model, without a guide, without artifice, I go to work and earn my living, my well-being, and my fame. What do I need more? With a goose quill and a few sheets of paper I mock the universe.

Early in his life Aretino acquired some knowledge in the art of painting, but his fame rests on the 'alchemy of his pen'. He lived, as he put it, 'on sweat of black ink'. But the sweating was done by his victims, whom he blackmailed with exposure of their private lives. Titian, whose paintings he sold to potentates and the rich nobility, was drawn to him and painted him many times. Michelangelo flattered him in self-defence, popes and princes feared the power of his pen. He was called the first bohemian and he certainly was the first gossip columnist and yellow journalist. To him there was nothing sacrosanct. But he was an excellent playwright, letter-writer, and the greatest erotic sonneteer of all times, a writer who turned from classic tradition to become a modern realist. Scorning society while profiting from its weaknesses

25  Albrecht Dürer ADAM AND EVE

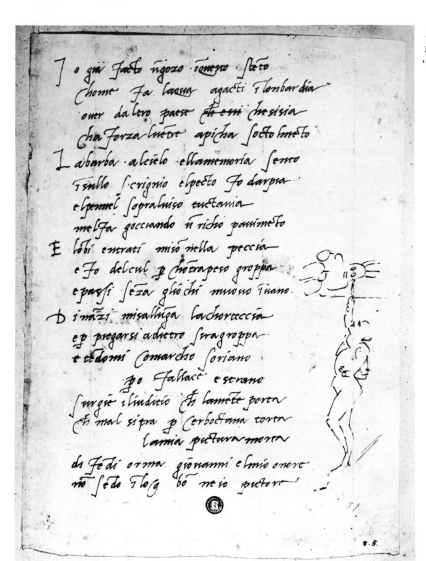

I o gia facto ūgozo ī mezo stēto
chome fa lacqua agacti ī lonbardia
ouer daltro paese chessisia
cha forza luētre apicha soctol mēto

L abarba alcielo ellamemoria sēto
īnullo scrignio elpecto fo darpia
elpennel sopraluiso tuctauia
mel fa gocciando ū ricco pauimēto

E lobi entrati misō nella peccia
e fo delcul p chotrapeso groppa
e passi sēza gliochi muouo īuano

D imāzi misallūga lachoraccia
ep piegarsi adietro sragroppa
e tēdomi comarcho soriano

po fallacē e strano
surgie īliudicio che lamēte porta
che mal sipra p cerboctana torta

lamia pictura morta
di fedi orma giouanni e lmio onore
nō sēdo īlo⸳g bō ne io pictore

27    Titian PIETRO ARETINO

29 Giorgio Vasari
PORTRAIT OF BENVENUTO CELLINI

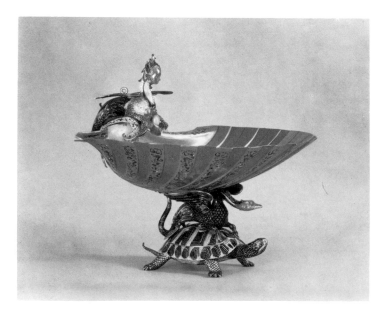

30 Benvenuto Cellini (?) THE ROSPIGLIOSI CUP

and corruption, he reflected the Borgia image of the Renaissance. Aretino lived a free, rich life, giving its sordid greatness a gesture of grandeur. He died laughing too vehemently about a bawdy joke.

It was no longer the Church alone which acted as the patron of the artist. The many small and large courts in Italy, the many cities growing in importance, competed with each other to show off their riches. The patrons endeavoured to cover themselves with honours and to advance their prestige as much as the artists did. But among the Italian patrons social snobbery was a dominant feature for a long time. They were prejudiced in favour of the scholar and poet, the man who knew Latin and could turn a phrase with elegance. He was invited for dinner, but not the painter and sculptor.

However, with the explorations came the complete re-orientation of the craftsman who worked with brush and chisel. He had to take to mathematics and physics to study the laws of perspective, he had to study anatomy in order to do justice to the needs of realism with which he began to approach the new aesthetic principles. *Nolens volens*, the Renaissance craftsman gradually combined encyclopedic learning and practical versatility which made him acceptable to the upper classes as an equal of the humanists. Embracing universality, as he did, he too became an *uomo universale*. And at the height of the Renaissance it was no longer the princes who bestowed favours on the artist, but the artist who granted a favour to the princes, potentates or popes by accepting a commission.

Of course, the encyclopedic knowledge and its reflection in artistic accomplishment was often troubled by dilettantism. With the exception of the extraordinary examples of Renaissance genius, most artists were better equipped in one field than in the many others they practised with equal fervour. Architecture, then based on such humanistic prerequisites as a thorough knowledge of Vitruvius' works, is a case in point. Most artists took up the architectural profession in their careers, and this was less due to a need for maturity than to the fact that this art was no longer acquired through practical study but through an academic education. To know about architecture had also become an intellectualized social game, like the habit of reacting to the slightest intellectual challenge with the writing of a sonnet. Most patrons were dilettante architects as they were dilettante poets. Sometimes this made the life of the real artist more difficult. On the other hand, it brought about an atmosphere which furthered the creative impetus and produced a general feeling of humanistic and artistic well-being. This was the mood of the time, and the *uomo universale* its unique and attractive window display.

This situation is best documented by Albrecht Dürer's (1471–1528) reaction when, in the autumn of 1494, he ventured across the Alps to Italy. He found his colleagues among the humanists, as he said, and not among the craftsmen. It was no doubt the humanistic influence of Italy that inspired Dürer to express himself verbally. There are three theoretical books in which he proves to be the northern counterpart of Leonardo da Vinci; furthermore, the diaries of his journeys and the records of his researches, the family chronicles and letters all testify to his verbal power. In his *Book of Memories* (Gedenkbuch), Dürer tells us of a dream with apocalyptic vision:

I saw how much of the big waters fell down from heaven. And all this fell to the ground only about four miles from me with such ferocity, with such tremendous rushing and gushing, drowning the entire land. I was so gravely frightened that I woke up, but then more waters came down . . . And some of the water fell far away, some of it nearer, and it came from so high above that in my thoughts I saw it fall but slowly. But as the water that first fell to the ground came close by, as it fell with such speed, wind and sweep, I was frightened and it was then that I woke up so that my entire cadaver trembled, and it took me long ere I came to . . . May God turn all things to the best.

*Plate 25*

Although he was a Renaissance genius, Dürer's entire mentality had the imprint of medievalism and was strongly keyed to the word of the gospels. The various sequences of his pictorial narrative of the Passion are the loud confession of his human and artistic experiences. Dürer, who had started out by learning the craft of a goldsmith from his father, had a very clear image of his own greatness, also characteristic of the Renaissance artist. In later years he saw himself as the reformer and innovator of the art of his country, and he reflected a great deal on what he was doing and why he did it.

Twice he went to Italy, which was then the country in which man was able and free to discover his potentialities. His Gothic-oriented world, with its disparity between body and soul, reality and symbolism, felt the impact of the Italian painter's sensuous approach, his harmony and ease of form, his realization of the classical ideal of beauty. But Dürer's pondering Nordic mind could never quite make its own what the heavens and the cultural climate of Renaissance Italy gave its artists with their birth certificate: the inner freedom with which to find the rhythmically motivated and harmonious *Gestalt* of man and his world. Giorgio Vasari recognized this to some extent when he wrote: 'If Dürer had been born in Tuscany and had he been able to study the Roman ruins as we did, then as he is now the best painter of the Germans he would have become the best painter of our country.'

There could be no better proof of the importance which the cultural climate can exert on the creative talent and on the multiplicity of creativity than the comparison between the atmosphere in Italy and Germany at that time. Dürer felt the difference between his position within the rigid order of the Nuremberg guilds and the creative freedom and the varied artistic opportunities of his Italian confrères, when he exclaimed in one of his letters: 'O, wie wird mich noch der Sunnen frieren, hie bin ich ein Herr, doheim ein Schmarotzer' – Oh, How I shall shiver for the sun. Here I am a lord, at home a parasite.

LEONARDO'S UNIVERSALITY

There are few men in western civilization who have so caught our imagination that an astounding number of volumes have been written about them: Jesus, Napoleon, Shakespeare, Goethe, and Leonardo. Far beyond their accomplishments, man's interest was aroused as much by the mystery of their secret power as by the secret power of their mystery.

Leonardo da Vinci (1452–1519) is the prime example of the artist as scientist and the scientist as artist. Combining artistic talent and scientific knowledge, he stands apart from all other geniuses, and this in spite of his fragmentary oeuvre. It is hardly imaginable that such universality in any one genius could have appeared at any other time than the Renaissance.

He left us less than ten paintings, some not quite finished, others, such as the *Last Supper*, fading while he was still alive.
*Plate 28* But there are many of his peerless drawings. Whatever fascinated his restless mind – from the study of horses and heads to that of drapery, the curling locks of hair or the play of light on a skull – was pursued by him in sketches, sometimes annotated by phrases or whole paragraphs in his notebooks which, more than anything else, are the key to his personality. Odilon Redon said: 'I have loved and shall always love the drawings of Leonardo: they are like the essence of life . . .'

Many of these drawings were sketches made for paintings he never started. Or he would begin a painting and then abandon it. Leonardo's mind was so rich that he was easily tempted to try many things. And the world has never quite forgiven his genius for having behaved like one. A great deal of psychological probing and twisting has been applied to the fact that the commissioned paintings had to be parted with, whereas most of his drawings remained in his possession. Sir Kenneth Clark speaks of Leonardo's 'inborn distaste for finality'. Finality also meant separation to Leonardo, and separation, death.

Twice he planned an equestrian statue, one of his great unfulfilled dreams. One he prepared for Lodovico Sforza when in the Duke's service in Milan. While procrastinating over its execution, the model was destroyed by Gascon soldiers. The casting of the monument would have cost a large sum of money, and the bronze readied for it was finally turned into guns.

Toward the end of his life Leonardo planned another equestrian statue, one of the then famous Captain Gian Giacomo Trivulzio, but nothing came of it. But as Vasari tells us, Leonardo 'showed his powers as a sculptor in the three bronze figures over the north door of San Giovanni'. Many drawings of plans and elevations for domed churches reflect Leonardo's interest in architectural problems, and about 1488 he worked on a model for the dome of the cathedral at Milan.

His literary work consists of a mass of fragments. The contents of his manuscripts at Milan, Paris, Windsor, and London prove the wide range of his interest in science and machinery, his literary mind and philosophical bent; they reveal him as an anatomist, mathematician, chemist, geologist, astronomer, botanist, geographer, physicist. Since his focal point in life was painting, we would expect him to outline his theories on the art of painting, and he did so in his *Trattato della pittura*. He was interested in music, played the lyre, had a pleasant singing voice and was also skilled in improvising verses. He arranged festivities, the trionfi for his lords, with the eyes of a painter and sculptor. There was hardly anything in which he was not interested, and all the things he did were done with surprising ease and a sense of perfection.

Vasari is not always the most reliable source, but he was Leonardo's contemporary – he was eight years old when Leonardo died – and must have learned about da Vinci from those who were close to him. Vasari stresses that Leonardo was handsome in appearance, that his penetrating mind could comfort and persuade, and that he was physically strong enough to withstand any violence. After having praised him for 'his many wonderful gifts', he adds in parenthesis, 'although he accomplished far more in words than in deeds'.

Vasari's description of Leonardo's last hour, in which he admitted 'he had offended God and mankind by not working at his art as he should have done', opened the endless flood of reproaches for having whetted our appetite without having given us enough to satisfy it, and the many investigations and speculations as to why Leonardo had done this.

A great deal has been made of Leonardo's illegitimacy, his lefthandedness, the mirror writing and homosexual tendency. His copious notes, of pertinency the very moment they were written, flashes of thoughts caused by or related to incidental events of the day, ideas resulting from meditation and observation, have now been closely scrutinized and analysed. The two most well-known men who tried to probe Leonardo's psyche and mind from the vantage point of our time were Sigmund Freud and Paul Valéry. Their analyses evoked a host of other treatises taking issue with theirs. And there is understandably not one art historian who, in his way, did not try to illuminate the artist and man.

It is as easy as it is dangerous to base analysis and conclusion on some known facts in the history of a man and on some of his utterances. It is very likely that Leonardo regarded his father as a person who neglected him. He may have identified with him to the extent that he neglected and abandoned his own children: his paintings. The lack of paternal authority may have helped to make his mind roam beyond all boundaries and fed his instinct to search for the unknown. Moreover, his over-eroticized relationship with his mother Caterina, a servant, are some of the strongest features in Freud's portrait of the master, with all of them contributing to Leonardo's neurosis, his inability to act decisively, as well as to his pursuit of knowledge and his versatility.

Paul Valéry, also fascinated by the ambivalence in Leonardo, by his Hamlet-like irresolution and indecision, relates the constant shift of focus in Leonardo's work to the concept of continuity. Valéry saw a singleness of purpose and unity of thought at the basis of the impressive variety of Leonardo's endeavours. Valéry came to the conclusion that Leonardo's miraculous mind was able to perceive an infinity of relations in whatever he saw.

We must not neglect the fact that, at the age of twelve or thirteen, Leonardo was apprenticed to Andrea del Verrocchio (1435–1488) and spent the following twelve years – his formative years of life – with this master. Verrocchio was a painter, sculptor, architect, engineer, and goldsmith. He was not only a great artist, but also a thinker and philosopher who, in Socratic manner, asked many questions and, in un-Socratic manner, pressed for answers. It was here, in a very congenial environment, that Leonardo's eyes were focused on a variety of artistic, aesthetic, and philosophic problems. It was also in Verrocchio's workshop that Leonardo's mechanical tendencies were fostered. And a desire to emulate the master has ever played a dominant role in Leonardo's life.

Whether or not we see in his preoccupation with flight a sex wish and consequence of repressed sexuality, the fact remains that a desire to fly has always occupied man's mind. Why should a curious and inventive mind whose drawings range from a mechanical excavator to an automatic file cutter not think of building a flying machine?

Leonardo's intense interest in water is only revealing when considered with the generally misanthropic trend in his notebooks. We find similes with water when he speaks of the human soul or of the organism of man or of the flowing of time. In essence, he saw the basis of all phenomena in change and movement, in the continuum of eternal flow. But drawings of water finally reach the stage of cataclysmic destruction in his old age.

There must have been moments in his life when melancholy threw him into despair and when he felt alienated in a world in which the cruelty of man to man hurt his sensibility. With the prophetic power of a poet, with the fury of a King Lear gone mad and talking to the elements, he translated the Renaissance ruthlessness into terms still fitting our own age:

Creatures shall be seen upon the earth who will always be fighting one with another with very great losses and frequent death on either side. These shall set no bounds to their malice; by their fierce limbs a great number of the trees in the immense forests of the world shall be laid level with the ground; and when they have crammed themselves with food it shall gratify their desire to deal out death, affliction, labours, terrors, and banishment to every living thing. And by reason of their boundless pride they shall wish to rise towards heaven, but the excessive weight of their limbs shall hold them down. There shall be nothing remaining on the earth or under the earth or in the waters that shall not be pursued and molested and destroyed, and that which is in one country taken away into another, and their bodies shall be made the tomb and the means of transit of all the living bodies which they have slain. O Earth! what delays thee to open and hurl them headlong into the deep fissures of thy huge abysses and caverns, and no longer to display in the sight of heaven so savage and ruthless a monster?

Another beautiful passage in his notebooks has been considered a meditation on life and death:

Behold now the hope and desire of going back to one's own country or returning to primal chaos, like that of the moth to the light, of the man who with perpetual longing always looks forward with joy to each new spring and each new summer, and to the new months and the new years, deeming that the things he longs for are too slow in coming; and who does not perceive that he is longing for his own destruction. But this longing is in its quintessence the spirit of the elements which, finding itself imprisoned within the life of the human body, desires continually to return to its source. And I would have you know that this same longing is in its quintessence inherent in nature and that man is a type of the world.

I see in this passage Leonardo's wish to speed up time, his fear and inability to cope with the constant pressures from outside and the threat of disorganization. His impatience with the slow process of growth and change coupled with an insatiable longing for change lay at the root of his restlessness, driving him from one unfinished task to another. Perfectionism and the setting of unattainable goals invited frustration, which added fuel to the inner fire of impatience. Then, his interest in whatever he did was soon exhausted, and he had to move on to something else, looking for fresh stimuli.

In spite of his inner struggles I do not see any real separation between art and science in Leonardo's mind. He could not draw a body before making a detailed anatomic study, and he could only create the picture of a battle after having been involved in an exact study of clouds of dust and whirlwinds, the geometric and dynamic progression of movement. Leonardo contended, with passion, that painting is a scientific activity and, at the same time, he claimed that painting is poetry made to be seen. The visionary and researcher in him were tied to each other, unified. In this light I see Sir Kenneth Clark's remark: 'Leonardo's mind passed without warning, and almost without consciousness, from fact to fantasy, from experience to imagination'. And vice versa, I would add. But it is the dreamer and visionary who leads the realist and scientist. There is a passage in Leonardo's notes: 'Since the eye is the window of the soul, the latter is always in fear of being deprived of it'. The visionary is always afraid of being unable to realize his dream. The quote is a poetic image in which death and blindness are equated in a traumatic manner, but through which also his realization of the total fusion between the inner and outer eye, between vision and sight, provides some understanding of his unified mind.

If prolificacy most often goes hand in hand with genius, then Leonardo is certainly the outstanding exception. What there is of his work either embraces the artistic achievement of the age while heightening it in a climactic and very personal way, or it delineates a final breakthrough which must be viewed in connection with his scientific alter ego.

With the exception of Ernst Cassirer, who sees in Leonardo the prototype of a modern scientist, the concensus is that Leonardo is at best no serious link in the development of science. Some of his inventions were directed toward immediate practical application, but mostly they were dreams to be realized in a remote future. Whatever his reasons were for turning away from the most important invention of his time, the printing press, the fact remains that there are no drawings or notes which show his interest in improving an invention which gave the world eyes to read – except the one reference among his anatomical notes, 'il modo di ristemparlo' (the manner of reprinting it), and a pejorative reference to printing in his *Trattato della pittura:* 'Questa non fa infiniti figliuoli, come fa li libri stampati', (It [painting] does not beget infinite progeny like printed books).

Leonardo owned a number of books. Did he pay so little attention to the printing and engraving process because of his lack of formal education or because he never seriously thought of writing books? Was he frightened of the finality of the printed word just as he feared to finish a painting? He played with the thought of writing a treatise or of collecting his thoughts jotted down in his notebooks over the years: 'To arrange them in order in their proper places according to the subject of which they will treat.' Apparently he even thought of collecting his tales, jests, and fables in the form of a book since one of his notes says, 'I will create a fiction which shall express great things'. But he never got around to doing it, and all his ideas remained fragmentary and aphoristic. ('Experience does not err; it is only your judgement that errs in expecting from her what is not in her power.')

His northern counterpart, Albrecht Dürer, was far more practical and organized. He arranged his thoughts and not only prepared the material to be printed, he did his own printing. Instead of producing a single drawing as Leonardo did, Dürer realized that a woodcut or engraving would make it possible to reach a hundred and more buyers with the same effort. Dürer established himself as printer, engraver, and bookseller. Each of his books bears the imprint: *Printed in Nuremberg by Albrecht Dürer, the painter.*

'The love of anything is the fruit of our knowledge of it, and grows as our knowledge becomes more certain', Leonardo wrote. Then, could he not trust his knowledge to live between the two proverbial covers? In comparison with Dürer, Leonardo was the more profound, even though impractical thinker. Like a bohemian, he did not care about the material end of whatever he did. He reacted like a dreamer and rebel, who states the cause of his discontent, but is too busy dreaming of truth and beauty.

His great gift was to record, as the first scientific researcher, every step of his pioneering ventures, to realize the intricate interrelationship of nature, its structure, mechanism, and deep revelations, with the arts and with philosophy. When to see is to be a poet, in Ibsen's definition, then Leonardo certainly was one of the greatest poets. To see the secret, the mystery behind natural appearances made him say: 'Paint the face in such a way that it will be easy to understand what is going on in the mind'. His demands on the artist are as unlimited as the creative power of nature, and it is in this light that Leonardo attributes the potentiality of a God to the artist: 'If the painter wants to behold beautiful things that he will fall in love with, he is the master who can create those things, and if he wants to see monstrous things that terrify, or comical and laughable or even piteous, then he is lord and God over them.'

The abundance of wonders of the world turned him into a fanatical observer. There is a remark in his notebooks, isolated, unexplained, the lonesome birth of a fragmentary thought: 'The sun does not move'. It was written long before Copernicus published his work, *De revolutionibus orbium coelestium*, in 1543. By then Leonardo had been dead for twenty-four years.

Leonardo scribbled on page after page of his notebooks during his later years: 'Tell me if anything at all was done'. A man of his analytic abilities must have been well aware of his potentialities and limitations. When therefore he questioned himself, he may have thought less of the few more paintings he might have done than of discipline and distraction ('Small rooms discipline the mind; large ones distract it'), of nature which 'is full of infinite causes that have never occurred in experience'. Or he may have contemplated once more what he had written previously: 'Where the spirit does not work with the hand there is no art.'

The totality of his personality made Leonardo a unique figure in the history of the world's achievement, in being the man whose mere existence illuminates the development of mankind. And when the full measure of his universal greatness is obscured by his failings as a human being, when the enigma of his versatility has been probed and interpreted and is left yet unsolved, Leonardo can easily silence his admirers and detractors alike with the simple words he once wrote: 'Naturally nature has so fashioned me.'

And there he goes by the grace of God, the archetype of this book, the most magnificent failure whose greatness has put us all to shame with so little that is so much.


MICHELANGELO'S SONNETS

Michelangelo was recognized and honoured as a poet by the Florentine Academy, which accepted him as a member, although he never thought of himself as a professional poet. When he grew up, the writing of sonnets and madrigals was in high fashion. The choice of the then newly awakened intelligentsia was between Dante, who could neither be imitated nor emulated, and Petrarch, who had inadvertently opened the floodgates to a deluge of facile sonneteers. An abundance of verses added to the visual lustre of the time, but little of what was written was poetry.

Dante was to the Italians of the fifteenth and sixteenth centuries the stern moralist of the past, and his work was viewed as the crowning testament of the Middle Ages, which they thought were better forgotten. It was Petrarch and his imitators who expressed best the mood of a people who had only recently discovered the joy and beauty of life. As a young man Michelangelo had heard Dante's echo through the thundering sermons of Savonarola and, in spite of his Renaissance dream of visual grandeur, there was something in him that was decidedly Dantesque.

Although Michelangelo employed the poetic forms then in fashion, sonnets, madrigals, octave stanzas or those in terzarima and some quatrains, they were different in form-feeling and melodic quality from those of his contemporaries. So were his thoughts. He rarely fell into the trap of pastoralizing, but where he could not withstand the lilt of the Petrarchan imitators, he became insecure. He added a note to a sonnet sent to Luigi Riccio:

Master Luigi, the last four lines of the above eight of the sonnet I sent you yesterday contradict themselves, so please send it back to me, or insert these in place of those, so it will be less awkward, and you polish it for me.

Or a telling remark accompanying a madrigal to Riccio reads:

Master Luigi, please send me the last madrigal, which you don't understand, so that I can polish it, because the squib carrier, who is Urbino, was so prompt that he didn't let me look it over.

His writing is, as he admitted, 'rough and rugged'; it shows an impatience with imperfection which often makes his poems appear fragmentary. Beauty in its perfection was all he looked for everywhere, and we must not forget that it was he who said that 'beauty is the purgation of superfluities'.

*Terribilità* was the word with which Giorgio Vasari described the work of this Titan, who considered himself a sculptor first and last, even adding the epithet *scultore* to his signature. Terrifying is the passion and fury which emerges from his work, and some of it overflowed into poetic lines which were written next to sketches, on the book of drawings, or on letters he received. The forming of shapes was foremost in his mind. To him God was a sculptor when he gave shape to Adam. This is why even his verbal expressions have a sculptural feeling, as in a poem on his father's death:

> *My brother's memory is painted in my mind,*
> *But yours is sculpted deep within my heart.*
>
> *It pales my face and pains my wound*
> *And yet, as for the debt, I feel quite calm.*
> *He paid so much for little. You had it all consumed.*
> *We must not mind to pay this debt when old.*

The following poem was written while Michelangelo painted the ceiling of the Sistine Chapel. Vasari wrote in his *Life of Michelangelo* that this work was done 'with utmost unpleasantness for he had to stay with his head up, and so badly had he ruined his vision that he could read letters and look at drawings only by raising them up above his head; and this lasted several months and I wonder how he could bear all that discomfort'. The poem is entitled: TO GIOVANNI, THE

*Plate 26*   ONE FROM PISTOIA, of whom little is known.

> *And now I have a goitre from this strain*
> *Like cats in Lombardy, or wherever it may be,*
> *From drinking dirty water in large quantity.*
> *My belly is pushed up as far as to my chin.*

*My beard is turned to the stars, the head*
*Pinned to the shoulder, I grow a harpy's breast;*
*And colour dripping from my brush*
*Has made my face a floor of many stains.*

*My loins pushed deep into my paunch*
*And my behind used as a counterweight,*
*And without seeing where I go I move.*

*In front of me my skin is being stretched*
*While in the back it lies in wrinkles and in knots*
*And I am bent like an Assyrian arch.*

*And yet my vision ought to grow,*
*Borne in the mind, however crooked and peculiar;*
*You cannot shoot a gun that isn't straight.*

*Giovanni, come and help to make*
*My painting live, my honour too with it.*
*This place is bad; I know I am no painter.*

Most of Michelangelo's poems were written at a ripe age, and therefore it is to be expected that death and old age will appear frequently as subject matter. When almost eighty years old, he wrote to Vasari: 'Dear friend, you too will probably say I am an old fool for wanting to write sonnets; but since many accuse me of senility, it is my duty to write'. And in a sonnet addressed to Vasari, the old man tries to account for his doings and realizes the many mistakes he has made in the name of his imagination and art. He also recalls the feelings and thoughts so full of gaiety and emptiness while being in love, and then ends the sonnet with the lines:

*To paint, to sculpt no longer stills the soul*
*Which now, returning to the only love,*
*Sees in those arms nailed to the cross its goal.*

The most often recurring motifs in his poems are God, love, beauty, and his own work. Christian faith, with a touch of medieval asceticism and the terrifying fear of the two deaths of body and soul, are curiously mixed with a strong sense of Greek fate.

Also, his concept of love is not easily definable. Love and beauty seemed to have been interchangeable to him, for we must reconcile his admiration for the male body – as exemplified by his friendship with many young men and as reflected in his work – with his ambivalent relationship to the most famous woman of his time, Vittoria Colonna. He met her when he was sixty-three. He was exalted as much by her spiritual qualities as by her attractive appearance.

To him Platonic love was not a trite conventionality hiding frustration behind a chivalrous gesture; it was an agonizing struggle against the temptations of the ultimate in reality because he could only see lasting beauty on a spiritual level. And if he refers to her even in the masculine gender he wants to express that she transported him beyond mere corporeality. It was said that in her presence he became a changed man, her magnetic power brought out the most tender feelings in him. His passion for her was often referred to as calm and noble. He felt he could come closest to the poetry of her being through the poetry he had in himself. In a madrigal addressed to her he said:

> *A God speaks through a woman's voice:*
> *And listening to her lips and*
> *To his words has made me such*
> *A man as never to be mine again.*
> *And ever since she stole me*
> *From myself I feel but pity*
> *For the wretched thing still left in me.*
> *The beauty of her face can take*
> *Me on a flight in vain desire*
> *So that all other beauty pales like death.*
> *O Lady, you who take the souls*
> *Through flame and water to their happiness,*
> *Help that I myself may not return to me.*

There are striking images in his poems in which we can see his mind repress flashes of sensual passion, as the beginning of a sonnet to Tommaso Cavalieri:

> *Violent passion for inspiring beauty*
> *Is in itself no mortifying error*
> *If, in a gracious mood, the heart is left*
> *To feel the piercing message of the holy missile.*

Reading Michelangelo's poems – he must have written many more which were lost and of which we only know from the few lines quoted by others – one cannot help sensing the tremendous struggle through which he must have gone. The medieval concept of the sin-crushed self was still alive in him and freed itself in the most personal and often fragmentary creations which, because of their violent power and disarming humanness, have such universal appeal and are unique even among the many great works of the Renaissance. Ice and fire were some of his favourite images, and so were hammer and

117

stone, the powers that defy man's will and feelings and challenge man's power to overcome them.

Michelangelo wanted very much to be a part of the humanistic circle of his time, and his acceptance as a poet by the Florentine Academy must have been a source of great satisfaction to him.

Several factors seem to have played their part in inducing him, the sculptor, painter, and architect, to write. There was a gentle lyricism locked within him for which he found no outlet when forcing stone and marble to yield the monumental figures of his imagination or when ceilings or murals retold the great phases of human destiny. There was his strong feeling for nature, his relationship to his family, to men and to Vittoria Colonna, his thought-feelings about such abstract notions as happiness, dreams, and death, which all evoked in him a need to put them into words.

The ceiling of the Sistine Chapel illustrates the Neoplatonic doctrine, 'so dear to Michelangelo, and so often expressed in his sonnets, that life must be a progression from the servitude of the body to the liberation of the soul', as Sir Kenneth Clark put it. Michelangelo was full of thoughts and theories that also found their way into his poetry, which often is didactic in its thought-provoking reflections as much as it is a verbal comment on his work.

In spite of his indifference to physical hardships and of his determination and willpower, he suffered from irrational fear which made him run away from confrontations with himself at times. Michelangelo seemed to have lived under tremendous tensions which caused the need for escape and relief.

With the years his religious feelings developed into a heightened sense of guilt. To free himself verbally from this burden of growing consciousness of sin was closer to confession than any sublimating process through painting or sculpting. Moreover, one of the loudest influences prompting him was very likely the intellectual habit of the time of expressing oneself through poems. For instance, Giovanni Strozzi, a member of the famous Florentine Strozzi family whose palace still stands as a sign of Renaissance splendour, was a minor poet. He once wrote a short poem, entitled *On the Night of Buonarroti*:

> *The Night which here so sweet asleep you see*
> *Was sculptured by an Angel into stone. How true,*
> *She is alive because she sleeps. Have faith in me.*
> *If not, then wake her up and she will speak to you.*

This fan letter in the shape of a poem was answered by Michelangelo with another short poem which he sent to Giovanni Strozzi:

*I love to sleep, but more so to be made of stone,*
*As long as wrong and shame remain.*
*To see not, nor to feel I call great gain.*
*Don't wake me up! Please, speak but in your softest tone.*

Michelangelo was a lonely man, seeking aloneness. This makes us understand why the image of darkness and night recurs so often. He, 'the son of night', is doomed to work and work on his art, 'the fruit of night', with the relentless fanaticism of a man who wants to get out of the darkness of life, following the path of light shown by his 'firefly'. It was, as one of his sonnets says, the night which created him and his art, and it was then that his body met his soul. Out of this torturing dualism of flesh and spirit, out of this lostness between fire and ice arose this Titan who hammered the stone to give it the shape hidden within. There was the vision of growing wings and the never-dying hope in man that he expressed in two fragmentary lines of a lost poem: '. . . This is how Daedalus awakened, and this is how the sun rejects the shadow'.

IN THE WAKE OF GREATNESS: VASARI AND CELLINI
Whatever one may think of Giorgio Vasari's (1511–47) *Vite de' piú eccellenti architetti, pittori e scultori italiani*, commonly known as *Lives of the Painters*, it remains one of the earliest prototypes of 'modern' art criticism. It contains some erroneous statements and plagiarisms, but it is a classic of its kind, a work of erudition and catholicity of taste, written by a man whose calling was that of a painter, muralist, portraitist, and architect. At the age of thirteen he was an apprentice of Michelangelo. Later he worked for and with Andrea del Sarto. He did a great many murals and paintings which are in the Vatican, in the Cathedral and Palazzo Vecchio in Florence and, at that time, he was also well known for his numerous portraits of the Medici. The Uffizi Palace and the tomb of Michelangelo in Santa Croce reveal his ability as an architect.

In any other age Vasari might have been one of the leading artists whose visual works would have given the time its imprint. Surrounded and overshadowed by so many titans, he is forced into the role of a third-rate artist. But his work as a writer on art is unsurpassed. In retrospect we can see that Vasari created a new type in the growing world of Humanism, a character later so well acted by Boswell and Eckermann. Vasari also was the first art reviewer who exercised an often frightening dictatorship by giving artistic and aesthetic value judgments.

In his journalistic manner he leans heavily on adjectives, and some of them became guide lines in his description of the artist. Thus, Fra Angelico is pious, Fra Filippo Lippi unscrupulous, Perugino irreligious, Sebastiano del Piombo lazy, Raphael eclectic, and Michelangelo divine. We must not forget Michelangelo was Vasari's first master, who felt induced to write him a flattering sonnet after receipt of his essays. Vasari also accepts local rumours as facts, a journalistic tendency, as in the case of Andrea del Castagno. He describes the artist's character as brutal and ill-tempered, an allusion to tales of homicide which later scholarship proved to be untrue. Castagno's alleged victim, Domenico Veneziano, outlived the 'criminal', condemned by the power of the printed word in a best-seller, by four years at least. True, Castagno's style is stark and forceful, and Vasari's judgment of the paintings influenced him to equate an aesthetic approach of the artist with an innate quality. In his cultural history Egon Friedell underlines that 'all those who dared to oppose Vasari's critical revelations were persecuted by him with utmost vengeance and unfairness'.

No one writing art criticism for a newspaper or magazine today would think of acting as an impresario or art dealer. But in the Prefatory Letter 'To the Artists of Design' Vasari speaks of a 'generous indignation that so much talent should remain concealed for so long a time, and still continue buried'. This was one of his reasons for wanting to write the *Lives of the Painters:* to recognize and record genius, to publicize works by lesser known artists. By the mere inclusion and praise of an artist, by the exclusion or harsh criticism of others, he arrogated and anticipated the power of the curator of a museum or modern art gallery in addition to playing the role of critic and consultant.

Of interest are Vasari's pretences in finding the right motivations for taking on the then formidable task of writing biographical essays on about 200 artists from the trecento to the mid-cinquecento. According to his own testimony, it was essentially due to chance that he became a writer. When decorating the Cancelleria in Rome in 1546 Vasari had supper with Cardinal Farnese and a few humanists. One of them, the scholar Paolo Giovio, had planned to write such a history, but Vasari criticized him for not having 'put things in their proper order'. He tells us how the Cardinal and other scholars and poets accepted his argument that a creative artist is better equipped to write such a book; and how they persuaded him to overcome his reluctance and to accept this challenge. The fact is, however, that for six years prior to this supper Vasari had been travelling a great deal and had filled his notebooks with anecdotes, ideas and sketches and, as he himself reveals, was able to turn to 'notes and memoranda which I had prepared even from my boyhood, for my own recreation, and because of a certain affection which I preserved toward the memory of our artists . . .'

A hundred and sixty-three years after Gutenberg printed the Bible, Giorgio Vasari wrote the first best-seller. The initial edition, soon sold out, was followed by an expanded second edition eight years later. It is the first great literary work on the visual arts in the history of modern man. None of his shortcomings can weaken the merits of this book. His is the classic example of a phenomenon so often encountered through the centuries of an artist's unfulfilled potentialities bringing forth the critic in him. Vasari attempted to picture himself as a creative artist – he was a successful man who made quite a fortune – as an artist who sacrificed his time to write the *Vite* in order to help and serve his fellow artists as well as the public. He could not have made a better psychological spectacle of his motivations and point to himself as the arche-type of the artist-turned-critic.

Vasari did not write about Benvenuto Cellini (1500–71), whose life and work best symbolize the late period of the six-teenth-century Renaissance. Cellini, however, wrote about Vasari in the most derogatory terms. They had their differences – Cellini seemed to thrive on disputes, quarrels, and brawls – but Vasari's judgment of Cellini's work, as much as is known of it, was fair and even lenient. Vasari also made a portrait of *Plate 29* him. It is the profile of a daring looking man, who seems to be bent on challenging the whole world in an almost Don Quixotic manner.

In chapter 86 of the first volume of Cellini's autobiography he tells us of having been denounced by Vasari at the Floren-tine court of Duke Alessandro.

Now this ill turn I owed to the painter Giorgetto Vassellario (who is Vasari) of Arezzo, perhaps in return for many good turns I had done him. For I had given him hospitality in Rome and paid his expenses, though he had been a most troublesome guest . . . Afterwards I got an opening for Georgio with the Cardinal de' Medici, and continued to help him. It was for this I had deserved his slanderous report to Duke Alessandro that I had spoken ill of his Excellency . . .

Cellini's remarkable account of his life is full of such minor asides, often exaggerated and put down with a flourish.

Cellini had begun to write this *Life* of himself with his own hand, but he soon lost patience. He realized how much time he could put to better use working on the various crafts he mastered so well. He engaged a fourteen-year-old boy to whom he dictated his story. 'And as I took no little pleasure in the thing, I worked all the more diligently and was the more productive.' By virtually *telling* the story, he gained a valuable vividness and immediacy in his descriptions. There is nothing laboured in his account, except the excesses of his verbal sallies and of his boastfulness. In his dedication to Benedetto Varchi, to whom he had sent some part of the manuscript, he states that the discourse of his *Life* is more pleasing in 'its first shape than were it polished and retouched by others – for then the truth of what I have written would show less clear; and I have taken great care to say nothing of things for which I should have had to fumble in my memory'.

Perhaps he would have had to fumble in his memory to tell us about two imprisonments during his middle age. The explanation for these punishments might have been emotionally painful for him. He also keeps from us that he took the first tonsure rather late in life only to withdraw from entering the Church. But he describes one of his imprisonments in Rome in great detail, probably because he could present himself in heroic feats. He is not a man given to introspection and soul-searching.

He casts himself in a role which epitomizes many traits common to the Renaissance man in the mid-sixteenth-century. His lines reflect the tumultuous zest for life which propelled Renaissance man to act and adventure into a world of unlimited beauty. He wallows in self-satisfaction, no matter whether he stabs an enemy or indulges in endless wrangles with his patrons. 'Men like Benvenuto, unique in their profession, stand above the law', said Paul III of Cellini, and Francis I, King of France, when he was shown the model of Cellini's famous salt-cellar, exclaimed: 'The man is a wonder! He should never lay down his tools.' In fact, Cellini never laid down his tools or his sword.

Although the autobiography is full of his brawls and love

affairs – he had eight children, two of whom were legitimate – of adventures and exploits which show him as a ruthless, vain and boastful man, we also have a consummate picture of him as the hard-working, tremendously ambitious and talented artist. He came late in the Renaissance, when a touch of decadence and violence, of mannerism and imitation had taken hold of the painters and sculptors.

Cellini had something of the Renaissance genius about him, that something which Vasari called 'truly terrible', the demon of energy, a lust for power, an uncontrollable intensity in living and creating. And yet he remained a minor figure as a sculptor though caught by the spirit of restlessness and the hectic drive to create something different and more unusual than the titans of former generations had done.

Cellini was born when Leonardo had reached his fiftieth year, and Michelangelo, who called Cellini 'the greatest goldsmith of whom the world has ever heard', was his senior by twenty-five years.

Neither Cellini's statue of Perseus nor his Nymph of Fontainebleau show complete mastery of the human figure or the inevitability and grandeur which characterized the works of the period immediately preceding him. In fact, his figures, such as the Nymph, were marked by elongation and mannerisms. His nude images had little of the chastity of classic form revived by the quattrocento artists. Cellini considered the human shape an ideal form which we cannot see often enough, and he helped spread the trend of adorning door-knockers, candelabras, forks and knives with representations of the nude. What was once a spiritual experience became cheapened by its utilitarian purposes. One no longer objected to cutting one's food or knocking at doors while fingering the figure of a Venus. Cellini's work anticipates the taste for the sumptuous *Plate 30* and richly ornamented image of the Baroque.

The artisan of the respectable workshop turned into the 'virtuoso', who hoped for popes and princes to compete for his favour. This is the very same quality Cellini's writing displays. There is something of the narcissistic bravura artist in him as a goldsmith, a sculptor, and a writer. He still personifies the multiple talent which we expect the Renaissance artist to reveal. His father taught him 'to play the flute and to sing music', because the father preferred music to any of his other interests. And Benvenuto tells us that his father was the first 'to work well in ivory', that he made 'wonderful organs with wooden pipes, and spinets the best and finest that had ever been seen, as well as violas, lutes, and harps, all of them

123

beautifully and excellently fashioned. He was an engineer, too, and showed a wonderful talent in inventing instruments for lowering bridges, for fulling, and other machines'.

The momentum of hereditary forces was at work, augmented by one more gift for writing which Cellini describes as 'a quiet vein of poetry', exemplified in his book by a prophetic and epigrammatic quatrain his father had written. Benvenuto did not take to music, but he soon excelled as a goldsmith, coin-maker and seal-maker. In chapter 26 of his book, Cellini also tells us how he became enchanted with the art of enamelling.

But though I found it no easy matter, yet such pleasure did I take in it that its great difficulties were a rest to me. And this sprang from a special gift lent to me by the God of Nature, a temperament so healthy and well-proportioned that I could confidently carry out whatever I had made up my mind to do. These arts I have been speaking of are entirely different from one another, so that a man skilled in one of them rarely attains to equal success in any other, whereas I strove with my whole strength after them equally; and in its own place I shall show that I succeeded.

When Cellini was fifty-eight years old he made up his mind to write the story of his life and he proved that he 'carried it out confidently', although he carried his story no further than to his sixty-second year. During the eight years in which he dictated his story his health was bad, and he did not receive any important sculpture commissions. But he was never idle, his work as a goldsmith was still in great demand. Perhaps he sensed that he had outlived his time; he certainly realized that his former patrons – at the risk of being less well served – preferred less troublesome artists to work for them.

In a mood of resignation thinly covering his ill-temper and irritability he set out to write his story. He finally found a haven in marriage with Piera di Salvadore Parigi, his former servant and mistress, and felt he was 'going on his way rejoicing'. Cellini always needed to assert himself, and when his prowess left him, when he no longer had the strength and inclination to challenge the world with his sword, he decided to do so with his word. In his prefatory sonnet to his autobiography he speaks of his high-aiming deeds –

> *and there I do remain.*
> *My cruel fate has fought me but in vain:*
> *Life, glory, worth, an all-embracing skill*
> *Within me found fulfilment and its will*
> *To best the many and the best to gain.*

## The Painter Reveals Himself

It is often said it is a sign of weakness if an artist must justify and explain his work. But this is belied by the many illustrious men who have tried to communicate what made them be the way they were. The reasons for it may include the artist's psyche, the circumstances in which he worked, the period in which he lived, the recognition he received.

One of the most common revelations of the artist's self has been the self-portrait. Artists have also used themselves as models in their paintings, a fact which is often more revealing than any writing could be, as in the case of Dürer, who cast himself as a Christ figure. The decision to do one's self-portrait goes beyond the convenience of having a model at hand, and the obvious narcissistic quality basic to all creative efforts. Moreover, it stands to reason that the painting of a self-portrait will occur when there is a psychological need for it. More likely than not, it may mark an important point in the personal development of the painter, as if he wished to have a long look at himself. Sitting as a model is sitting in judgment on oneself. In other words, the process involved in self-portraits is close to imaginary dialogues with oneself; it affords the opportunity to ask the most urgent and ultimate questions. When many artists take pen in hand (I cannot visualize a painter sitting at the typewriter, except for Andy Warhol or Robert Rauschenberg), they replace the self-portrait with an autobiography.

*Plates XII, XIII*

The manner in which the artist explains himself is significant. He may want to empty his heavy heart while writing a letter. He may wish to explain himself to himself, one part of his mind communicating with another. Or the painter may simply use the writer's tool to talk shop. This is most often done in form of diaries or treatises. To be an artist does not necessarily exclude being a teacher; on the contrary, some artists may have the urge to share their experiences with their contemporaries or even with posterity. A man like Leonardo may, in the course of his experiments, consider it vital to notate his thoughts and register his findings as meticulously as possible. A conscious innovator, standing at the crossroads of history and his own life, may feel forced to take up the pen to fight for his ideas. Or he may be a born raconteur or a gossip who uses his idle hours to indulge in his weakness. Or the visual artist may be a poet who cannot help writing too and turns his convictions into confessions, documenting his visions and thought-feelings with the written word.

From William Hogarth (1697–1764) to Ben Shahn (1898–
1969) some painters have concentrated on recording the social
scene of their time as commentators and critics. Their strong
interest in the daily event seen against its political and socio-
cultural background gives their work a journalistic tinge. If
their visual art, however, is journalism, then it is visual
journalism at its artistic best.

Both painters[1] found it necessary to put their aesthetic
principles into words. Hogarth lived in an age of reason;
reasoning about the aesthetic values of one's craft, contributing to the scientific truth of one's art was the thing to do
in the first half of the eighteenth century. Ben Shahn has
witnessed the turbulent changes of the twentieth century,
living though the age of anxiety which was, at the same time,
an age of analysis. As an artist-teacher at various American
universities, he was forced to formulate his artistic concepts.
Shahn opens the most important of his books, *The Shape of
Content*, based on his Harvard lectures, with the pertinent
questions:

What can an artist bring to the general knowledge or the theoretical
view of art that has not already been fully expounded? What can
he say in words that he could not far more skilfully present in pictorial form? Is not the painting rather than the printed page his
testament? Will he not only expend his energies without in any way
increasing the general enlightenment? And then, what can an audience gain from listening to an artist that it could not apprehend far
more readily simply by looking at his pictures?

He comes to the honest conclusion that such a 'verbal Odyssey'
above all serves the artist in clearly defining things which may
be of some value to himself.

There are certain parallels between Hogarth and Shahn
despite the obvious dissimilarities of the cultural climate of
their centuries, their personal backgrounds, their emotional
reactions and sensibilities. But both artists are mainly stimulated by the immediacy and dramatic contrast of life. Their
interest is invested in the frailty and social plight of human
beings as victims of social circumstances. Hogarth's satire
turns with merciless accuracy against the follies and manners
of his time when he shows the sore wastefulness, rather than
the wickedness, of his harlots and rakes, when he depicts
the miseries and vices of rich and poor. Nor is the event
itself, however disastrous, in the foreground of Ben Shahn's

126                                   [1](see page 341).

creative interest. Instead, his intentions are 'to create the emotional tone that surrounds disaster; you might call it the inner disaster'. Hogarth's paintings were the result of direct experiences, but the artist's imaginative re-creation saved them from being mere records of social scenes. Most of Shahn's work is derived from factual material which the artist then discards in order to reach from the immediacy of the event toward its universal meaning. ('The universal experience is that private experience which illuminates the private and personal world in which each of us lives the major part of his life.')

*Plate 32*

Hogarth's initial inspiration came from the theatre, from the satiric tableaux of John Gay's *The Beggar's Opera*. Moreover, his was an era in which sentimentalism had the better of sentiment and in which a certain flair for theatricality was in the air. We learn from Hogarth's reminiscences how strongly he was influenced by the theatre when he says that he was determined to 'compose pictures on canvas similar to representations on stage', expecting them to be 'tried by the same test, and criticized by the same criterion . . . Let the figures in either pictures or prints be considered as players dressed either for the sublime – for genteel comedy, or farce – for high or low life. I have endeavoured to treat my subjects as a dramatic writer: my picture is my stage, and men and women are my players, who by means of certain actions and gestures, are to exhibit a *dumb show*'. And theatricality remained Hogarth's trademark as a painter.

Not so as a writer. Many reminiscences of other painters were written with more dramatic intensity than Hogarth's, and his treatise, *The Analysis of Beauty*, has an unmistakable academic tone. Against the general contention of most art critics, among whom Jonathan Richardson was most powerful, that a painter must raise his ideas beyond what he sees, Hogarth insisted on a very intimate relationship between nature and the creative artist, extolling 'the beauties of nature unimproved'. In a mood of restlessness and defiance, Hogarth decided to give his own ideas literary form and, at the end of 1753, his book appeared: '*The Analysis of Beauty*. Written with a view of fixing the fluctuating *Ideas of Taste*'. In an engraving he indicated the Line of Beauty by two eels on a dish, and he depicted himself as Columbus Breaking the Egg.

*Plate 31*

The book is written in a conventional manner belying his artistic temperament but conforming to the tenets of his time. There are chapters on Fitness, Variety, Uniformity, Simplicity,

Intricacy; he deals with a new method of acquiring easy and graceful movements of parts of the body and even talks about dancing, especially the minuet. He discriminates between a two-dimensional Line of Beauty and a Line of Grace, being superior to beauty in its three-dimensional scope. He prescribes the ideal of pyramidal – vide the Laocoön group – and serpentlike form, the economy of simplicity, the gracefulness of the undulating line, and the importance of variety ('Simplicity without variety is wholly insipid . . . There is no object composed of straight lines, that has so much variety, with so few parts, as the pyramid . . .').

The importance of his writing lies in the fact that his was the first attempt to define beauty in empirical terms and to make formal values the basis of an aesthetic system (as pointed out by the book's editor, Joseph Burke). Fortunately for Hogarth's work, he himself did not rigorously adhere to his own theories which often border on the absurd. But basically his concept of the Line of Beauty symbolizes eternal movement in space and continuity in time. In this context one must refer to Giovanni Paolo Lomazzo, who wrote in 1584 about Leonardo advising his pupils to give his figures a pyramidal or serpentlike shape since 'the greatest grace and life a picture can have, is, that it express motion . . .' and that there is no form better suited to express motion than 'the flame of fire which according to Aristotle . . . is an element most active of all others . . . so that a picture having this form will be most beautiful . . .'.

Hogarth stood between the Baroque and the Rococo, tending towards the more restless, mobile and wanton expression of the new form, and abandoning the voluptuous and dramatic solemnity of the Baroque. Seen in the light of this period of transition, the strong and weak points of his aesthetic principles bring *The Analysis of Beauty* closer to our understanding.

About two hundred years later Ben Shahn, thrown into a tumultuous transitional period, tries to formulate his ideas in the often Freudian spirit of his time. He too does not necessarily adhere in his own work to the ideal concepts he postulates. But does not the greatness of an artist rest in spiting all rules, even his own?

Ben Shahn's essay, *The Biography of a Painting*, however, affords insight into the creative process. He reveals how many different ways are open to the artist's mind, how many are

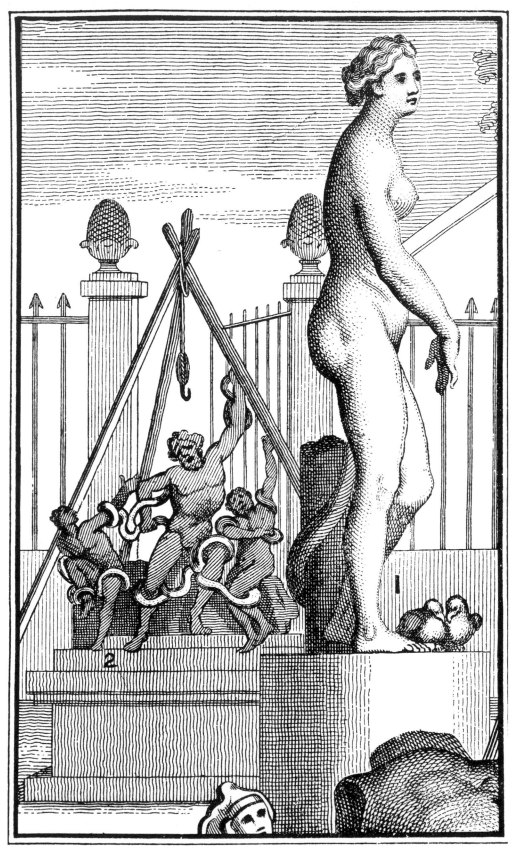

31   William Hogarth PAGE FROM 'THE ANALYSIS OF BEAUTY'

32  Ben Shahn FATHER AND CHILD

33  Odilon Redon HEAD OF A MARTYR

rejected and what is finally chosen, perhaps out of a compelling emotional reason which often lies hidden in the artist's memory.

Reading Shahn we are left with the realization that the many sources of imagery which seemed to have disappeared 'into the limbo of the subconscious, or the unconscious, or the instinctive, or the merely biological' could be traced and followed as they crystallize into the image on the canvas. These sources are always there, whether or not the artist can consciously rationalize them; in Ben Shahn we find this ability. Of course, there are many more factors at work which modify and shape the final image. The duel fought between the enthusiastic creator in the artist and the restraining hand of the critic in him (playing the role of the Id and Superego in his unconscious) is, or ought to be, one of the great battles within the creative process. Ben Shahn recreates this battle between the critic as ruthless destroyer and the artist's need for an ecstatic feeling to materialize his inner visualizations.

The central point in Shahn's aesthetics seems to lie in this struggle between the creative will and the scientifically minded analyst trying to control the artist's Dionysian drives (Shahn intended to become a biologist before turning to the visual arts). But, in its variations, this conflict is common to all serious artists, although it may not always be properly and so consciously employed as by Ben Shahn. The other pivotal point lies in the 'war between idea and image'. Shahn learned to reject the notion that the first law of creation should be the artist's 'disengagement'. On the contrary, he found aesthetic gratification in unfolding a great deal of his 'most personal thinking and feeling without loss of simplicity'. He is convinced that only the realization of something intensely personal leaves no spectator untouched. ('I think of a di Chirico figure, lonely in a lonely street haunted by shadows; its loneliness speaks to all human loneliness'.) Shahn's analysis of the artist's growth, of his changing views and his personal attitudes to social implications, seeing the suffering being as his real artistic concern, is a rare and moving statement.

In the early thirties Shahn rejected the conception of art as based on aesthetic sensation and felt a need for the artistic recreation of the social scene as a commentary on the mores and manners of his time. He recognized nonconformity as the basic precondition of art, but he also warned against the desire of artists to be in the swim of things and to try always to be ahead of everyone else, which too often pushes a work to meaningless extremes. ('Of course when such a work becomes dated, its emptiness emerges, for nothing is so hard to look at as the stylish, out of style.')

As a contemporary of surrealism and all the other -isms of our time, he realized the fruitfulness of tge vast inner land-scapes with their unconsciously ready-made symbols and images. But Ben Shahn's aesthetic feelings for the creative process have always seen the artist's triumph achieved with the help of his 'intending self', the artist's scope and ability dependent on his conscious, creative will.

FROM NOTEBOOKS TO SONNETS:

REDON, COROT, DELACROIX , DEGAS

About 1905, when Art Nouveau was on its way out, Odilon Redon (1840–1916) found himself on a plane of magic symbolism, expressing a secularized religious ecstasy in varied colour symphonies. His *À soi-même* and some of his letters and journals are small masterpieces of self-revelation through which the struggle of the creative will in man is brought closer to our appreciation. He states that 'after hard work to copy a stone, a leaf of grass, a hand, a profile, or anything else of nature, alive or dead', there comes a point when he feels 'a mental rebellion within me; then I become creative and must yield to the creation of the imaginary. Nature, taken in the right doses and inspiration, becomes source and ferment to me'.

*Plate 33*

But when, as Redon relates, a young Englishman once came to see him in order to learn the genesis of his works, he re-turned disappointed because 'I replied to him with a smile'. It seems that in spite of all attempts at articulation and soul-searching, very few artists will ever be able to say what the sources of their art are. And if they do, will they be able to recognize the real sources of their creative will with an approximation of objective truth? In his journal we find Redon's answer:

The truth is that one can say nothing about one's self, nothing about what the hand brings to birth, at the anguished or passionate hour of gestation. It is often a surprise; one has simply gone beyond one's goal, that is all there is to be said. What more can one say? To what avail analyse this phenomenon; it would be in vain. It is better to relive the experience for its own joy.

Paul Valéry wrote that any painter who aspires to greatness, who seeks the liberating and gratifying sensation of achieving the best, the new, 'by more ambitious combinations of will, knowledge and power – such a painter is led to sum up his experience, to be strengthened in his own "truths" as well as to define the vaster or more complex works of his dreams'.

Jean Baptiste Camille Corot (1796–1875) felt the need to see his precepts solidified by writing and thus, filling his notebooks, he increased his faith in himself. 'But with him', Valéry thought, 'between life, sight, and painting, there is little or no "intellectual" intermediary.' Jean Auguste Dominique Ingres (1780–1867) also put down on paper his often too cryptic thoughts in an imperious manner.

Eugène Delacroix's (1799–1863) *Journals*, kept from 1822 to 1824 and from 1847 to the end of his life, are among the most informative and best written diaries of any painter. His reflections show the totality of the man in the artist who has a grasp on all the arts, on history and politics, and who, despite the informality of his prose, achieves a very personal style, lucid and direct, colourful and often dramatic.

The most outstanding quality of his *Journals* is the feeling he conveys that he is searching for *his* truth, however wrong it may be, and that he is utterly sincere in his statements, even though he keeps his mind open to be able to change it. His entries are heightened by flashes of intuition. Although he often expresses his likes and dislikes without mincing words, he rarely permits himself to make such biting remarks as the one about Ingres whose work, he declared, is the 'complete expression of an incomplete intellect'.

Delacroix could be intuitive and rational, impetuous and sceptical, naive and sophisticated. Most of the subjects he painted were romantic, and yet he hated Romanticism all his life, as revealed in his *Journals*. His Romanticism seemed closest to Stendhal's who, in Julien Sorel, created the first modern hero of fiction in a cool, analytic fashion. Delacroix's work also displays a flair for theatricality as hardly manifest in any painter preceding him. Apollinaire sensed this when he said that Delacroix 'was passionately in love with passion and coldly determined to search for means to express passion in the most visible terms'. This remark points to the dualism in the painter's nature which also becomes obvious in his writings. Baudelaire, who considered Delacroix essentially creative, as a man with a wide frame of reference, a good mind and the habit of reflection, recognized this dualistic quality in him when he likened him to 'the crater of a volcano artistically concealed by bouquets of flowers'.

Delacroix rejected Berlioz as 'heroic mess', but adored Mozart whose 'technique was always up to the level of his inspiration', the very same thing he demanded from himself.

Music meant a great deal to this painter, and he once observed that colour has a purely 'musical' quality, a statement which we find in Kandinsky's aesthetics – and one could not imagine two more diametrically opposed painters.

To compile a Dictionary of the Fine Arts was one of Delacroix's desires, but he never found time to finish it. This is only registered as proof of how intellectually inclined he was. He always tried to grasp the artist's problems as several of his entries show. In 1824 he spent an evening with friends:

Interesting discussion between genius and unusual men. Dimier thought that great passions were the source of genius. I think that it is imagination alone, or better still, what amounts to the same thing, that delicacy of the organs that makes one see what others do not see, and which makes one see in a different way. I was saying that even great passions joined to imagination lead most often to disorder in the mind, etc. Dufresne said a true thing: what made a man unusual was, fundamentally, a way utterly peculiar to himself of seeing things . . . So, there are no rules for great souls: rules are only for people who have merely the talent that can be acquired. The proof is that they do transmit that faculty. He was saying: 'How much reflection is needed to create a beautiful, expressive head, a hundred times more than for a problem, and yet at bottom, the matter is merely one of instinct, for it cannot explain what brings it about . . .'

In 1853 he noted that '. . . it is much more important for an artist to approach the ideal that he carries within himself and which is peculiar to him, than to be satisfied with the fleeting ideal that nature may offer'. Toward the end of his life he made the deeply-felt statement: 'The foremost merit of a painting is to be a feast for the eye'. And as if his cerebral alter ego had to write on the margin of his feelings, he added: 'That is not to say that reason should not find its place in it'.

Edgar Degas (1834–1917) was certainly a man of letters, but in his whimsical manner he most often declined to talk shop, particularly with the literati. However, he too kept notebooks, proved himself very expressive in his letters and was known for his biting wit. We find his bon mots and epigrammatic statements in the journals of his contemporaries.

He was known as a fanatic worker ('Do it again and again, ten times, a hundred times. Nothing in art must seem to be an accident, not even movements'). He was obsessed with movement. From his many sporting pictures, mainly of race horses, which allowed him to capture the ecstasy of motion on canvas, he turned to the ballerina and the ballet scene. In the movements, poses and relaxed positions of the dancers he

*Plate 35*

saw a replica of his horses. There he found again the flawless function of limbs, the perfect pose, the synchronized motion of groups. Over and over again we see the same stereotyped elements of an animal nature in these dancing creatures, who, in action, look like marionettes. ('They call me the painter of dancers. They don't realize that for me the dance has been a pretext for painting pretty materials and delineating movement.').

Of course, one could claim that Degas, the perfectionist, afraid of the imperfection of the finished painting, could not help but leave the dancer's facial expression nondescript. His compulsion for perfection made Degas write about twenty sonnets. He chose the sonnet form because of its being the most difficult form of poetry. This was in the years 1889 and 1890. The outside stimulation, however, came from Mallarmé, who had asked Degas to illustrate a volume of his poems.

Impressed by Mallarmé's formal perfection – were not the dancers' tireless exercises at and off the barre the road to perfection too? – Degas worked with his usual intensity on sonnets. Paul Valéry and André Gide recalled that Degas once complained about the difficulty of writing poetry: 'What a profession! I've wasted the whole day on a damned sonnet without progressing one step. Not that I have not got enough ideas! I am full of them, I have too many'. Mallarmé replied quietly: 'One does not write poetry with ideas, Degas, but with words'.

One of Degas' sonnets, *The Dance*, shows his preoccupation with structure and idea, with whatever art form he visualized:

> *It seems that languid Nature – long ago –*
> *sure of her body's beauty, fell asleep*
> *and still would sleep, if Dance, on nimble toe,*
> *had not, with one compelling breathless leap,*
> *awakened her. With her expressive hands,*
> *alive with pulse, and with her weightless feet*
> *that twined in intricate design, dance stands*
> *atune with time and space, and in a suite*
>
> *of turns makes Nature turn with her. And you,*
> *in spite of your so common looking face,*
> *move boldly – all you goddesses of grace!*
> *The dance lends you the magic of her sheen.*
> *And you must know from your own stagebound view*
> *that paint and distance make you seem a queen.*

## VAN GOGH, GAUGUIN

*Plates III, IV, 34*    Both Vincent Van Gogh (1853–90) and Paul Gauguin (1848–1903) verbalized with rare brilliance the trauma of their lives, the anguish which penetrated the process of their creative frenzy. During their brief but tormented relationship, Vincent wrote: 'Gauguin interests me much as a man – much . . . Now here without the slightest doubt one finds oneself in the presence of a virgin-being with the instincts of a savage. In Gauguin blood and sex prevail over ambition'.

I do not think that anyone else has drawn the image of this man with fewer words and more precision. Gauguin reciprocated with a portrait of Van Gogh, who accepted it: 'Yes, it's me all right, but me mad'. He also recognized: 'Between the two of us, he like a volcano, I boiling inwardly, a struggle of some sort was inevitable'. The story of how Van Gogh attacked Gauguin, who then left him and shortly afterwards exchanged Western civilization for life in Tahiti, is well-known.

They were both desperately lonely men who could not resist withdrawing from the superficialities of sophistication, from the seduction of expanding mechanization in society. Both artists sought to rediscover the source of life, the self-evident object, the pure and earthy image. And both found it in a different way. Gauguin had to make a long journey to reach the vision of rapture. Van Gogh found rapture of vision by staying with himself.

Both painters have expressed themselves without inhibition in their medium and both have had the need and gift to put into words their visual experiences. They had the sensibility for and the touch of poetry, a feeling for the meaningfulness of the slightest simile. Van Gogh's letters and Gauguin's journals are full of poetic passages, descriptive impressions, spontaneous outcries.

Gauguin seems to have been the far more self-conscious of the two when writing. His autobiographic records from Tahiti *Noa Noa*, however tender and unpretentious they may appear, have the literary finish of a knowing hand. ('I am no longer conscious of days and hours, of good and evil. The happiness is so strange at times that it suppresses the very conception of it. I only know that all is good, because all is beautiful.')

We know that Gauguin often wrote letters of great anxiety to his wife in Copenhagen or to friends in Paris, but nothing of his doubts, afflictions, and unhappiness can be found in his description of the sensuous beauty of man and nature and the poetic innocence which he found on this island. In taking leave from it for a short return to France, Gauguin summed up with a few ecstatic words his feelings for this 'mysterious world', words which are somewhat remote from a painter's imagery and show the literary skill in finding the final phrases which turn his personal experiences into a universal message:

Oh mysterious world of all light, thou hast made a light shine within me, and I have grown in admiration of thy antique beauty, which is the immemorial youth of nature. I have become better for having understood and having loved thy human soul . . .

We often encounter Van Gogh's spiritual anguish in his letters, with no purposeful consciousness of phrasing. They are rare poetic documents of his suffering soul. But he also had a compulsive need to explain or describe what he so brilliantly conceived in flaming colours. Above all, he realized the intimate interrelationship between the various art forms: 'There is Rembrandt in Shakespeare, and Correggio in Michelet, and Delacroix in Victor Hugo, and then there is Rembrandt in the New Testament, and the New Testament in Rembrandt, as you like, it amounts very much to the same thing'. Vincent's desire to compare painting with poetry and even with music sometimes misled him to use too obvious a simile. ('And then my brush goes between my fingers just as a bow would on the violin.')

In spite of its primitive intensity there is a human message in all his paintings. They are a product of nature and express a simple philosophy of nature which he enjoyed in Japanese colour prints:

. . . isn't it almost a religion these simple Japanese teach us, who live in nature as if they themselves were flowers? You cannot study Japanese art, it seems to me, without becoming much gayer and happier, and we must return to nature in spite of our education and our work in a world of convention . . . Their work is as simple as breathing, and they do a figure in a few sure strokes with the same ease as if it were as simple as buttoning your coat. Oh! I must manage some day to do a figure in a few sure strokes.

In his desire to speak about his paintings or to describe what he saw in his finished work, he often created a poetic extension to his colour visualizations. His words often added an emotional emphasis here, a philosophic and moral idea there. From the insane asylum of Saint-Rémy he wrote to Émile Bernard in 1889 about a canvas picturing 'a view of the park of the asylum where I am':

You will realize that this combination of red ochre, green saddened by grey and the use of heavy black outlines produces something of the sensation of anguish, the so-called *noir-rouge*, from

137

which certain of my companions in misfortune frequently suffer. Moreover the effects of the great tree struck down by lightning and the sickly greeny pink smile of the last flower of autumn merely serve to heighten this idea.

Van Gogh instinctively knew the colour and shades of feelings, the forms and levels of existence. How beautifully expressed is 'the green saddened by grey' and the 'blackened red' melancholy of the patients! Sometimes his exaltation eloped with his imagination, and he said about his painting, *Road with Cypresses:*

*Plate II*

. . . a cypress with a star, a last attempt – a night sky with a moon without radiance, the slender crescent barely emerging from the opaque shadow cast by the earth – a star with exaggerated brilliance if you like, a soft brilliance of rose and green in the ultramarine sky across which are hurrying some clouds. Below, a road bordered with tall yellow canes, behind these the blue *Basses Alpes*, an old inn with yellow windows, and a very tall cypress, very upright and very sombre.

Van Gogh had the genius of not only turning his visions into an apotheosis of colour and form, but also saying what his inner eye saw.

THE WRITING OF AUTOBIOGRAPHIES
*Marc Chagall*
Marc Chagall (1887–), the painter from Vitebsk in White Russia, was the child of a Jewish worker in a herring depot. His mother, who had never been to school, was a world in herself, self-contained and, at the same time, outgoing, and embodying the mysterious forces that are form-giving, life-shaping. 'Our mother had a style that was rare', wrote Chagall in *My Life* in 1922. He realized that his talent 'lay hidden somewhere in her, that through her everything had been passed on to me, everything except her spirit'. She smiled his smile, he tells us.

*Plate V*

His work has an unmistakable style all its own, whether it is a painting, a drawing, a stained glass window, a book illustration, a piece of ceramic, a mural, a stage design or a curtain. His is a world of colourful dreams with cows and horses gaily flying through the air, with time ticking clocks and fiddlers who seem to have just escaped from the *Tanzhaus* of centuries ago. There is a quiet sadness and a dancing joy in his work, the reality of a non-real life that tells a tale without being literal. There is chaos and distortion of form, but his colours sing. His images have a haunting quality, but his

I   Alwin Nicolais SOMNICOQUX
II   Alwin Nicolais SANCTUM

III   Vincent van Gogh ROAD WITH CYPRESSES

IV   Paul Gauguin MAN WITH AN AXE   →

imagination is coherent. His vision is rooted in myth. The Chassidic's joyful embrace of and submission to the divine spirit is in Chagall's work; it embodies the Chassidic dancing rhythm with which he tries to feel the omnipresence of God rather than the spiritual heaviness of the Talmudic interpretations of the almighty will. Such exuberant joy and sensual rhythm in theme, design and colour are the key to his work. And it was he – more than anyone else among the twentieth-century painters – who followed the path of revolution without abandoning the specific ties with his past and who fully succeeded in translating poetry into painting.

When in 1910 cubism was at its height in reducing reality piecemeal to geometric forms, Chagall felt very revolutionary:

I got the impression that we were still scratching at the surface of things, that we were afraid to plunge into the chaos, afraid to smash and trample that surface underfoot . . . Down with naturalism, impressionism and realistic cubism! Welcome to our new madness! An expiatory bath, a revolution up to the hilt, not just on the surface.

But with all his distortions, with heads put on bodies upside-down, people flying over town, with his famous goat sitting at a tilted table, the colours hold everything together. Moreover, here is method in the madness of his composition:

If, in a picture, I have cut off a cow's head and put it on upside-down, or occasionally even painted the whole picture topsy turvy, I have not done so in order to make literature. I want to introduce into my picture a psychic shock, which always operates through pictorial factors, in other words to introduce a fourth dimension. Therefore let people cease talking about fairy tales, of the fantastic, of Chagall the flying painter, when they speak of me. I am a painter who is unconsciously conscious.

Art is to him above all a state of the soul. ('Everything in art must come from the movement of our blood, from the whole of our being, including that part that is unconscious.')

Chagall's paintings are a form of personal biography. But in Russia during 1921 and 1922, struggling with the purely physical miseries of daily life, with the gross misunderstanding of what art ought to be to the people, with his attempts to free stage design from the naked images of reality, he began to write his autobiography, *My Life*, and finished it in Moscow before leaving for Berlin and Paris. It was published ten years later.

That he sat down to put his reminiscences on paper must have been the result of deep-felt disappointments, of unfulfilled days, of a feeling of being lost in a vacuum. These

V   Marc Chagall LE TRAPEZISTER

143

stories of his life were written in an almost expressionistic, often telegraphic style, with half-line paragraphs, but with the rich colours of a visual imagination. He closely related his writing to his painting and on the last page says: 'These pages have the same meaning as a painted surface. If there were a hiding place in my pictures, I would slip them into it . . . Or perhaps they would cling to the back of one of my characters . . .' Henry Miller once described Chagall as a poet with painted wings. His poetry is also in his writing. The images and colours are there. Only his form does not shock as much as his paintings: the heads of most people are not upside-down, the primitive joy of flying lovers is far more earthly. And yet, his prose speaks in painted pictures.

A wounded soul cried out at the end of his book: 'Neither Imperial Russia, nor the Russia of the Soviets needs me. They don't understand me. I am a stranger to them. I'm certain Rembrandt loves me'. He felt akin to Rembrandt and Cézanne, who are both included among his relatives together with his mother, his grandfather, who was a rabbi, and his wife Bella, immortalized in his gentle paintings of love and lovers ('. . . a painting is not much more than another way of loving'). I am certain that Rembrandt would have loved him.

## George Grosz

In *A Little Yes and a Big No*, the autobiography of George Grosz (1893–1959), one is not quite sure of how much the writer conveniently forgot or what he chose not to say. For in his preface he warns the reader not to expect to hear the truth, the whole truth, and nothing but the truth. On the contrary, 'If I had all this material in front of me: notes about the First World War, letters, passports, family photographs, love letters – everything that attaches itself to one during the course of a turbulent life . . . I still would not resort to them. I cannot and will not write a profile of myself'. Apparently he wanted to avoid writing a profile, a sharply focused picture of his personality, and preferred to exhibit only snapshots. George Grosz obviously wanted to make sure that the reader would be aware of his consciously faulty memory, although we do not expect any autobiography to be true to the letter of each experience.

Grosz's life was clearly divided in two sections, the pre-exile period which he spent in Germany until 1933 and which is also the longer and far richer time of his career, followed by his emigration to America where he stayed almost the rest of his life and where he wrote his book about himself.

The title of the book telescopes the whole tragedy of our time and the tragedy of the artist and man, George Grosz. We must read into it his reaction to life as a whole. He found little affirmative in it and wanted to shout his big No into the world. The big No is indicative of Grosz in post-war Germany, a period in which he reacted to the physical and moral collapse of society with drawings of a merciless vitriolic satire. When the nightmare world of the twenties turned into the Hitlerian inferno, Grosz came to America where he desperately desired to find new roots. It was as if he wanted to forget his own most terrifying indictment of post-war Europe. He began to paint, mainly the American landscape in which he wanted to re-plant his roots. His little Yes speaks to us from the work he did in America. When he shouted his protest in post-war Germany, he was heard all over the world. When he whispered his little Yes, a small circle listened with understanding.

His was the tragedy of the exiled artist. But he was not only a refugee from Hitler's Germany; he became a refugee from himself, from his time. He denounced his own denunciation of a corrupted and phoney world. When he entered America and swore allegiance, vowing to do nothing that would help to overthrow the government, he took his oath more than literally. Some time later he wrote:

. . . my friend Alexander King . . . was the only one who took me for what I was, an analyst and interpreter, and did not pull his punches. He would say: 'Scratch their eyes out, George, the sharper the better'. But, for me, something of that spirit had died.
I wanted to be a 'free' artist, but I was apprehensive. The new visions and dreams were no longer distortions or caricatures. They were not created or designed to improve or educate man. They were now composed of apocalyptic fire and intimated the duality of the world.
We travel along strange paths. I did some thorough thinking and discarded many former ideas as illusions. I was still capable of changing my mind . . . Now I sharply rejected my previous work, and caricature in general. Lacking inspiration from man and things, I found new worlds were available. Nature came closer to me in its greater simplicity, unity, beauty and inexorable permanence.
Yes, the second phase of my life began in America, but with it came an inner conflict over the break with my past . . .

In his descriptions of the period after 1917 when he had become one of the leaders of German Dadaism, Grosz makes light of the movement. Disparaging remarks fill these pages ('If Dada made no sense to the masses, it at least served as an

145

outlet for the rich playboys who financed our movement. We simply mocked everything . . . Nothing was holy to us . . . We spat upon everything, including ourselves. Our symbol was nothingness, a vacuum, a void . . .'). Grosz wrote that he was simply reporting what he experienced, that he was not attempting to make or seek any explanation.

His autobiography is full of confessions – particularly because he tried to avoid taking issue with his life and life in this age – and one of the most indicative confessions tells of his secret enjoyment in drawing 'natural, normal illustrations' while he 'travelled the paths and bypaths of insane Dadaism'. In his second phase he embraced the sober reality by which he found himself surrounded, he enjoyed the glorification of the small middle-class in real life and in the illustrations of the American magazines.

Strangely enough, he chose to illustrate his *A Little Yes and A Big No* with those devastating drawings which damned the same society for whose understanding of his dilemma he pleaded in his book. Strangely enough, he finally felt drawn back to Berlin and returned to the place in 1958 where the real unreal George Grosz was once at home. A few months later he had a fatal accident.

*Plates 36-38*

## Salvador Dali

*The Secret Life of Salvador Dali* (1905–) is an apotheosis of narcissism. His spiritual perversions often reach the grotesque. On four hundred large and closely printed pages, interspersed with several visualizations of his eccentric fantasy, Dali professes to pour out his innermost thoughts and feelings. But he writes with the nerve and voice of a barker at a fair, who confesses that 'it has often become impossible for me to know where reality begins and the imaginary ends'. And one looks into the recesses of his mind and the receptacles of his emotions, exposed in black and white, with the same fascination of incredulous belief with which one looks, astounded, at his limp and shape-lost watches hanging down melancholy from the edges of eternity.

*Plate XII*

The invisible and inaudible alarm in those watches awoke Dali one day to his fame. From that time on he lived the ensuing hours with the consciousness of one surprised, who is out to surprise the world. He is a craftsman par excellence, but he is an equally good showman who knows how to whip up his extraordinary artistry into utilitarian ecstasy. The poetic fullness of his colours and his technical proficiency of the painstaking detail mingle with the weird imagery of his

146

dream-life. The result is a deliberately conceived replica of man's divine madness, revolting and enchanting, beguiling and perplexing.

Dali developed some beautifully varnished idiosyncrasies such as his predilection for watches and his pet hatred for the telephone:

Telephone frappé, mint-coloured telephone, aphrodisiac telephone, lobster-telephone . . . Edgar Allan Poe telephones with a dead rat concealed within, Boecklin telephones installed inside a cypress tree (and with an allegory of death in inlaid silver on their backs), telephones on the leash which would walk about, screwed to the back of a living turtle . . . telephones . . . telephones . . . telephones

His images are steadily in search of their fetishistic verifications. ('All my life I have been preoccupied with shoes, which I have utilized in several surrealist objects and pictures to the point of making a kind of divinity of them'.) In his work living organisms are often made to function like machines, while the inanimate takes the active part of the living. If such contradictory ideas are put to work and forced into the straitjacket of symbolic meaning, we find the catastrophic absurdity of our time in the title of his painting, *Debris of an automobile giving birth to a blind horse biting a telephone*. The painting literally translates Dali's triumphant fury over the tyranny of mechanization. Or: The image of a woman's beautiful torso casting a huge shadow on the sand of endlessness is called *Sphinx Embedded in the Sand*, and Dali's own descriptive words are: 'with a woman's slippers and a glass of warm milk underneath the skin of her back – the most active fetishes in my life'.

Salvador Dali is quite conscious of his craftsmanship and the absurdities of his time which, not being receptive to any traditionally meaningful form of artistic expression, forces such artists as he into the avenue of 'novelty – which is after all what you are after', as Dali says about himself. His work shows in sincerest self-revelation that he deeply believes in tradition which, in his opinion, holds the key to invention. To let the world see the wonders of his secret life was always a necessity for him. He himself issues his own passport for his many voyages of artistic adventure. If he should ever be stigmatized as a master counterfeiter of the current money he needs for these journeys, then he can rightly claim that his imitations are more genuine than the original values used for his fraudulent fancies.

He is always true to himself, no matter whether he visualizes himself in embryonic nakedness in an eggshell, or whether he jumps through the window of a bookstore where he is supposed to sign copies of his *Secret Life*. True to himself, he tends to outstrip all mental stripteasers, who use their pens for this purpose. ('Since 1929 I have had a very clear consciousness of my genius and I confess that this conviction, ever more deeply rooted in my mind, has ever excited in me emotions of the kind called sublime'.)

Dali writes with the joy and ease of a verbal juggler. He admits that he has always admired conversationalists. Since he became a 'talker' after having overcome 'the remnants of my pathological timidity', his admiration for himself seems to be unlimited, and to some extent deservedly so. It is a characteristically Dalinesque idea to write an autobiography at the age of thirty-seven. But, after all, it begins with intra-uterine memories and exposes the surrealistic life of 'the most representative incarnation of post-war Europe', as Dali in a flashing moment after four hundred pages of self-reflection confesses in all modesty.

How entertaining humorous madness and surrealistic aggressiveness can be! 'I am completely naked', he writes in his epilogue, 'and look at myself; my hair is still black as ebony, my feet have not yet known the degrading stigma of a single corn . . . I want only two things: first, to love Gala, my wife; and second, that other inescapable thing, so difficult and so little desired – to grow old.'

When we come to the last page of Dali's autobiography, we have seen – in his uninhibited nakedness – an artist of stature and a tortured human being crying out for love and faith. He wrote another book and may still write a third. But in whatever he does, whether he paints, draws, or writes, Dali involuntarily acts and lives with the mocking seriousness befitting our time. From its tombstone I can visualize Salvador Dali's watches hanging down in nonchalant boredom and telling eternity of a moment in which Dali was one flashing facet of time's many incarnations.

## The Turn of the Century

When history books about the twentieth century are written from a greater perspective, it may be said that the first half of this epoch began in 1895 and lasted until 1945 when the atom bomb was dropped on Hiroshima. These fifty years have undoubtedly been a preparatory period leading to a new era which may run under such headings as the electronic or atomic age. These fifty years will probably be marked as important decades, as were the latter half of the fifteenth and sixteenth centuries.

By 1900 the world was completely conquered and colonized by white man, divided and redivided. A saturation point was reached which, by its own momentum, had to lead to combustions within, to cataclysmic events without. Our century was destined to reap the results of the Industrial Revolution with mass movements, mass communications, refrigeration, synthetic food, radar, antibioticized bodies and 'air-conditioned nightmares', as Henry Miller said.

Man enjoyed playing with the toys of technology. He became speed-mad. In his Futurist Manifesto of 1909, the Italian poet Filippo Marinetti hailed those puffing and fuming automobiles which began to invade the landscapes like raging cockroaches demanding more and better roads, as 'more beautiful than the Nike of Samothrace . . .' Ever since, man has moved at a frightening speed to improve the condition of whatever is before letting it mature to full ripeness. Among the technological wonders were the silent movies which, at the very moment when they had reached almost artistic perfection were made to talk and to talk themselves out of their own achievement. When the Wright Brothers took off from the ground in 1906 and when, twenty-one years later, Charles Lindberg triumphed with his lone flight across the Atlantic, the skies shrank in fear of man's daring. The thin voice of the French mystic Simone Weil said that it was immoral to reach a destination without having made a journey.

But mankind was much too busy to listen, it had to stem one of those many tides which always turn everything upside down, it was about to erase an evil it had helped to grow. Meanwhile, theologians and philosophers studied God's obituaries, and scientists proclaimed that tomorrow they would be able to stop death, to create artificial life and reveal the mystery of creation by hauling the cosmos down to earth.

The germ of change became manifest at the turn of the century. At that time, man was aware of having a new destiny but did not quite know when or where it was to be. Not since the Renaissance days had man been so conscious of his own power, his own greatness as when he woke up to the realization that this was a new epoch. Of course, he could

149

not foresee the many moments of frightening darkness through which he would have to move before watching the mushrooming clouds of his atomic blasts. Then, he did not know that one day he would push buttons and turn on gadgets relentlessly, would see and hear what happens at the very moment it was happening all over the world; that he would have perfected communication but would suffer from noncommunicativeness. Then, he could not know that forty or fifty years hence W. H. Auden would say to him 'Aloneness is man's real condition', and Jean-Paul Sartre's voice would shout 'Hell is other people!' Man, at that early date, could not be aware of the dangers that lay ahead: that the more magnificent his cars and roads became, the more easily he might lose control over his destiny.

When this century was young, we were sure of ourselves and of our task to rebuild the world in the image of the twentieth-century gods. However, not quite sure of what this image was, we tried and groped from one -ism to the next: Imagism, Fauvism, Orphism, Futurism, Vorticism, Cubism, Expressionism, Dadaism, Surrealism; after the second World War Existentialism had opened the gates, futility and nihilism dispatched, in sardonic joy of their prolificacy, an endless variety of –isms into the land of the absurd.

Man's awareness has constantly grown and with it man's denial of himself. With the years he became frantic in the search for his own identity. While penetrating his subliminal being, he discovered his spiritual isolation. While tearing down the old world he tried to cope with and stem the avalanche of crumbling values. He looked for the meaningfulness of meaning, and finding none he decided to make a virtue out of the void. An angry young world shouted that it did not want to be punished for the follies of its fathers. Man was finally caught in paroxysms of negation and, since he could not get out of them, he wallowed and still wallows in their interpretations.

In spite of all this, and to paraphrase Shakespeare, I would say: 'I do not come to bury our time, I come to praise it'. Not since the Renaissance did man have such greatness offered to him. And he did make the best of it, even though the times were confusing and confused. Charles Péguy said in 1913 that 'the world has changed less since Jesus Christ than it has in the last thirty years'. Although such a statement is exaggerated, it also carries a great deal of truth. This statement assumes greater justification if we look at the drastic changes of the last seventy years or so.

34  Paul Gauguin HEAD OF A YOUNG TAHITIAN

35  Edgar Degas DANCER LOOKING AT THE SOLE OF HER RIGHT FOOT

36   George Grosz NUDE

37   George Grosz A SONG OF YOUTH

38   George Grosz GOD WITH GASMASK

The poetry of our science, the hard-hitting prose of technology will be written about in the next century. People will marvel at the ingenuity of our architecture. They will hardly wonder why the dance – always closely related to architecture – was so prominent in a world which had become so visual-minded. In this light, the film will be considered the great invention of the century as a new artistic medium, and with it the mass media, radio and television. Some of the arts may be found lagging in their struggle to adjust to the dominance of the electronic in life.

As indicated in the chapter, *Environment as Creative Stimulus*, versatility cannot be in doubt in our age. The temptation to find new manners or forms of expression in new fields has been too great. What can be doubted is whether the level is sufficiently high on which the multiple talent unfolds. It is comforting to know that in an age in which science and technology dominate, some scientists feel the need to break out of the prison of specialization and join the artists who try to be jacks of all arts, if only to protest, to counteract, to spite, and to escape the total mechanization of our existence. We encounter such scientists as Buckminster Fuller, whose horizon is wide enough to encompass architecture, philosophy, and *belles lettres*, or Lord Bertrand Russell, a philosopher and mathematician, writer and professional reformer, educator and political revolutionary.

*Plate 41*

There was Le Corbusier, one of the greatest and most influential architects of the century. His real name was Charles Édouard Jeanneret and he was born in Switzerland in 1887. He was a leading architect in industrial design and city planning. He was a fine poet, painter and sculptor, and he was an articulate pamphleteer:

A town is a tool.

Towns no longer fulfil this function. They are ineffectual; they use up our bodies, they thwart our souls.

The lack of order to be found everywhere in them offends us; their degradation wounds our self-esteem and humiliates our sense of dignity.

They are not worthy of the age; they are no longer worthy of us.

A city!

It is the grip of man upon nature. It is a human operation directed against nature, a human organism both for protection and for work. It is a creation.

Poetry also is a human act – the harmonious relationships between perceived images. All the poetry we find in nature is but the creation of our own spirit. A town is a mighty image which stirs our minds. Why should not the town be, even today, a source of poetry?

There was Albert Schweitzer, musician, physician, writer, one of the great universal geniuses whose realistic attitudes to the burning problem of our time had a saintly connotation.

Physicians who entered maturity at the beginning of this century, showed a trend toward writing, beginning with Anton Chekhov, who, however, did not see too many years of the twentieth century; Arthur Schnitzler wrote prose and plays at the time when Freud began to probe man's psyche in Vienna; Axel Munthe, the Swedish physician, who practised psychiatry in Paris, became world-famous with his book, *The Story of San Michele*.

'To be more than a man in the world of man . . . to escape from the human condition', wrote a vibrant Promethean figure of universal gifts, André Malraux, adventurer, revolutionary, traveller, linguist, politician, and a poet, novelist and art critic, as well as one of the last great conversationalists. 'The monuments in a man's life do not add up in orderly accumulation. Biographies which run from the age of five to fifty are false confessions. It is his experiences that situate a man.' Nothing could more fittingly describe Malraux.

*Plate 51*

His novels, *Man's Fate* and *Man's Hope*, have become classics. His three works on the arts, *The Voices of Silence*, *The Imaginary Museum of World Sculpture* and *The Metamorphosis of the Gods* have made art history. No other man has experienced more in so many diverse areas of activity than he has. His autobiography testifies to it. 'If I can say to myself, on dying', he was quoted to have said, 'that there are 500,000 young people who, thanks to my work, have seen the opening of a window by which they can escape the rigours of technocracy, the aggressiveness of advertising, the need always to make more money for leisure activities which are, for the most part, violent or vulgar – if I can say that, I will die happy . . .' Among the din of voices Malraux's voice is the most unique one of this century.

Basically, Malraux is a man of letters, whose creative mind is also an active and restless mind, who lives with the concern of a man for the meaningfulness of life. In a different way and in a different area we find an artist of our time showing a similar concern. This century saw a multiple genius emerge together with an art form which could have only come into existence in our technological age. The art form is the film, and it brought forth the greatest comedian of silent movies, Charlie Chaplin.

We may assume that he would have excelled all comedians even without the help of this medium. But the fact remains that the silent movies gave him the opportunity to unfold his talents for the benefit of millions of people, from China to Chile, from Sweden to South Africa. Humour, and particularly satire, is intrinsically tied to the peculiarities of a culture and nation. Chaplin, in the disguise of a tramp, with his uncanny cane, boots and hat, transcended all boundaries of geography and time.

The film has been a new incentive to multiple creativity. Even if the director does not write the scenario, which often he does, he dominates the scene. There are skilful cameramen, but, essentially, it is the director who has learned to see with the eye of the camera, to paint the background, to sculpt the living images. In comparison to the actor on stage, who develops a character in front of the audience, the movie actor, however much talent and personality he may bring to his part, is a puppet in the hands of the director. There have been many directors who have genius, but Ingmar Bergman is particularly distinguished through the poetry and psychology, through the daring and penetrating subject matter which he invents and to which he gives cinematic life in an artistically most persuasive manner. Sergei M. Eisenstein, an architect and engineer before he began his film career in 1924, probably gave cinematic art its strongest impetus. He expounded his montage theories and techniques in a book, called *The Film Sense*. Eisenstein, who drew and painted, exemplifies the idea of the one-man film creator.

But no director has ever embraced the totality of this new art as Charlie Chaplin did. He is his own leading actor, director and composer. And he certainly is a dancer since movement is basic to every moment of his acting. His direction is choreographically orientated. If there ever was a creative entity in the performing arts, then it is his. *The Gold Rush, City Lights, Modern Times* are works of a multiple genius in a medium which was the genial medium of his early years.

Chaplin began with the knock-about comedy of slapstick and farce, but he worked himself up to the heights of classical satire. His 'fun' did more than create laughter. He started with an individual case, enlarged its validity and then reduced it to its skeleton. There is nothing more ridiculous than to be exposed to the world in one's own nakedness. This is the function of satire. But the laughter thus generated leaves a sting in our soul. We discover that we are part of this world which

e. e. cummings
Charlie Chaplin

Chaplin scourges with our laughter. True, it is fun but fun in a subtler sense of the word. Without being pathetic, it is pathetic fun because of its definite aim and instructive value, of which we are unconsciously aware. We learn by laughing about ourselves, without being compelled to admit that we are the target of our contempt. It is the inaudible pathos in Chaplin's fun which marks his work as great satire.

The lonely figure of The Tramp who walked through the incongruities of life and who reacted to them with a puzzled and puzzling innocence was a universal character with whom one could easily identify. Every one of his little gestures and every bit of his suffering, however fun-provoking, grew in its dimensions of meaning. The habit and habits of this tramp, his involvement with society in all its tragicomic consequences, were detailed in devastating symbolism. The invention of this figure was a stroke of genius. There are very few characters in world literature who have caught the imagination of the people through the centuries; the Don Quixote of the late Renaissance, the Don Juan of the Baroque, the medieval Faust of Romanticism.

Chaplin's tramp who, at the end of his travails and our amusement, trailed off hopefully towards the distant horizon and into an unknown tomorrow, was the classic figure of a time caught in the callousness of technology. He was the last and lonely individualist pitted against the movement of the masses. He was the ironic and satiric reflection in the broken mirror of an aching time.

WHISTLER'S WIT

The story has been told that James Whistler and Oscar Wilde were together at a banquet. In the course of the animated conversation Whistler dropped one of his amusing *bon mots*, whereupon Oscar Wilde said: 'James, I wish I'd said that!' Whistler's reply was: 'You will, Oscar! You will!'

James Abbott McNeil Whistler (1834–1903), the American painter and etcher, first went to Paris where he scored a signal success at the Salon des Refusés with his *Little White Girl* in 1863. Then he took up headquarters in London and defended his credo of *l'art pour Whistlerien art* in lectures and polemics. His eccentricities and acid wit made him notoriously known long before he became famous as a painter. Disgusted with the ugliness and squalor of daily life in its Victorian surroundings, he became inspired by the delicacy and dreamlike woolliness of Japanese prints. He was a master in blending purely decorative elements and atmosphere with poetic subtlety. He was as little an impressionist in the true sense of the word as was Degas, or Rodin. Capturing atmosphere did not mean to him achieving a maximum effect of light and colour. His concern was with the design of delicate patterns and the avoidance of literary interest. He loved to play with subdued tones without becoming sentimental.

The irony of history played an evil trick on him: he became known to the multitude, generation after generation, as the portraitist of his mother, by a painting which has become the picture postcard ideal of the Victorian sentimentality that Whistler loathed all his life. At the same time when he exhibited this work, in 1871, it was called *Arrangement in Grey and Black*, and Whistler probably thought of it as the perfect expression of his maxim that what matters in painting is not the subject but the manner in which colour and form evoke a feeling. But the very subject he chose expressed the drama of a mother's resigned loneliness, and his choice of subdued colour composition enhanced the drama to cliché-like obviousness.

John Ruskin, painter, essayist, and art critic, the champion of Pre-Raphaelitic beauty, was as much incensed by the materialistic standards of Victorian England as Whistler was. Yet Ruskin and Whistler went different ways and became bitter enemies. Many people thought of Whistler as an imperious, arrogant, and quarrelsome person. The fact is that his life was not only blessed with success but also with lawsuits, of which the one against John Ruskin was the most publicized. Whistler, who knew how to promote a good as well as a bad cause, gave a detailed account of the proceedings of his libel suit in his book, *The Gentle Art of Making Enemies*.

*Plate 39*    In 1877 Whistler's series of night-pieces which he called *Nocturnes* were exhibited, and the painter had priced each of them at 200 guineas. John Ruskin wrote:

For Mr. Whistler's own sake, no less than for the protection of the purchaser, Sir Coutts Lindsay ought not to have admitted works into the gallery in which the ill-educated conceit of the artist so nearly approached the aspect of wilful imposture. I have seen, and heard, much of cockney impudence before now; but never expected to hear a coxcomb ask two hundred guineas for flinging a pot of paint in the public's face.

'That passage, no doubt', Whistler contended, 'had been read by thousands, and so it had gone forth to the world that Mr. Whistler was an ill-educated man, an impostor, a cockney pretender, and an impudent coxcomb.'

Essentially, the cross-examination turned around the question of whether these pictures were finished products or mere sketches since Whistler admitted that he 'completed the mass of the pictures in one day'. Ruskin's attorney claimed that the defendant had the highest appreciation for completed pictures; and he required from an artist that he should possess something more than a few flashes of genius. When Whistler was asked whether he really demanded the enormous sum of 200 guineas for the work of a day or two, he replied: 'No, I ask it for the knowledge of a lifetime'. This libel suit ended with 'Verdict for plaintiff. Damages one farthing'.

*The Gentle Art of Making Enemies* is filled with satiric diatribes, venomous assaults, and whiplashing gestures against friends and foes. As in Whistler's other book, *Ten O'Clock*, his hostility and aggressiveness found a convenient, and probably wholesome, vent in his verbal wit, pungent polemics, and epigrammatic attacks against whoever crossed him. When Dante Gabriel Rossetti once laboured hard on a picture and sonnet simultaneously, with the sonnet actually treating of the same subject matter as the painting, Whistler is said to have told him: 'If I were you I would take the picture out of its frame and put the sonnet into it'.

Whistler's epigrams had the polish of Oscar Wilde's prose at its best:

Industry in Art is a necessity – not a virtue – and any evidence of the same, in the production, is a blemish, not a quality; a proof, not of achievement, but of absolutely insufficient work, for work alone will efface the footsteps of work.

The masterpiece should appear as the flower to the painter – perfect in its bud as in its bloom – with no reason to explain its presence – no mission to fulfil – a joy to the artist, a delusion to the philanthropist – a puzzle to the botanist – an accident of sentiment and alliteration to the literary man.

Nature sings her exquisite song to the artist alone, her son and her master – her son in that he loves her, her master in that he knows her.

Algernon Charles Swinburne, taking Whistler to task for his *Lecture on Art*, referred in Fortnightly Review, June 1888, to 'the light and glittering bark of this brilliant amateur in the art of letters', which 'is not invariably steered with equal dexterity of hand between the Scylla and Charybdis of paradox and platitude; it is impossible that in its course it should not once and again touch upon some point worth notice, if not exploration'. Whistler was more often than not wrong with his apodictic pronouncements which he gave forth during his many lectures. Swinburne tried to do him justice when he spoke of 'an artist of Mr Whistler's genius and a writer of Mr Whistler's talents'.

Whistler's work as a painter, etcher, and lithographer was distinguished by an evocative atmospheric quality; it was brilliantly executed in its fine luminosity and poetic delicacy. In contrast to it, his writing and lecturing was provoked by a flamboyant and exhibitionistic streak in his nature. He could not have chosen a more fitting symbol with which to sign his visual work than a butterfly in its iridescent beauty. A gadfly should have been his signature under his polemics and lectures.

As a reaction to Whistler's famous Ten O'Clock lecture on art in the Prince's Hall, London, on February 20, 1885, Oscar Wilde wrote in the *Pall Mall Gazette* of Whistler's 'really marvellous eloquence', and described him as 'a miniature Mephistopheles, mocking the majority' and the lecture as a masterpiece. Oscar Wilde ended his review with great insight into the creative process of a versatile man when he said:

As long as a painter is a painter merely, he should not be allowed to talk of anything but mediums and megilp, and on those subjects should be compelled to hold his tongue; it is only when he becomes an artist that the secret laws of artistic creation are revealed to him. For there are not many arts, but one art merely: poem, picture and Parthenon, sonnet and statue – all are in their essence the same, and he who knows one knows all. But the poet is the supreme artist, for he is the master of colour and of form, and the real musician besides, and is lord over all life and all arts; and so to the poet beyond all others are these mysteries known; to Edgar Allan Poe and to Baudelaire, not to Benjamin West and Paul Delaroche.

Whereupon Whistler answered Wilde in a letter printed in the *World* a few days later:

I have read your excellent article in the *Pall Mall*. Nothing is more delicate, in the flattery of 'the Poet' to 'the Painter', than the naiveté of 'the Poet', in the choice of his Painters – Benjamin West and Paul Delaroche!

This prompted Wilde's reply in which he warned 'the painter in Whistler' not to fret his energies away with exhibitionism:

Dear Butterfly, – By the aid of a biographical dictionary, I made the discovery that there were once two painters called Benjamin West and Paul Delaroche, who rashly lectured upon Art. As of their works nothing at all remains, I conclude that they explained themselves away.
Be warned in time, James; and remain, as I do, incomprehensible. To be great is to be misunderstood.

Butterfly
James McNeill Whistler's
signature

159

When Wilde said in his review 'that an artist is not an isolated fact; he is the resultant of a certain milieu and a certain entourage', he also characterized Whistler as a phenomenon of the *fin de siècle*, a symbol of the fastidious elegance and arrogance of Dandyism. Whistler could easily have been a figure in one of Oscar Wilde's plays in which the characters indulge in wit for wit's sake. Perhaps Whistler did recognize some of his wit in the epigrammatic banter of Wilde's characters. At least, he often insinuated that he was plagiarized and made this clear when Wilde attacked him in a letter to the newspaper *World* on November 24, 1886, by saying: '. . . With our James vulgarity begins at home, and should be allowed to stay there', to which Whistler replied: 'A poor thing, Oscar! – but for once I suppose "your own".'

THE POET PAUL KLEE

The world of Paul Klee is a world all by itself. You can only *Plate IX* enter it with the wonder of the innocent, with the eyes of someone who can see the reality behind the unreal. His pictures have often been called fables, but they are no sanctuary for escapists, they do not reflect a dream life in a vacuum, they are not a means of evading reality for reality's sake. Others have pointed out that Klee was an excellent musician, that music meant to him as much as colour, form and poetry, and to them his pictures are graphic images of musical rhythms. His work has puzzled and perplexed a great many people; sometimes it is compared to the outgrowth of a child's imagination, and Klee himself refers in his *Diaries* to 'the legend of the childishness of my drawings'.

However his drawings and paintings may strike us, their irrational images regain the validity of rationality through Klee's artistic sleight of hand. Poetry can sing between the lines, music and some theatre dance are able to touch upon and to reveal universal truths by the simplest creative means. Klee's microcosmic world of poetry-made-visual also achieves that reality in the intangible.

A visitor to Klee's studio in Munich described it as 'an alchemist's laboratory'. Klee was often working on several paintings at the same time and, in explaining some of them, he spoke with great simplicity: 'I had to do it that way so that the birds could sing'. His world is full of birds and flowers, of fishes and waves, of houses, trees and some people. They are there in the most abstracted form of life – to be what they are, to mean what we see in them. Klee's poetry lies in the magic of his self-imposed limitations, in the art of creating a whole out of the minutest elements and of reaching from the particular into the universal.

In their symbolism, his paintings are reduced to the essential, to allusion rather than any statement. They are poetic in their suggestiveness, in their ability to transform reality into a remote poetic image which becomes more real than concrete reality. It is through the poetic image that his paintings and drawings evoke sensations the scope of which is as varied and wide as our perception and imagination.

All his life Klee was addicted to words as much as to colour, lines and shapes. The writing in his *Diaries* shows the remarkable way he had with words. He was about twenty when he wrote a love poem in prose to Eveline. 'By Eveline', he wrote, 'I meant fulfilment, the ideal'.

> *Finally, Eveline becomes the Muse of all my desolation . . .*
> *I call Eveline a green dream under foliage, the dream*
> *of a naked child on the meadow.*
>
> *March threatens us with summer as you threaten my soul*
> *with burning love, Eveline!*
> *May still waxes green. These are still cradle songs.*
> *I sharpened many a steely word. I wanted to be a rock*
> *in the tide.*
>
> *Do not flee from my proximity! Trust! Recognize! You have*
> *dried up the swamps of my soul, now you are hidden in*
> *clouds Your victory will be complete.*
>
> *When reality is no longer endurable, it appears as a*
> *dream dreamt with open eyes. Continue, dreadful dream,*
> *with Eveline. O deceptive illusion, that you yourself,*
> *singed and burnt, seek shelter and consolation with me.*
>
> *This is the great day, aglow with nothing but love. Will*
> *there be an end here too, a twilight? Will a goddess fall?*
> *Still it is day, still aglow with nothing but love.*

Klee took his ability as a poet very seriously and often gave it a more than passing thought: 'Many poems should have given form to my newly gained creative strength. Of course, this intention was not realized. For to be a poet and to write poetry are two different things. However, that strength and tranquillity has remained dear to me even in my later life, I would not like to have anyone making fun of it'.

He did not seem to have been an avid, but rather a selective, reader. In 1901, when he was twenty-two, we find in his *Diaries* the entry: 'That Aristophanes! I wish I too might write a good comedy'. Attempts in that genre followed.

It was a year later that he projected the being he wanted to become when he noted:

The main thing now is not to paint precociously but to be or, at least, to become a human being. The art of mastering life is the prerequisite for all further forms of expression, whether they are paintings, sculptures, tragedies, or musical compositions. Not only to master life in practice, but to shape it meaningfully within me and, by doing so, to achieve as mature an attitude as possible. It is obvious that this cannot be accomplished with a few general precepts but that it grows like nature. I also wouldn't know how to find any such precepts. *A Weltanschauung* will come of itself; the will alone doesn't determine which direction will yield the clearest path, this is partly settled in the womb and is predetermined by fate.

In many ways 1902 was a turning point in Klee's life and work. His Italian journey was behind him. He looked critically at himself and, as he expressed it, he felt 'some spiritual development' taking place. It seems that from then on he began to think more and more in similes and symbols, and turned them into the visions of his life. In December of that year he wrote a poem, most indicative of his *Lebensphilosophie*:

> *While looking at a tree:*
> *The birds are to be envied,*
> *they avoid*
> *thinking about the tree and its roots*
> *and all day long, agile and satisfied, they swing*
> *and sing, perched on the very tip of the branches.*

Trees continued to be of great significance to him in his work and in his thoughts. 'Let me use a simile, the simile of a tree', Klee said in a lecture he gave at Jena in 1924 in which he tried to convey his artistic experience. 'The artist is like a tree. He has dealt with this bewildering world pretty well and he has managed to cope with it, we shall assume, in his own quiet way. He has found his bearings well enough to set order into the flight of appearances and experiences. This orientation among the things of nature and life, this order with all its ramifications, I liken to the roots of the tree. From these roots comes the sap that streams through the artist and through his eye, for he is the trunk of the tree. Under the pressure of this mighty flow, he channels what he visually experiences into his work. And just as the foliage spreads out in time and space, visible from all sides, so grows the artist's work.'

To him 'art is a simile of Creation. Each work of art is an example, just as the terrestrial is an example of the cosmic'.

In his *Creative Credo* he gives a vivid account of how his inner vision and conscience as an artist built his world of lines and dots and colours. He invites us to enter this world as if we were to take a journey: 'Let yourself be carried on the invigorating sea, on a broad river and also on an enchanting brook such as that of the richly diversified, aphoristic graphic art'.

His must have been a very strong urge to express himself through words, and time and again the written word found its way into his graphic pictures as much as into his paintings as another kind of symbol beside colour and form. They all became interwoven into the unified realization of a dream.

The choice of his titles which are either unusual or poetically suggestive also shows his sensitivity to verbal imagery and sound. *Harbinger of Autumn; Pious Northern Landscape; Revolution of a Viaduct; This Star Teaches How to Bend; Laughing Gothic; Dance, Monster, to My Soft Song; Virgin in a Tree;* or *Flower Myth* are some examples. In his watercolour *Once Emerged from the Gray of Night . . .* he created a colourful picture out of little squares which he filled with the letters of a poem. The immediate impact is similar to the one of a medieval illuminated manuscript page. The letters function here as in many other of his paintings as a compositional element, fully integrated with the pictorial concept.

The letter R in his oil painting *Villa R* plays a dominant role in the structure of the picture. The letters in his gouache and gesso on canvas *The Vocal Fabric of the Singer Rosa Silber* seem playfully distributed when, in fact, they are intricately conceived in the spirit of the entire pictorial image. The isolated letters lose the banality of their alphabet reality and are the answer to an artistic need. They are not used in order to embellish or symbolize anything, but to convey the inner realization of the vocal fabric of a singer called Rosa Silber. In Klee's manner of microcosmic reduction, her personality is anagrammatized visually.

Antonin Artaud wrote about Klee that 'in his work the objects of the world fall into order, and it seems he was only taking down their dictation'. Artaud went on to say that Klee searched 'for the hidden sense', for 'an illumination of visions in the mind'. These visions often found expression in little poems which, as it seems, he did not write apart – dissociated from his drawings and paintings – but rather as a part of his creative needs.

His poems were not published during his lifetime. Some of them were found in a blue notebook, others were jotted down in his *Diaries*. They reflect his work as a painter in their

deceptive simplicity, in being cryptic and mystical, humorous
and ironic, philosophic and playful. With a touch of imagism
he wrote a poem in a self-reflective mood into his diary in
August 1917 while serving with the army:

> *Because I am, blossoms opened,*
> *Fullness is everywhere, because I am.*
> *My ear conjured for my heart*
> *The nightingale's song.*
> *I am father to all,*
> *All on the stars,*
> *And in the farthest places.*
> *And*
> *Because I left, evening came*
> *And mists of clouds*
> *Robed the light.*
> *Because I left,*
> *Nothing threw its shadow*
> *Over everything.*
> *O*
> *You thorn*
> *In the silver swelling fruit!*

Paul Klee's poem *A & B*, written in 1905, has a Brechtian
quality. Bertolt Brecht was then seven years of age.

> *A & B have been arguing long over a bottle*
> *of wine about their opposite points of view.*
> *In the stage of drunken sentimentality*
> *they meet half way in reconciliation.*
>
> *Each one delivers such a fiery speech*
> *that B finally reaches A's point of view*
> *and A the point of view of B.*
> *Surprise in their eyes, they join hands.*

Some of his poems display form and imagery close to, if not
identical with, the visual forms and pictorial images we have
come to see as essentially characteristic in his work. Two
examples, written in an interval of eight years, make it clear
that his inner vision was prompted by the same impulses and
directed in the same manner regardless of its visual or verbal
means of expression. We can readily translate *Poem* (1906)
into a graphic image:

> *Water,*
> *Waves upon it,*
> *a boat upon them,*
> *a woman upon it,*
> *a man upon her.*

The other *Poem*, written in 1914, is even more interesting since, with its surrealistic overtones, it covers more ground visually and has a decided point of view:

> *The big animals mourn at the table*
> *and are not satiated.*
>
> *But the small cunning flies*
> *climb mountains of bread*
> *and dwell in Buttertown.*
>
> *One thing alone is true:*
> *a weight in the self, a little stone.*
>
> *An eye that sees,*
> *another one that feels.*
>
> *Animal–Man:*
> *Clock of Blood.*
>
> *The moon*
> *in the railway station: one of the many*
> *lamps in the woods; a drop in the beard*
> *on the mountain:*
> *that it doesn't roll down!*
> *that it is not pierced by the cactus!*
> *that you do not sneeze the bladder to bits!*

Paul Klee was an individualist, untouched by any fashionable -isms, free from everything that went on around him. He said: 'I want to be as though newborn . . . knowing no pictures, entirely without impulses, almost in an original state'. And when he wrote his own epitaph he verbalized better than anyone could have done the goal of his earthly journey, the artist's dream fulfilled and yet unfulfilled:

HERE RESTS THE PAINTER
PAUL KLEE
BORN ON DECEMBER 18, 1879
DIED ON JUNE 29, 1940

I CANNOT BE GRASPED IN THE HERE AND NOW
FOR I LIVE JUST AS WELL WITH THE DEAD
AS WITH THE UNBORN
SOMEWHAT CLOSER TO CREATION THAN USUAL
AND STILL FAR FROM CLOSE ENOUGH

Looking at Alfred Kubin's work one feels transported into a dream world, but into one which is quite different from Paul Klee's. It lacks Klee's loftiness and lightness, the transparency of an illumined imagination. Kubin was referred to as 'a dream artist' as early as 1903. But the dream world he recreates deals with the raw material in which the psychiatrist is interested. He admits in his autobiography that he tried 'to capture dreams in picture form as they are still reflected in one's memory immediately after awakening'. He made a methodical study of dreams, he claims. Whatever clinical images this study may have yielded was at once fully embraced, absorbed and worked on and over by his fantasy.

*Plate 40*

'Fantasy is fate', he wrote, having been only too well aware of its potentialities in his own case. To begin with, it was a morbid fantasy which indulged in romantically weird or eerie images. As a boy he developed a burning curiosity for corpses. While he lived in the Austrian mountains, in Zell am See, the gravediggers often dragged decomposed bodies out of the lake in which many persons drowned, either by suicide or accident. 'This was the origin of my admitted interest in grisly scenes.'

Out of shreds of an imagined dream world and an innate tendency towards exaggeration Kubin developed a vision of a very unreal reality. He tells us that as a child he loved to draw cows with four horns and that his 'childish drawings . . . teemed with magicians, comic and terrifying cattle, landscapes consisting entirely of fire' – in short, the seed of the later Kubin was contained in them.

He was given to great excess. He could only grasp ideas when they were accompanied by 'an aura of sensualism'. At times he could completely shut himself off from the outside world and could obtain inner illumination in a state of indescribable quietude 'like a being for whom physical objects, the room and all my familiar past experiences, existed only as a delusion'. He once tried to immerse himself in Buddhism and lived for ten days like a Buddhist monk in self-styled isolation and meditation. But the exacting breathing exercises caused heart pain and frightened him into returning to his ordinary life. Also, there was a pessimistic undercurrent in his make-up which must have been responsible for some of his bizarre nocturnal attitudes. He devoured Schopenhauer and 're-velled in his ideas', in the pessimistic *Weltanschauung* which found a friendly echo in his mostly low-keyed, often desperate, mood.

Kubin was possessed of a strange power. He was fully aware of it and explained it best in his autobiography:

'I wandered aimlessly in the dark streets, overcome and literally ravished by a dark power that conjured up before my mind strange creatures, houses, landscapes, grotesque and frightful situations. I felt indescribably at ease and I exulted in my accursed world . . . I went into a small tearoom . . . As soon as I entered it, it seemed to me as though the waitresses were wax dolls actuated by God knows what mechanism, and as though the scattered guests . . . who appeared to me as unreal as shadows – had been surprised at some satanic rite . . . With a few bold strokes I put down in my notebook all that I could retain of these impressions.'

When he was thirty years old he put the short period behind him in which he painted with strong, lively colours. It was then that his father died. In the last years of his life he had become very close to him. His death stirred him 'to the depths as the intellectual realization that a whole chapter of my intensive emotional life had suddenly been turned into nothing'. Kubin's melancholy deepened and he lost all desire to work. In the months that followed he painted little but read a great deal, particularly old mystics, both Occidental and Oriental, to whom he had always been attracted. When working he sketched rather than painted. He felt he had to find a way out of his depression and decided to make a journey to achieve the impetus he needed. He travelled with a friend of his to northern Italy.

On his way home he felt a tremendous desire to occupy himself again with drawing. He was full of new ideas and images and he thought that what happened to him was a new world of inner splendour. He returned home, impatient and eager to start drawing. But when he sat down to begin work nothing happened to his fingers, his pen and paper. He was unable to put down any intelligible, coherent lines. He was frightened by being frustrated while, as he himself said, he 'was inwardly bursting with the need to work. In order to do something, no matter what, to unburden myself, I now began to compose and write down an adventure story. The ideas came flooding into my mind in superabundance; they forced me to work day and night, so that in twelve weeks' time my fantastic novel *Die andere Seite* was finished. During the next four weeks I provided it with illustrations'.

*The Other Side* was the work of a visionary. He himself thought of it as the turning point of his spiritual development. Written in 1907, it anticipated the cataclysmic events of the twentieth century. His gory visions pictured an Orwellian Dream Kingdom in which one man ruled dictatorially. He could not be seen or reached, but his image was hourly on the mind of the people whose life he dominated. Behind the artificial aura of Kubin's descriptive passages stood the cruel reality of our era. In this Dream Kingdom – hidden and completely shut off from the outside world, situated somewhere in the midst of Asia near Russia – an American appeared. He was as symbolic and unreal-real as the Master of the Kingdom. He appeared as the ruler's antagonist to start a revolution in the course of which, through the Master's ruthlessness or through unforeseen circumstances and events due to the illusionary life in the Kingdom, an inferno of nightmarish intensity broke loose. Horrors were piled upon horrors, climaxed by scenes which only the wildest and most morbid fantasy could dream of. But the behaviour pattern of animal and man and the consequences of a sick society with existentialist connotations carried a symbolism of Kafkaesque proportions.

This 'fantastic novel', as its subtitle says, was written long before Kafka was published, but it fully, and only in a more grotesque way, visualized his world. Later, when Kafka's writings became known, Kubin recognized his spiritual kinship with Kafka. It is unfortunate that Kubin had no opportunity to illustrate Kafka's work. A passage in his autobiography refers to it: 'I should also have liked very much to provide illustrations for one of Franz Kafka's novels, which touch me so intimately . . .'

What made Kubin write his novel, *The Other Side*? It was written as he expressed it, 'out of an inner compulsion and psychological necessity . . . in an extraordinary state of mind that was literally comparable to intoxication. I felt as though actually possessed of true clairvoyance'. Was Kubin at an impasse as a graphic artist at that time because, quite unconsciously, the notions, images and visions that gathered and gained propelling force to be shaped, to become alive could not be put down on paper as drawings but demanded verbalization? Or did this crisis make those notions, images and visions grow in a manner which did not lend itself to pictorial representation?

Immediately after he had put the story to paper he felt exhausted and irritable, mainly because he had misgivings about his daring to divert his creative urge into writing. He had not written anything before and thought he had insufficient self-criticism as to the literary quality in this alien medium. But

39 J. A. McNeill Whistler NOCTURNE. BLUE AND SILVER − CREMORNE LIGHTS

40 Alfred Kubin WATERHOLE AT NIGHT

41   Le Corbusier SELF-PORTRAIT

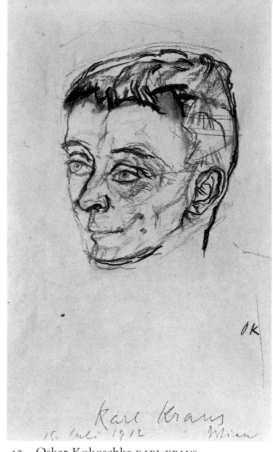

42   Oskar Kokoschka KARL KRAUS

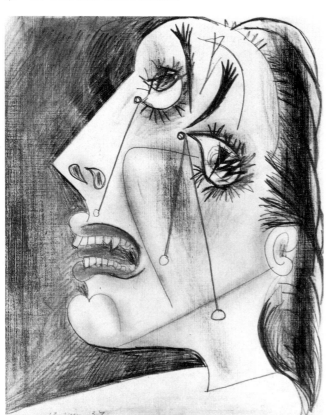

43   Pablo Picasso HEAD – A STUDY FOR 'GUERNICA'

44   Egon Schiele FRAU DR. H.

45 Oskar Kokoschka PAIR OF LOVERS WITH CAT – STUDY FOR A PAINTING

46 Ernst Ludwig Kirchner BATHERS

47   Paul Klee THE VOCAL FABRIC OF THE SINGER ROSA SILBER

his novel is amazingly well constructed and written, as the critical reaction to it proved. In this 'uncongenial activity' he only lacked economy. But he saw in the publication of this novel some danger to his artistic reputation 'since some people already believed that they detected literary elements in my drawings'.

Not only are there literary elements in his drawings, but his novel betrays the visual artist in him. This is not to be found in the imagery of his simple style as much as in the plastic and symbolic power of the scenes and in the dramatic sequence of events. Those familiar with Kubin's style of drawing can – while reading the novel – easily translate his verbal expression into his visual images. His drawings accompanying the text help stimulate the reader.

In writing this novel he was more ahead of his time than with his drawings, however unusual they were. His novel expresses the mentality of the sixties, the feeling of indifference after a series of cataclysmic crises, the strange mingling of anxiety with futility, and the glorification of the banal. Kubin felt very acutely what he expressed in his novel when he said: 'During its composition I achieved the mature realization that it is not only in the bizarre, exalted or comic moments of our existence that the highest values lie, but that the painful, the indifferent, and the incidental-commonplace contain these same mysteries. This is the principal meaning of the book'.

Kubin was very self-conscious and almost apologetic for having written this novel. He tried to explain, and his explanation was quite revealing: 'The fact that I wrote instead of drawing lay in the nature of the problem; this happened to be the right means to discharge my thronging ideas more rapidly than would otherwise have been possible'.

After having written *The Other Side* and gained some perspective to it, Alfred Kubin felt relief and a renewed desire to return to his drawings. It was an interlude for him. Through it he regained the necessary measure of inner calm. Later in his life he returned to writing. A collection of illustrated stories, called *Peep Show*, was published in 1925, and fourteen years later appeared a volume, *From the Desk of a Draughtsman*. It was real labour for him to write these two books, and they often sound laboured. The publishers had urged him to do them, and he tried to oblige – perhaps trying to test himself without taking the test too seriously. They do not have the inner motivation, the demonic experience, the compulsive drive of *The Other Side*, which remains a unique literary document of the tortured soul of a great painter.

There are very few titans among those whom we call geniuses. Pablo Picasso (1881–) has raged through this century, changing his face whenever he felt ready and creating with untiring energy one work after another. The focal point from which his energies expand is probably painting, but the universality of his genius has left its mark in the field of sculpture, drawing and etching, of murals and ceramics, of designs for the theatre and cinema. This only indicates the scope of the visual artist, whose hand is the tool of his genius.

His art is described as the mirror of our time and has been analysed from all aspects. The power of its vitality and violence gave the world a new vision and understanding of what art is; its insight gave us a deeper insight into our own being and a more profound feeling for our own time. His influence has been inestimable. If those who looked up to him or looked to him for guidance learned nothing else than that any artist must be true to himself, they learned a great deal.

*Plates 43, 49*

Painting has always been Picasso's passion, but we must not ignore that his paintings have an inherent sculptural quality. Even more important is the fact that Picasso has always thought in terms of total expression which in one medium reveals all other media. His entire oeuvre exemplifies this thought. The scope of his work also includes the writing of poetry and plays. This is not to say that had he been a writer only he would have been Pablo Picasso, but he is Pablo Picasso because he also writes. His urge to explore, to yield to the lure of uncovering the unknown, his curiosity and strength to please his curiosity had to lead to writing as another way of painting – painting with words. It is to be expected that in this medium also, he would break all rules and circumvent the obvious.

One day Picasso told Braque that 'punctuation is a *cache-sexe* which hides the private parts of literature'. He abandoned the traditional rules of punctuation and created monolithic entities made up of words which, whatever lyric meaning they may have by themselves, create a Picassoesque image of plastic poetry. Or as André Breton said in his essay in the *Cahiers d'Art* this is 'a poetry that cannot help being plastic to the same degree that (his) painting is poetic'.

André Breton was the first to have brought Picasso's poetry to the understanding of the public (or a relatively small intellectual élite). Since Picasso wrote his poetry in Spanish, the problem of translation was surmounted by Picasso himself who gave a word-by-word translation of some of his poetry to Breton. In his essay, Breton pointed out that Picasso as a painter desires 'to represent all that belongs to music'. 'We learn from this the necessity of a total expression by which he is possessed and which compels him to remedy in its essence the relative insufficiency of one art in relation to another.'

As Roland Penrose explains in his biography of Picasso, this 'new discovery was not a sideline or a hobby. It was a means of translating into words his intimate visual life'. For Picasso it is logical to choose a manner and medium for artistic expression which he feels is closest to what he has to say. 'Different motives inevitably require different methods of expression', he once explained. The temperamental mood of the artist must not be overlooked. His friend Jaime Sabartès tells us that one day while he was setting the table for lunch, Picasso came from the adjoining room saying: 'Look! Here is your portrait!' In contrast to earlier portraits he had made of Sabartès, this one was painted with words.

Picasso depends on and is inspired by his surroundings. He paints the way 'some people write their autobiography. The paintings, finished or not, are the pages of my journal . . .', he is quoted by Françoise Gilot. Whatever the artistic medium, the immediacy of reality is his point of departure, even though the final product may seem to be a departure from reality. Picasso sees mediocrity in the Apollonian achievement of harmony and seeks the unstable balance, the precariousness in his creation which, he feels, is then closest to the dramatic image of life.

> *In secret*
> *be silent say nothing*
> *how the street is full of stars*
> *and the prisoners eat the doves*
> *and the doves the cheese*
> *and the cheese the words*
> *and the words the bridges*
> *and the bridges the gazes*
> *and the gazes the bowl full of kisses*
> *in the orchata*
> *how everything hides in the wings*
> *the butterfly the night*
> *in a café last summer*
> *in Barcelona*

When instead of uniting he dissociates the partial images of the total image, he achieves a surprising and dramatic effect by upsetting our mind and by forcing our eyes to deviate from the channels of habit. His destruction of the obvious is the construction of the unusual. Violence and tenderness are not juxtaposed but interpolated, no matter whether in his colour or word composition. Picasso said, 'Painting is poetry and is always written in verse with plastic rhymes, never in prose. Plastic rhymes are forms that rhyme with one another or supply assonances either with other forms or with the space that surrounds them, also, sometimes, through their symbolism, but their symbolism must not be too apparent'. Then we may also say that his poetry is painting and always created with the plasticity of colours which harmonize or clash, which have symbolic meaning without making the meaning apparent. André Breton quotes a fragment of one of Picasso's poems:

*Listen in your childhood to the hour that white in the blue memory*
*borders white in her very blue eyes and piece of indigo of a silver sky*
*the white glances run cobalt through the white paper that the blue ink*
*tears away blueish its ultramarine sinks so that white enjoys blue rest*
*agitated in the dark green wall green that writes its pleasure pale green*
*rain that swims yellow green in the pale forgetfulness at the edge of its*
*green foot the sand earth song sand of the earth after noon sand earth*

He takes off from the immediate sensation of his surroundings with the power of recreating the inner vision he gains from seeing reality. It rarely happened that he painted the same subject he was writing about, although he might be occupied with certain images that, on another occasion, might force themselves into verbal expression. But when he did the etching and aquatint, *Dream and Lies of Franco*, the urgency and fury he felt about his subject matter compelled him to break out into verbal cries of despair, a torrent from a tormented soul. It turned into a powerful prose poem which also anticipated his *Guernica*. Here is the final part of the poem:

*the street rises to the clouds tied by its feet to the sea of wax which rots*
*its entrails and the veil which covers it sings and dances wild with pain –*
*the flight of fishing rods and the alhigui alhigui of the first-class burial*
*of the moving van – the broken wings rolling upon the spider's web of*
*dry bread and clear water of the paella of sugar and velvet which the*
*lash paints upon his cheeks – the light covers its eyes before the mirror*
*which apes it and the nougat bar of the flames bites its lips at the wound –*
*cries of children cries of women cries of birds cries of flowers cries of*
*timbers and of stones cries of bricks cries of furniture of beds*
*of chairs of curtain of pots of cats and of papers cries of odours which claw*
*at one another cries of smoke pricking the shoulder of the cries which*
*stew in the cauldron and of the rain of birds which inundates the sea*

*which gnaws the bone and breaks its teeth biting the cotton wool which*
*the sun mops up the plate which the purse and the pocket hide in*
*the print which the foot leaves in the rock*

During the Nazi occupation of France Picasso lived and worked in Paris relatively unmolested by the Germans who were well aware of his political leanings. His studio was often searched by Gestapo officers and, although Picasso's work certainly belonged to what the Germans then called 'degenerate art' or 'Kulturbolschewismus', they did not prevent him from working, only from exhibiting. An incident has become well-known in which Picasso answered a German officer turning to the photo of *Guernica* and asking: 'Did you do this?' 'No, you did'.

A man so strongly attuned to living as Picasso must have suffered from the mental and physical deprivations caused by war and occupation. But he did not accept any favours and was supposed to have replied to the suggestion of accepting an extra allowance of food and coal with the words: 'A Spaniard is never cold'. But the shortage of food occupied his mind, and with devastating humour he responded to the sordid misery of poor lighting and meagre meals with a

*Plate 49*

*Still Life with Sausage*, an oil painting in which a blood sausage is extolled as a rare dish. A fascinating feature of the picture is the aggressive attitude of forks and knives looking out of the drawer.

This painting was preceded by a playlet which Picasso wrote in four days in January 1941. He often claimed that he only wrote when he was unable to paint, sculpt, or draw, but he did write some of his poetry during fertile periods of painting. His biographer tells us that, one evening, after a vigorous day's work on his canvases, he began to write. On the fourth evening, the play *Desire Caught by the Tail* was finished. Essentially, it dealt with cold, food and love. André Breton hailed it as a poetic play which is 'like a theatre in an earring' and telescopes everything, from the fantastic to the super-real, in the framework of Picasso's world.

This play could be easily rejected as an outgrowth of Picasso's annoyance with the physical conditions under which he then existed and as an expression of playfulness. He did not mind telling the world that he tossed this play off within four days and more likely in four cold winter evenings. It is a tragic farce in six short acts and several shorter scenes. The dialogue is between disembodied feet and other dehumanized characters, such as Silence and The Curtains. The leading character is Big Foot, a writer living in an 'artistic studio', apparently in love with the heroine, called Tart, and rivalled by his friend Onion.

*Desire Caught by the Tail* is full of Dadaist crudeness and surrealistic overtones of irony. In one scene Tart enters the room of Big Foot, beginning her long speech with: 'Hello and good evening! I'm bringing you the orgy. I'm stark naked and dying of thirst . . .' And she ends her speech with: 'Now go and get me some tea. Meanwhile I'll cut off the corn on my little toe that's annoying me'.

At certain points of the play Picasso forgets himself and has a moment of lyricism when, for example, Thin Anguish looks at Big Foot and says: 'How beautiful he is, like a morning star! A dream painted with watercolours on a pearl. His hair is artistically intertwined as the arabesque in the halls of the Alhambra, and the colour of his skin has the silvery tone of the bell which sounds the evening's tango to my love-filled ears. The light of a thousand glowing electric bulbs radiates his body'. Some of the best Dada and gibberish fun is found in the stage directions and in such ideas as 'the two feet of each guest are in front of the doors of their rooms, writhing in pain' and lamenting in a monotonous chorus: 'My chilblains, my chilblains, my chilblains . . .' The scene is set in 'A corridor in Sordid's Hotel'.

This play is only interesting because Picasso wrote it and because, in its preoccupation with food, it has a great deal of what we find in Alfred Jarry's *Ubu Roi*, a play written at the end of the last century and now considered to be the prelude to the twentieth-century revolution in playwriting. Alfred Jarry, whose paintings, etchings, and designs are also quite impressive, inspired Guillaume Apollinaire to create his surrealistic play, *Tiresias's Breasts*, and Apollinaire was an intimate friend of Picasso. Both plays are the classic forerunners of The Theatre of the Absurd, and Picasso's playlet must be seen as one of the earliest attempts at mixing Dada and surrealism in dramatic form with a bit of existentialism added. Of course Picasso was not aware of playing a link in a chain that should lead to such a formidable movement as The Theatre of the Absurd. All that Picasso did was to express his anguish at the absurdity of his condition in those years, and he found writing in dramatic form a better or more appropriate articulation for his helpless feeling of disgust than painting.

On March 19, 1944, still in occupied Paris, *Desire Caught by the Tail* had a public reading: Albert Camus directed, and among the actors were Jean-Paul Sartre, Simone de Beauvoir and other well-known artists. In London it had performances and a reading in which Dylan Thomas took part. It was produced together with another painter-poet's play, *The Island in the Moon*, by William Blake.

In 1952, when Picasso was busy decorating the chapel at Vallauris with the theme of war and peace, he took time off to do a series of light, idyllic drawings of girls dancing, gracefully skipping and turning somersaults. It seems that Picasso needed to divert himself, and it was then that he wrote another, yet unpublished, play in six acts, *The Four Little Girls*, to which Roland Penrose refers in his biography. The play caught something of the mood found in the aforementioned drawings. It is described as 'a fantastic rambling picture of the desires and antics of four charming and precocious children. In the spontaneous joy of their games, their ecstatic dances and their erotic songs, the instinctive violence of their desires breaks through. Disquieting screams season the sweetness of their kittenlike play, in which the claw is scarcely hidden beneath the softness of the fur'.

This play too, is full of soliloquies and stage directions which are important, since they depict more action than is found in the scenes themselves. They are spiced with puns but also with serious thoughts about vision, life and death. When one of his stage directions speaks of 'a winged white horse . . . surrounded by wings', it evokes an image similar to the one he drew for the curtain of *Parade* in 1917. He took Pegasus in disguise from this painting and made it appear in his play again.

'It is my misfortune – and probably my delight – to use things as my passions tell me.' Picasso never stopped to think why he was doing what he did. But whatever he does lives the life of a living creature. Even non-objective objects live, everything changes into forms and colours: visual shapes as much as words. The means and manner of expression matter little for the real genius. 'What is important for me now is to be', Pablo Picasso once said, 'and to leave the trace of my footsteps . . .'.

FROM THE CABARET VOLTAIRE TO THE BAUHAUS
The importance of Dada may only be fully understood when its assaults on the aesthetics and ethics of its time and its repercussions have run their course which, after more than fifty years, is still unforeseeable. Dada received its name when, in 1916, a few malcontent and enraged artists found this word in the dictionary. But it was not by mere chance that Dada as an anti-art art movement came into being. The artists, in

their violent attack against established principles and in their desire to create art to end all art, were not riding on 'hobby horses'.

Dada was born at a time when the world based on the vestiges of Renaissance ideals was in the painful process of collapsing. Therefore Dada was the first reaction to, and reflection of, the twentieth century's trauma. Dada was a glorified invective spat into the face of a world which asked for it. The entire movement is a collective expression of artistic hostility. Seeing the horrifying result of man's behaviour 'As if he had created the world and could play with it', as Hans Arp said, the Dadaists took refuge in total destruction and, at best, in a defiant detachment. One of its founders Richard Huelsenbeck, expressed this feeling in his poem, *End of the World* (1916), whose first few lines say

*This is what things have come to in this world*
*The cows sit on the telegraph poles and play chess*
*The cockatoo under the skirt of the Spanish dancer*
*Sings as sadly as a headquarters bugler and the cannon lament all day*
*That is the lavender landscape Herr Meyer was talking about*
*when he lost his eye*
*Only the fire department can drive the nightmare from the*
*drawing-room but all the hoses are broken*

The artistic shock generation was most active between 1916 and 1924. It was then that Dada was partly absorbed by Surrealism, partly by the Bauhaus movement. The victory of Dada lies in the single and signal fact with its message that anything can be art and art can be anything it prepared the public to accept its own spiritual defeat and the art of non-art as the image of our time. To judge by the various art movements in the late fifties and sixties, by the works of an Andy Warhol or Robert Rauschenberg, the wrecking is still going on and Dada, under whatever name, is playing its artistic games on the debris of the past.

*Plates XXII, XXIII*

Surrealism added poetry as substantial image to Dada's radical opposition to pure, traditional, and representational art. Despite seeing in art an 'alibi', in André Breton's words, surrealism often succeeded in giving Hieronymus Bosch's fantasies the Freudian lyricism of the colourful unconscious. Both Dadaists and Surrealists are drawn to literature. There are many reasons for it. One may be a lack of conviction in their own artistic *raison d'être* because their attitude is nihilistic. Another, and perhaps more important, reason can be found in their intimate relationship with cerebral concerns, with

*Plate 50*

psychological and philosophical concepts. Thus, everything literary becomes second nature to most of them. And some have embraced more than one medium outside their 'own'. Vistas in many directions open up as soon as all barriers of rules and aesthetic principles fall. Where there is no inhibition created by heritage and tradition, where no comparison and analysis is likely to check the flow of expression, it easily spills over in all directions.

It lies in the nature of these two art movements to indulge in excesses of experimentation. The results must have been more amusing and startling at the time of their creation than they are now when our senses have become adjusted to, or dulled by, some of the consciously built-in irritations. Most works of these artists reflect a casual lightness, a flair for satiric seriousness; in short, the atmospheric qualities of the literary cabaret. It was in the Cabaret Voltaire in Zürich in 1916 that Dada began to crystallize as a movement. Tristan Tzara, Hans Arp, Richard Huelsenbeck, and particularly Hugo Ball, gave Dada its literary and visual image then and there. It was some time later that strongly political elements were added by their comrades-in-revolt.

Hugo Ball owned the beer parlour in the Altstadt of Zürich. He wanted to make it more attractive to his guests (one of whom was Lenin) by creating a novel type of artist's cabaret. He played the piano and engaged singers, Tristan Tzara read his poetry, and Huelsenbeck, a medical student and pacifist, blackened his face and danced pseudo-African dances. Paintings were hung on the walls. Ball also introduced his *Verses Without Words*, which are phonetic poems or sound paintings, perhaps the literary equivalent to the Dada collages. Ball, clad in a fantastic-grotesque costume which he designed for himself, read his verses. He intended to rescue the language from its threadbareness, he 'wanted to penetrate the alchemy of the word' and created a Dada image which was endlessly imitated and varied. Kurt Schwitters played with these sound paintings most successfully. In 1932 he wrote his *Ursonate* which began with the line:

*Fümms bö wö tää zää Uu...*

Tristan Tzara said Kurt Schwitters was 'One of those figures whose inmost being, whose second nature was always Dada'. He would have been dadaistic, even if Dada had never been invented. On the other hand, Schwitters knew he never quite belonged to the Dada movement, that he was a thinker,

181

a constructor of things, Cubist-inspired. He had a touch of the clown, of Tyll Eulenspiegel, who translated his humorous ideas and practical pranks into unconventional (and sometimes very conventional) art. His versatility was so all-embracing that in many aspects he remained a highly gifted dilettante. He painted, sculpted, made collages; he wrote poetry, novels, essays, and composed; he was a recitationist; he edited and published magazines and books; he theorized about the theatre, architecture, and photography; he was known for his typography and lithographs. He created the concept of what he called Merz [rhymes with Schmerz (pain) and Herz (heart) and is the root of the verb ausmerzen (eradicate)], and he became identified with his Merz pictures, collages, sculptures, buildings ('. . . the whole fraud people call war came to an end. I felt free and had to shout my jubilant feelings into the world . . . One can also shout with garbage, and that's what I did, glued and nailed refuse together. I called it Merz . . . everything was kaputt, and now we had to rebuild something out of bits and broken pieces . . .').

*Plate VIII*

He loved to write phonetic poems. Here is his *Furor of Sneezing* which needs no translation:

> *Tesch*
> *Haisch*
> *Tschias*
> *Haisch*
> *Tschiaa*
> *Haisch*
> *Haisch*
> *Happaisch*
> *Happapepaisch*
> *Happapepaisch*
> *Happapepaisch*
> *Happa Peppe Tschaa!*

But he could also be conventionally legible and wrote a series of poems in the vein of Christian Morgenstern:

> *SO – SO*
> *Four masons sat on a roof.*
> *The first one said: 'Goof!'*
> *The second: 'Is this possibly fair?'*
> *The third: 'That the roof can be still up there?'*
> *The fourth: 'When there is no pillar anywhere ! ! !'*
> *And*
> *In a flash*
> *Down came the roof with a crash*

Schwitters exploded with versatility. But most of the artists of the shock generation combined paintings, collages, sculptures with their writings. Yet, in a way, they seemed to remain visual artists while writing, the word being alive only because it paints a pictorial image. Paul Eluard, speaking about the versatility of these artists, said in his *Notes sur la poésie* that the word is less important for them than the object itself, the event, the essence of being. Henri Michaux, who has many poetic books to his credit and is a visual artist of great merit, was even more explicit when he maintained that in our taxing century the poetic material is no longer the word that sings but the everyday language; the poet is no longer expected to be the virtuoso on a violin, but a mechanic who knows how images are put together. The magic beauty of a doll when a child plays with it is different from the magic surprise when the doll is taken apart. Schwitters was such a mechanic and constructor par excellence. He enjoyed, with the innate mischievousness of a child, putting a doll together again with the skill of making it look like a non–doll still displaying the essential parts of a doll in its bareness.

Each of the artists of this ilk has his own way of violating ordinary language while trying to give it new meaning. Max Ernst loves to play with the distortion of phrases and creates surprises with a satiric undertone making it clear nothing is to be taken seriously. What a surrealistic word painting are the opening lines of his *Some Data on the Youth of M.E.*! 'Max Ernst had his first contact with the sensible world, when he came out of the egg which his mother had laid in an eagle's nest and which the bird had brooded for seven years.' Sometimes his prose has an ironically lyric touch to it:

January 1926. Stretched out, I lie on my bed and see standing at my feet a tall slender woman in a glaring red gown. The gown is transparent, and so is the woman. I am surprised how tender her bones are. I am almost tempted to pay her a compliment.

In some of his poems he plays havoc with idioms and creates hilarious images which, however, become untranslatable. How close everything visual and verbal was in these artists is best shown by Max Ernst's comment on his first one-man collage exhibit:

Under the title 'La Mise sous Whiskey-Marin' I assembled and exhibited in Paris (May 1920) the first results obtained by this procedure, from the *Phallustrade* to *The Wet Nurse of the Stars* . . .

183

What is a Phallustrade? It is an alchemic product, composed of the following elements: the autostrade, the balustrade and a certain quality of phallus. A phallustrade is a verbal collage . . . a typical product of black humour . . . The quantity of black humour contained in each authentic collage is found there in the inverse proportion of the possibilities for happiness (objective and subjective). This invalidates the opinions of those who wish to see, in the pretended absence of all humour in surrealist painting, the essential difference between surrealist and dadaist works: can they believe that our epoch is any rosier than the years 1917–1921?

There are many more who have taken to writing. Giorgio de Chirico composed beautifully elusive prose pieces. Kurt Seligmann felt drawn to black magic and wrote a book about it. There are the rather factual writings of Jean Helion ('It was actually a good thing for me that I had the urge to write. Writing brought home the limitation of my approach to painting. Most abstract painters write and talk very well. They need to talk. The restrictions they adopt in their pictorial language leave them a lot to express in another medium'.) Joan Miró complemented his visual work with playful poems:

*Plate 52*
*Plate 53*

> *A scarlet red butterfly builds his nest in the décolleté*
> *of my friend. She runs barefoot*
> *across the ocean and grows peonies over there.*

There are the essays by Piet Mondrian dealing with a subject vital for the *Liberation from Oppression in Art and Life* ('I think the destructive element is too much neglected in art'). And there is the phenomenon of Marcel Duchamp.

It was Duchamp who gave the Mona Lisa beard and moustache ('Don't let yourself be hypnotized by the smiles of yesterday; rather invent smiles of tomorrow'). Witness his *Nude Descending a Staircase* ('A painting which doesn't shock isn't worth painting'). In his *Large Glass* he is drawn to the lucid display of the organic ('There is no solution because there is no problem'). Also, a linguistic triumph of transparency can be seen in his compulsive play on words. Like Hugo Ball he may have searched for a new language, for the uniqueness of primary words, but basically his desire for detachment and his mathematical logic needed this exercise in decomposing the means of communication as he had to decompose form.

'Mirrorically' he called himself an 'unfrocked artist' who made of 'A . . . rrose, c'est la vie' his pseudonym Rrose Sélavy. It also appears in one of his most Freudian suggestions: 'Rrose Sélavy and I believe that an incesticide must sleep with his mother before he kills her; bed bugs are indispensable'. While in Munich, Duchamp wrote critiques which remarkably hit their targets. As a near-chess-champion he wrote a book on how to keep one's king from escaping his checkmate. His notes, speeches, and interviews reveal the man and artist of whom it was said that he 'swings like a pendulum between the inertia-acceptance of reality and suicide-refusal, which gives him his dynamism'.

Some of these iconoclasts became 'masters', a title for certain teachers at the *Bauhaus* which, in the early twenties, became a rallying point for *Neue Sachlichkeit* (New Functionism). The *Bauhaus* was founded by Walter Gropius who 'sought a new synthesis of art and modern technology'. It turned into a centre of experimentation, exploring and teaching the new and daring. Two of its teachers were Josef Albers and Wassily Kandinsky.

*Plate VI*  Albers paid *Homage to the Square*, he was the creator of the three-dimensionality of straight lines and right angles, the painter who saw colour in motion and found the greatest possible economy in form-colour-space effects. In his poems and philosophic statements we find the same pithy attitudes. His philosophy is presented at right angles:

> *My earth*
> *serves also others*
>
> *my world*
> *is mine alone*

Or as designer of the objectively beautiful he can write such lines:

> *More   or Less*
>
> *Easy   to know*
> *that diamonds   are expensive*
> *good   to learn*
> *that rubies   have depth*
> *but more   to see*
> *that pebbles   are miraculous*

*Plate VII*  Kandinsky created some of the first and most important abstract paintings which are the basis of our understanding of this art form and which have given us a deeper understanding of our time. What makes him stand above so many of the shock artists is the fact that he saw with the rare freshness and intensity of a first impression, that all his senses were alive all the time and reacting from a focal point while embracing the totality of artistic sensibility. He was convinced that the artist should have a message to convey, a message revealed to him

185

by an inner voice, and that he can never fail when he reacts out of an inner spiritual need.

Although this sounds old-fashioned or like the credo of expressionism, Kandinsky felt strongly that his inner feelings were most clearly expressed when they were free from representational intentions. He went through several phases of artistic expression, but the idea of mystery, the concept of the 'hidden' never left him. Seen from a psychological viewpoint, his abandonment of objective painting may have been the answer to his reluctance to disclose his inmost being ('I hate it that people should see what I really feel').

Kandinsky could not separate images in colour from feeling the sound of colour as abstract as a piece of music, and he could not help sensing both colour and sound so intensely, with almost religious ecstasy, that words easily reshaped the seen and heard. There were several Kandinskys, and it is difficult to visualize the play of balance and counter-balance functioning in him. But function it did, and it seems to me that the myth, the religious and poetic core was so strong in this artist that he could go as far as he did in reducing the objects of reality to hear their abstract elements which he turned into structural compositions ('. . . we are fast approaching a time of reasoned and conscious composition, in which the painter will be proud to declare his work constructional').

His poetic writings reveal his sense of colour and music in every passage. One must see and listen when reading his description of Moscow, the city which to him was the epitome of Russia and the source of his artistic inspiration ('I have the feeling that it has always been so and that at bottom I have always painted this single "model" merely strengthening the expression and perfecting the form over the years'):

The sun melts all Moscow into one spot which, like a mad tuba, sets one's whole inside, one's whole soul vibrating. No, this red unity is not the loveliest hour! It is only the final note of the symphony which brings every colour to its greatest intensity, which lets, indeed forces, all Moscow resound like the fff of a giant orchestra. Pink, lavender, yellow, white, blue, pistachio green, flame-red houses, churches – each an independent song – the racing green grass, the deep murmuring trees, or the snow, singing with a thousand voices, or the allegretto of the bare branches, above, towering over all like a cry of triumph, like a Hallelujah forgetful of itself, the long white, delicately earnest line of the Ivan Veliky Bell Tower. And upon its neck, stretched high and taut in eternal longing to the heavens, the golden head of the cupola, which is the Moscow sun amid the golden and coloured stars of the other cupolas. To paint this hour, I thought, would be the most impossible and the greatest joy of an artist.

In contrast to his theoretical writings, particularly his *Concerning the Spiritual in Art or Point and Line to Plane*, whose logic and clarity are strengthened by emotional conviction, some of his poems and most of his plays are highly experimental. His preoccupation with music is manifest in his first volume of poems, *Sounds* (Klänge) and his almost abstract 'composition for the stage', *Yellow Sound*, both falling into the period between 1909 and 1911. His stage directions are close to the style of landscapes he painted at that time, and the five light-yellow giants with blurred faces could have stepped out of his canvas into the play script. In this mystery play in which the giant turns into the symbol of a cross, Kandinsky tried to synthesize all the arts. Other plays of his written about the same time carry the significant titles *Violet*, *Black and White*, and *Green Sound*, mostly written for musical composition, neglecting the human element and experimenting with nonrealistic visual effects.

Kandinsky's development moved full circle from his early colourful mythical landscapes, followed by romantic improvisations, to the highly experimental Bauhaus period of the logically cold structures, and from there to the imaginative flight of new shapes and colours, recalling the beauty of the inner melody, and then becoming myth again. Kandinsky never ceased writing poetry, and one of his poems, *Chalk and Soot*, may serve as coda to a movement, tortured in its expressions, powerful in its destructive consequences, its echo of despair:

> *Oh, how slowly he walks.*
> *If only someone were here, who could tell the*
> *man: Faster, go faster, faster, faster, faster, faster.*
> *But he is not there. Or is he?*
> *This black face with the white lips, quite white lips*
> *as if painted with chalk, smudged, made-up.*
> *And the green ears!*
> *Were they green? Or perhaps not? Or were they?*
> *The trees lose their leaves each fall, their garment,*
> *their jewels, their body, their crown.*
> *Each fall. And how many yet? How many falls yet?*
> *Eternity? Or not? Or yes?*
> *How slowly he walks.*
> *And each spring violets grow, and smell sweetly, sweetly.*
> *They always smell sweetly. Do they never stop to smell*
> *sweetly? Or do they? Would you rather have him a white*
> *face and black lips, as if painted with soot, smudged,*
> *made-up? Would you rather?*
> *Or is there someone after all, who will tell the man*
> *and maybe already tells him: Faster, faster, faster.*

I never intended to entertain my contemporaries with the tricks of a juggler, in the hope of being recognized as an original . . . I consider myself responsible, not to society, which dictates fashion and taste suited to its environment and its period, but to youth, to the coming generations, which are left stranded in a blitzed world, unaware of the Soul trembling in awe before the mystery of life.

Oskar Kokoschka wrote this statement in 1948 looking back upon more than six decades of his life and forty years of a turbulent career.

*Plates X, 42, 45*

His quest for the mystery of life has never stopped. It began when this century and Kokoschka were still very young. It began in Vienna a city which, on the surface, was gay and carefree, but which, at that time, brought forth some of the great rebels destined to give our time its fascinating, though often perplexing and irritating, face.

The splendour of the Habsburg dynasty, with Vienna as the radiant centre of a multi-coloured monarchy, nurtured daily its own decay. The aristocracy, with its estates in Hungary and Bohemia or as far as the Dalmatian coast, resided in Vienna where the Emperor also lived, a lonesome and sad figure with an impressive beard and nothing to say, separated as he was from his people by a huge bureaucratic apparatus. The officer of His Majesty's army, stationed in the Vienna garrison, in his striking uniform, became the dream of a people that drowned its proverbially golden heart in wine and phony *gemütlichkeit*, that stuffed itself with sweets and *Sacher Torten* and suffocated in sentimentality and songs.

It was the right atmosphere for the Count to deceive his mistress, usually a famous singer or dancer at the even more famous Opera, with the chambermaid of his wife, the Countess. It was the time when duels were fought over virtually nothing because it was part of the pattern of life; when every gentleman entering a barber's shop was greeted with *Herr Baron* or, at least, *Herr Doktor*, though he may have been helper to a lackey of a rich man who had bought the lowest aristocratic title, *Herr von Soandso*, from the venal clerks of the Imperial Ministry. But music was played everywhere. The glitter of gaiety, the beauty of the Gothic and Baroque buildings, gardens and fountains, uniforms and pretty women dazzled the common people in accepting their lot. After all, they lived in a great cultural city.

The Vienna of that time created a cultural atmosphere in which everyone was proud of 'his' composers and writers, 'his'

48   Joan Miró DUTCH INTERIOR I

49   Pablo Picasso STILL LIFE WITH SAUSAGE

50   Tristan Tzara SNOBS

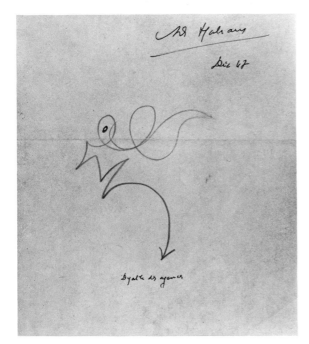

51   André Malraux DYABLE DES AGENCES

proof    meditation                              K. seligmann    1952

52    Kurt Seligmann MEDITATION

53   Jean Hélion COMPOSITION

theatres and museums. But there was only a thin layer of people who actually participated in the richness of a spiritual splendour, accumulated over several centuries. Most of those people who often gathered in the salons had their headquarters in the coffeehouses where one went not only for coffee and pastry. There you read all the magazines and newspapers or you brought your own book with you, there you sat for hours in heated discussions and there you withdrew to write your own poetry at a corner table, cut off from the world by the mist of cigarette smoke.

This was the atmosphere in which Oskar Kokoschka grew up. During the first decade of this century the works of several artists reflected the mood of a romanticized life, of the aesthetically appealing and superficially beautiful which could be found everywhere in Vienna. Hugo von Hofmannsthal, who wrote the libretto to some of Richard Strauss's operas and whose version of *Everyman* became a summer institution in front of the Salzburg *Dom*, was the foremost representative of a decadent, but always elegant and subtle tradition which was as doomed as the Habsburg monarchy. The physician Arthur Schnitzler skilfully dramatized the perfumed eroticism of a dying society and did it with psychological insight and great interest in its social ramifications. Peter Altenberg was the romantic rebel against society; his gentle and ecstatic lyrical prose extolled the beauty of innocence which he saw in the streetwalkers as much as in the girls of Lolita age whom he watched playing ball in the public gardens of Vienna or looking dreamingly at their balloons vanishing in the sky.

Egon Friedell, philosopher, actor, cabaretist, dramatist, essayist, and cultural historian was a characteristic specimen of multiple creativity in the coffee-house atmosphere of Vienna which never gave up its claim to being more baroque than any other city of Europe.

And then there was the unique recitationist, actor of his one-man theatre, the biting satirist and poetic pamphleteer Karl Kraus who, in brilliant writings, held a mirror up to the real nature of the Viennese and, in particular, to the follies and failings of their journalists as symbols for moral disintegration and the corrupted mind. His Cassandra cries were unfortunately to be echoed by the thunderous reality of history. Together with Gustav Mahler and Arnold Schönberg, with Gustav Klimt and Sigmund Freud, an unknown frustrated painter walked through the streets of Vienna at that time and tried to sell his watercolours. His name was Adolf Hitler.

Anon
Egon Friedell

This contrasting environment of a city with its fading glory helped shape many artists, among them Oskar Kokoschka. From the very beginning – he started to attend the Arts and Crafts School in 1904 – Kokoschka would not fall in with any demands of convention. First, of course, he could not help being under the influence of the fashionable *art nouveau* and its great exponents, the Viennese Gustav Klimt and especially the Swiss Ferdinand Holder, whose symbolism and expressiveness pointed the way to the realization of emotional values. But Kokoschka immediately turned these influences into channels of a very personal approach which even found expression in the fans and postcards which he had to do for the *Wiener Werkstaette*. In 1908 he was commissioned by this famous institute for applied arts to write and illustrate a book for children.

He proved that his ability to verbalize his experiences and impressions was in no way inferior to his visualizations in form and colour. *The Dreaming Boys* was the title of the book which was hardly suitable for children, although only a youth's highly imaginative mind could have produced such verbal and visual images. The lyrical prose runs in the margin next to the tapestry-like pictures. Everything in this illustrated book takes place on a heightened level of imagery with a hidden erotic symbolism as its propelling force. Some of his phrases have the quality of an ecstatic flight into nowhere:

> *I reach into the sea and plunge myself into your hair/ like a dreamer am I in the love of all being . . ./ it is strange around me/ somebody ought to answer/ everything follows its own traces/ and the singing gnats tremble above and beyond all cries/ . . . and I was the one who staggered/ when I discovered my flesh/ and I was an all-embracing lover/ when I spoke to a girl.*

Most of the pictures in this book are medieval in character, but seen through the eye of the *fin de siècle* artist. There is the unrestrained quality of surrealism in *The Dreaming Boys*, a book written twenty-six years before André Breton issued his *Manifesto du surréalisme* in 1924. This book was displayed at the *Kunstschau*, now in retrospect a historically important exhibition which took place in Vienna in 1909. *The Dreaming Boys* was accepted on its aesthetic merits while Kokoschka's other works, a sculpture of a girl, a painting, and a clay bust shocked the reactionary circles and the most powerful critics into frantic attacks.

It was a decisive moment in his life and if for no other reason than that he became Adolf Loos's protégé. Loos, who also wrote essays of clear, architectonic structure but dramatic power, built houses at the turn of the century which would be accepted today as 'modern' because of their simple cubic shape without any ornament and based on the principles of utility. Loos was a forerunner of the new functionalism, a fanatic of simplicity of style and living habits. This great Viennese pioneer (whom history has almost forgotten by now) took Kokoscha under his wing. It would be truer to say that he discovered Kokoschka. He influenced the artist's growth through his first seven years. They certainly were not lean years.

Under Loos's guidance (particularly between 1909 and 1913) Kokoschka, who was often referred to as the 'talented terror', went through profound changes in his artistic outlook. He had written another book, similar to the first one, which he called *The White Animal Slayer*, also with illustrations, but it was not published before 1913 and then with new illustrations under the title *The Chained Columbus*. The main theme of this long poem deals with the imaginary love of mortal man for the Moon Lady with whom he can only be united in death.

The motif of cruelty, even murder and love, became dominant in his writings. Whether this was due to the literary fashion of the time, or whether is was part of his romantic search for the female is difficult to say. But for him beyond this search was the final realization that spiritual and physical struggle is followed by disillusionment and symbolic or actual death, that ultimate union is only achieved through an ecstatic moment of death.

All this is borne out by two playlets which Kokoschka wrote in 1907. A few years later both were rewritten and enlarged upon, but did not change in their essential message and retained their key sentences. They were published and produced by the group of Dadaists in Zürich during the First World War and immediately after the war by the Dresden Schauspielhaus and Max Reinhardt's Kammerspiele in Berlin. From their original fragmentary form they developed into playlets of average one-act play length in which emotions and ideas were freely expressed, often in an explosive form or staccato stammering, and in which everything was only symbolic of reality in order to reflect the inner subjective state of a character. This is why Kokoschka was often described as having created the very first expressionistic play. But it is usually overlooked that there is a great deal of intentional obscurity in his writings, also the creation of dreamlike realities, of images loosely tied together without conscious control; all this is mingled with a defiance of the known aesthetic laws and any organized social existence. These approaches and principles anticipate the much later-formulated Dada and surrealistic movements.

Of course, many of these points can be found in his paintings too. Thus, he defies conventional accuracy in his portraits. He dissects and analyses a person until he hits upon the hidden face in man. It was the inner likeness he looked for, and the models did not recognize themselves. Karl Kraus said of his portrait: 'Kokoschka has made a portrait of me. It is quite possible that those who know me will not recognize me. But it is certain that those who do not know me, will recognize me'. The truth is that an objective observer will recognize the real image of the man, the inner likeness projecting his work and what it stands for in life. In whatever Kokoschka painted, one could see the fearless searching for the real nature of things, his affinity to the unusual, his urge to express through form and colour what words could not say.

*Plate 42*

One of his early plays was called *Sphynx and Straw Man.* Later it was retitled *Job.* The hero of the play is man in conflict with woman: his destroyer and wife, Anima, his breath and soul. The Rubberman is Job's antagonist. Healthy, plain, uncomplicated ('I don't understand a word!' he says, 'Ha, what joy to live . . .'), he takes possession of Anima to whom Job refers as 'Anima, my soul!' Job shouts at the Rubberman: 'You opportunist! What seemed to her a trampoline for leaping from lust is – alas – vulgarity that procreates itself!' Anima seems to explain her *raison d'être*: 'One feature I would take from this man, another from the next. To my lover I offered lips of resignation, and to my husband mocking mournfulness. From one to the other! Like a bee fickle while garnering the pollen! Until Lord Eros is arrived!' Kokoschka obviously deals here with surrealistic symbols when naming Job's and Anima's little son Eros. Precociously, Eros interprets the universal concept of man's genesis: 'From Papa's tears in Mama's womb arose a little boy'. The hardy Rubberman woos Anima with the following statement: 'Adored lady – stay . . . Besides, your Eros stimulates me too! . . . Purely objectively I wish to remark that the genetic development of your mythological son urges me toward an explanation by natural causes'. This three-act playlet is full of ironic twists and heavy with symbolic meaning. A parrot plays the part of Job's pathetic echo. The gardener in Job's house is called Adam. And Job himself, isn't he Kokoschka's self-caricature?

When, in the third act, Anima drops like a ripe apple down from the window, scantily clothed, and falls with her buttock on Job's head, he collapses under Anima's weight and dies. While Mr Rubberman is still after her virtue in an obvious way, Adam turns gently to the dead Job: 'You've placed your wife too high in the heavens. Only now when she falls can you see through her and view her bottom'. Ten mourning gentlemen appear for Job's funeral and end their speeches with the final apotheosis: 'I believe in the genius of man! Anima – Amen!' Adam, who plays the stage manager, turns off the lights: 'Good faith is a green eyeshade! It screens the light of truth for sickly eyes. The only good I still can do is blow out the light so that it needn't shine at all'. While he exits with Anima, we hear her voice out of the dark: 'Perhaps Job could never help but bear a heavy cross. I, with my own eyes, have seen here how they slandered me. Perhaps I alone slander myself. And perhaps Anima, who settled the heavy cross on Job's shoulders, is truly Eve'.

An even briefer one-acter, also written in 1907, was called *The Women's Hope* and later *Murderer the Women's Hope*. A man and a woman meet and perform a ritual of love, passion, murder and resurrection. The encounter is between a woman and a man in blue armour, with a pale face and a bandage around his forehead covering a wound. The chorus of men indicates that he is a leader and then saying, 'Our master is like the moon that rises in the East', they indicate that he is a saviour, the light – dimmed by the cruelty of life – that comes from the East. Like life itself he comes to kill and to perform miracles. The woman whom he meets is Kokoschka's ideal female image, tall, with loose yellow hair, wearing red clothes. She too is endowed with the powers of a sorceress, she divines what no one can understand, she can sense what no one can hear or see, and shy birds flock to her. As if hypnotized, man and woman are drawn toward each other. He stigmatizes her and while screaming in pain she knifes him. He is carried away, seemingly dead, but she cannot forget or leave him. She gives her blood to save him and while she lies dying he rises. The men and women who try to flee from him run into his path to be killed. From very far away we hear the crowing of cocks. A new day begins.

Although Kokoschka was not aware of what he was doing, he rejected the psychological and narrative theatre which is preoccupied with a personal problem. Kokoschka's attempts at playwriting captured what Antonin Artaud consciously strove for in the Thirties, namely to create a Theatre of Cruelty

Oskar Kokoschka
*Mörder, Hoffnung der Frauen*

197

which is based on action and returns to myth and magic in order to expose ruthlessly the deepest and most basic conflicts of the human mind. In *The Theatre and Its Double* Artaud says: 'Before our eyes is fought a battle of symbols . . . for there can be theatre only from the moment when the impossible really begins and when the poetry that occurs on the stage sustains and superheats the realized symbols'. In Kokoschka's ritualistic play *Murder the Women's Hope* Artaud's essential demands are fulfilled.

A few years later Kokoschka returned to the same theme in another play which he called *The Burning Bush*. Again man and woman face each other and the struggle between the spirit and the flesh becomes a focal point. Again there is no narrative in the conventional sense, only a situation, a confrontation between the sexes. She exclaims: 'My body is a burning fire-bush, and you are its nourishing wind . . . my hands are hot wings, my feet burning coal – white and red – white and red I burn; in a fire garment of long pain, glowing with shame I burn but do not perish. Come to me, extinguish the fire and redeem me'. Then realizing that he has crushed her with desire and has become her enemy and jailer, she is seized with passionate fury and throws a stone at him. He falls and cries out: 'You who have loved me injured me. Look how my life escapes with my blood! The earth can hardly drink up the strength which runs from me. Now you leave me to die'. They are united again when she says: 'I suffer with you'. The final union is achieved through the realization of their common guilt and suffering.

In 1918, after the end of the war, he had finished his most conventional play, *Orpheus and Eurydice*. For the first time he writes an idyllic love scene. But then, when Psyche warns Orpheus not to ask Eurydice any questions, Kokoschka's story assumes a very personal note. The events of the years she has spent in the home of the dead must not be evoked, but his curiosity grows. He cannot overcome the feeling that she knows something he cannot share with her. She tells Orpheus how she resisted Pluto for five years despite her great longing for the lord of the underworld. When, defeated by her faithfulness to Orpheus, he finally gave her her freedom again, she suddenly felt that she belonged to Pluto. But, she says, at that moment Orpheus appeared to save her and from that moment on she had been divided in her feelings for both of them. After her confession, Orpheus drowns her and himself.

Kokoschka's war memories dominate the scenes of the third part. Orpheus is back home as a ghost. Kokoschka, having returned from the front, projects himself into Orpheus's place. He is full of self-accusations of having murdered, of having killed what life has to offer: happiness and unhappiness. Eurydice's ghost appears to win him back. He calls her a stranger for whom he feels as little as for his past: 'What tie binds man and wife together? Our imagination . . . When I thought of you my heart stood still, my throat felt choked, I turned pale'. She kneels before him and implores him: 'Once more let me embrace you!' But he confesses with devilish joy that he now hates her. He goes mad, confuses his wife with his mother, and, in a symbolic parallel, his own tribulations with those of the world. She strangles him and, while he dies, she murmurs: 'Thus embracing you in a last struggle I free myself . . .' As in his first play, *Job*, woman triumphs over man.

His *Orpheus and Eurydice* emerged from very personal experiences. Kokoschka wrote it after having received serious injuries during World War I. At a later time he said about this play that it was 'spoken, whispered in ecstasy, in delirium, I cried, implored, I howled in fear and in the fever of mortal dread'. Kokoschka identifies himself with Pluto whom he sees as a propelling force, as a life-giving principle, as the eternally regenerating power. Orpheus, the man, lost to his confusion and errors, must yield. In contrast to the traditional story, he loses Eurydice because she is tied to Pluto forever, not because he tried to bring her back to the world.

As an artist Kokoschka is a total man as much as the man is a total artist. He cannot see life divided and compartmentalized. Basically, he is a painter seeing with a painter's eye. But there were periods in his life fraught with emotion and full of dramatic conflicts for which the linear-visual reaction on canvas seemed insufficient realization and relief to him. Experiences which touched the raw end of his nervous system exploded in such plays as *Murder the Women's Hope* or led to such dramatic lyricisms as *Orpheus and Eurydice*.

With *Murder the Women's Hope* as well as with *Job* Kokoschka made the first attempts at a new kind of theatre of which he himself could not have been sure where it was going. He isolated words or short groups of verbal images which became outcries of dramatic intensity, violent, volcanic, dissociated in bits of dialogue and scenes. But the visual element dominated his language. We hear such phrases as 'an arc of shy light', or: 'We were the flaming wheel around him', or: 'Time after time the wind blows wandering'.

Almost all his writing is confession. He was obsessed with the thought of the separation of the sexes, with their eternal polarity. As characterized in his play *The Burning Bush*, man and woman appear to him almost as mythical symbols going back to sun and moon cults. Kokoschka realized that man is a sexual and political animal. But above and beyond these primary facts that make men live together or apart the way they do, he has always been aware of the wonder that is nature, of the mystery that is life.

In December 1945, when the war had come to an end, Kokoschka wrote 'A Petition from a Foreign Artist to the Righteous People of Great Britain for a Secure and Present Peace' and began this long essay with the paragraph:

I am indeed grateful that the opportunity for physical survival was afforded to me in Great Britain when many an unfortunate friend of mine had been left behind in a Europe overrun by Hitler. Now, recovering from the first enthusiasm which has followed the defeat of Fascism, I pause for a moment of lucidity in which to find MY WAY BACK TO A CIVILIZATION suspended during the war.

In this essay he showed his well rounded historical and sociological knowledge and how he, as an artist, had learned to 'see' the world. He turns against the ruling mechanistic and dogmatic mind and pleads with the big powers to release some of their control, if not all of it, and to use compassion and a greater imagination to permit the perception of reality.

An early essay, a lecture given in 1911 under the title of *On the Awareness of Visions*, reveals the philosophy behind his work. Kokoschka only wrote when he had to say something that could not be expressed through form and colour. He is a phenomenon, a painter whose dramatic attempts anticipated in this century's opening gambit the writing trends of future decades. However imperfect his plays may seem today – Carl Zuckmeyer and Thornton Wilder among many other playwrights thought highly of them – they were perfect in their prediction of plays to come. Painting or writing, Kokoschka has always been many steps ahead of his contemporaries, and his only wish has been to teach them how to see.

GOD, NATURE, AND EGON SCHIELE

Seen from the vantage point of the latter part of this century, Oskar Kokoschka's plays and poetry may appear as rather puerile efforts. Also, they may have been written mainly because Kokoschka could not help being influenced by the stimulating Viennese coffee-house atmosphere which was not only full of smoke but also full of literature. Kokoschka, however, will never be judged by posterity as a writer. But

VII   Wassily Kandinsky CIRCLES IN A CIRCLE

VIII   Kurt Schwitters DER WUNSCH DES KÜNSTLERS

IX  Paul Klee VILLA R

X   Oskar Kokoschka VIEW FROM THE VICKERS BUILDING

it must be recognized that his plays will retain their historic value as the verbal expressions of a painter who was able to anticipate trends and –isms which found artistic fulfilment years and even decades later.

Egon Schiele (1890–1918) emerged from the very same atmosphere against which he rebelled in his way as much as Kokoschka did. Arthur Roessler, the Viennese art critic, discovered and furthered Schiele, as Adolf Loos had discovered and furthered Kokoschka. Roessler was a far more parochial figure than Loos, who was internationally known, a fact from which Kokoschka profited. Schiele's genius was tragic, and so was his life. At the very moment when he had exhibitions everywhere in Europe and his significance as an artist was recognized, he died. The First World War was over, but the influenza epidemic of 1918 still demanded more victims and Schiele was one of them.

In his paintings he gave us many stunning visualizations of himself. We also find several verbal sketches for a self-portrait. Once he wrote:

Ancient German blood flows within me and I often sense the nature of my ancestors . . . My early childhood impressions which still live with me vividly I received from vast plains of country roads in spring and from raging storms. In those first days it was as if I could hear and smell the enchanted flowers, the speechless gardens, the birds in whose bright eyes I saw myself mirrored in a rosy light. Often I was close to tears when autumn came. When it was spring I dreamt of the all-embracing music of life. Then I rejoiced in the wonderful summer and laughed when in the midst of its splendour my mind painted the whiteness of winter. Up to then I lived in joy, in a joy alternating between serenity and wistfulness. Then came the empty hours, the lifeless schools. Grammar School at Tulln, Realgymnasium in Klosterneuburg. I lived in rather endless and seemingly dead places and grieved for myself. At that time I experienced the death of my father. My brutal teachers were always my enemies. They – and others – could not understand me. Religion and art are the highest perceptions. Nature has purposes; but God is there, and I sense him deeply, very deeply, most deeply. I do not believe that there is such a thing as modern art; there is only art, and it is everlasting.

At the famed *Kunstschau* exhibition in Vienna of 1909 – where Kokoschka was also showing for the first time – Schiele's paintings had a sensational, though mostly negative, impact on public and critics alike. Some realized that here was an original talent, but the majority of those who came to see the exhibit were either puzzled or frightened by what they thought was the manifestation of a sick mind. Serious-minded critics called his work a caricature of reality without seeing that what they objected to was the nakedness of reality. This reality became more pronounced and defined in Schiele's work when, a year or so later, he freed himself from the decorative style of Gustav Klimt. The clear line, the simple colour configurations, the growing emphasis on over-sized hands with their almost anatomical bone and knuckle structure became a distinctive characteristic of his work.

Unconsciously, he must have seen in the human hand the mirror of man's soul which he wanted to reduce to its bare nakedness. At the same time, he felt like a child – 'I am eternally a child', he once wrote – and in his paintings he mostly hid the thumb like an infant wishing to go back to the womb. In spite of many sophisticated overtones, there are compulsively naive features in his designs, as there can be sophistication in naiveté as much as naiveté in sophistication. And in his obsession with sex we find a curious, exploratory approach to man's nakedness – 'Have the grown-ups forgotten how this frightening passion burnt in them and tortured them when they were children?' he cried out. 'I did not forget it because I have suffered terribly from it. And I believe that man must suffer from sexual tortures as long as he is capable of sexual feelings.'

There are compulsively naive phrases in his writings as well. His preoccupation with sex is verbally channelled into orgiastic descriptions of nature and colour. Egon Schiele's inclination to write seemed somewhat influenced by the 'literariness' of his environment. Since most of his poetic writing was done between 1909 and 1911, such encouragement may have come, however indirectly, from some of the important literary personalities with whom he had contact after the *Kunstschau* exhibit. One of the centres of the rebellious Viennese artists and writers at that time was the bookshop and gallery of Richard Lanyi, who also handled some of Schiele's works. Anyone spending an hour there could not help but become a part of the surging spiritual and artistic forces which wanted to escape the very same Viennese atmosphere which nourished them. But it seems that Schiele was well aware of writing and painting as two different disciplines since he wrote: 'I am everything at the same time, but never would I do everything at the same time'.

His diaries written during different periods of his life shed light on his very private personality. His entries not only show his potential greatness as an artist, the purity of his artistic approach and a fanatic will to succeed, but also the crucified human in him, his narcissistic obsession with his own being and his urge for a meticulous recording of his daily experiences. This is borne out by the frequently appearing marks in his diaries – either circles or crosses – which register the days in which Schiele had intercourse with his wife.

After absorbing the influences of the great art movements in his youth, of which Klimt and Hodler were most significant, he soon found his own style, as he realized that every work of art is a piece of the artist's life and must reflect 'a great ex--perience in his existence'. Also he felt that 'the artist must be of his time'. He sensed very acutely the pulsebeat of his time, which, recoiling in fear of the catastrophes and anxieties to come, forced the artist to spit his vomit into the face of the world, to empty his heart haunted by a nameless Kafkaesque terror, to stammer a denial of reality. Expressionism became the only manner in which Schiele could express himself. That so many painters of that period also wrote must have had to do with the form of expression, the impatience of the artists with their world and life, and the need for spontaneity. When one studies Schiele's writings, one comes away with the feeling that he did not write for the sake of writing, but rather that he sometimes used words to fight the enigma of the outer world and to explain himself as a painter. Some of his verbal expressionistic images found the form of prose poems which were published in literary magazines at that time. They are interesting for more than their personal statements of emotionally ecstatic moments. His lyricisms are the mirror reflections of a painter's visual power. They are shreds of images, as if lost and found again in parts, such as his

### LADY IN THE PARK
*. . . Thus I walked on along the sun-white path, I who was red. I saw the blue lady in the green, green garden, – she stood still, she looked at me with round dark eyes, and her face was almost white.*

Or:

### APPROACHING STORM
*Everywhere black mourning storm clouds rolled high above, warning woods of water, whispering huts and humming trees. – I walked toward the black brook. Bird flying like yellow leaves in the wind.*

Or sections from

### VISIONS
*I liked everything: I wanted to look with love at the angry people so that their eyes would have to respond. And I wanted to give a gift to those envious people and tell them of my own unworthiness . . . The white pale girls showed me their black foot and red garter and spoke to*

*me with black fingers. – But I thought of the wide worlds, of finger-
flowers, and of wet mornings. I saw the park in yellow green, in blue
green, in red green, in trembling green, in sunny green, in violet green
while listening to the blooming orange blossoms.*

No poet would ever use such descriptions which are a palette
full of weird, wet colour images. The early expressionism
found in Schiele's prose poems a fortuitous manifestation of
its crude distortion of reality by the inner eye, the dynamic,
almost volcanic, externalization of all unconscious drives.
Undoubtedly, Schiele was strongly impressed by the writings
of Arthur Rimbaud.

Strongest and poetically most valid are some passages in his
letters which – in contrast to his diaries – seemed to have
escaped Arthur Roessler's editorial pen. Schiele certainly did
not write his letters with the thought of getting them published
one day. Filling those pages he was alone with himself,
pouring out the pain of his being, giving spontaneous expression to his desires and despairs. More so than in his prose poems
we find in these letters a poetry, earthbound, untutored, and
untrimmed. There is as little artifice in them as in his drawings
and paintings. There is the same tormented expression, the
same sensuousness and sensual quality of joy in the naked
being, in the ecstatic beauty of sex, the nude as reflection
of the god-given creative power of man. (In 1912, when
arrested and imprisoned for twenty-four days on charges of
having drawn pornographic pictures, he wrote in his diary:
'He who denies sex is full of filth and, in the meanest manner,
dirties his own parents, who procreated him'.) His was an
incessant struggle to find and grasp the poetry in life, in all
areas of existence.

After the public reaction to one of his exhibitions, he wrote
to his friend and brother-in-law Anton Peschka:

Peschka!
I would like to get away from Vienna rather soon. How ugly it is
here! – All people are jealous and cunning; there is falsehood in the
eyes of former colleagues. A shadow lies over Vienna, the city is
black, everything is done according to prescription. I want to be
alone. I want to go to the Bohemian woods . . . I must see new things
and explore them, I want to taste dark waters, I want to see creaking
trees, the wild air, I want to look in surprise at rotting garden fences,
how they all live, those young birch groves, and I want to hear
trembling leaves, to see light, sun and to enjoy wet, green-blue
valleys in the evening, I want to feel how the goldfish glistens,
watch white clouds grow, I'd like to speak to flowers. To look in
earnest at leaves of grass, at pink human beings, to know what

dignified churches, little domes say, I want to run away without stopping through vast plains towards the fields on the round hills to kiss the soil and to smell the flowers of soft, warm moss; then I will shape beautifully colourful fields.

The old houses are warmed through by the Siena-like air, everywhere are sunburnt shades, white, red . . . and an old barrel-organ plays haltingly – the big and heavy, year-long coat of the blind musician is old green brown, faded and threadbare. – I call to you in order to show you all I want you to enjoy; there you can hear large and small eyes of children laugh at me and speak with loud voices about me. Up there in the garden there are all green colours and flowers which look like human beings. Out there in a meadow of colours colourful shapes have melted, brown bushy peasants on brown roads, and yellow girls in the meadow full of flowering May. Do you hear it? In the leaves of the tree an ardent bird is sitting, its colours are dull, it hardly moves and does not sing – a thousand green leaves are mirrored in its eyes – and it cries.

He had to write his friend what he would like to experience if he could only escape Vienna. He wanted to share it with him, to make him see. Because to see it is to be a poet. In another letter written in 1911 he said: 'I am so rich that I must give myself away!'

When Peter Altenberg died, Karl Kraus said in his eulogy: 'Ein Bettler ging von uns, wie sind wir arm!' (A beggar went from us, how poor we are!) This could have been said when Egon Schiele died in the autumn of 1918.

Anon
Caricature of Peter Altenberg

## Sculptors as Writers

In selecting four modern sculptors, whose background and approach to their art are strikingly different, I am showing above all how varied variations on a theme can be.

Neither the inner affinity of sculpture to dancing, when it is an arrested movement, nor the actor's art as a plastic realization on stage seems to induce the sculptor to find the way to release through acting or dancing. It is rather the other way round, with the dancer and actor feeling a need to put shape into stones, to play with the plastic growth of inanimate material. It is undoubtedly another mirror image he seeks, the unconscious desire to give the fleetingness of his own movement and existence on stage a more enduring counterpart. While, from the archetypal Michelangelo to Arp and Barlach, the sculptor has shown a strong predilection for the word as another means of expression.

In a latent or overt form music plays a stimulating, even though peripheral, part in the life of an artist, as Sir Jacob Epstein (1880–1959) admits. As a writer he belongs with those visual artists who accepted the challenge of the written word to reveal and explain themselves. However, Epstein soon found out that he easily tired of writing. Only the opening chapters of his autobiography convey a compelling feeling to communicate with the unknown reader, to impart his story because it has interest beyond the mere explanation of his self. This is the story of his life on the Lower East Side in New York where he was born and reared. And how from there his way led via Paris to London where he was destined to awaken an awareness for sculpture in the British public, a deed for which he was knighted.

After the opening chapters of his *An Autobiography* lacklustre and unevenness in the writing make us easily accept the known fact that Epstein's wife helped finish the book, which had become a burdensome job for the artist. However, he must have greatly enjoyed the polemic parts of it, citing many quotes from scathing reviews with the relish of knowing how history proved his critics wrong. He also sketched with great verbal skill the profiles of some of the famous personalities who modelled for him and for their own immortality. His account of the wise-cracking George Bernard Shaw is particularly amusing. Shaw is shown as a man with little knowledge of the real problems a sculptor faces. 'I would say that Shaw was not really interested in the plastic Arts', Epstein concludes in spite of the fact that Shaw had reacted to an earlier version of the sculptor's autobiography with a long letter on art and the artists, dealing with the problems involved in the characteristically Shavian manner of his prefatory epistles, ending with the passage: 'Your book was very well written to get all this out of me'.

*Plate 55*

Although it is not that well written, it contains many sections of great interest. In the second chapter, Epstein tries to defend his own approach to the art and becomes quite articulate:

There are infinite modes of expression in the world of art, and to insist that only by one road can the artist attain his ends is to limit him . . . Personally I have always been for freedom of expression, and I am amused at the intolerance of some of our later abstractionists, who, claiming the utmost freedom of expression for themselves, yet look with disdain upon all who diverge from them. I daresay that to the dancing dervish the monotonous twirlings have their ecstasy, but not to the onlookers.

I also found his reference to the superficialities in the world of art, infested with 'schemers, sharks, opportunists, profiteers, snobs, parasytes, sycophants, camp-followers, social climbers', a world which he sees as a 'jungle, into which the artist is forced periodically to bring his work', quite refreshing. It seems that whenever the polemicist was aroused in him he wrote well. It is our loss that he did not recognize his talent for the art of criticism and did not practise it more often. (Apparently it was not in his make-up to become a gadfly à la Whistler.)

The chapter, *I Listen to Music*, shows the strong influence music had on him. His comparisons of Beethoven's music with Rembrandt's works, his translation of music into terms and images of the plastic art are revealing. It proves the so often unexplained closeness of an artist excelling in one discipline to another art form. Epstein seemed to have lived so much with music within him and, out of his own experience was so convinced of its stimulating and wholesome effect as an art concomitant with sculpture that he closed this chapter of his autobiography with the words:[2]

I have often, when showing my larger works, wished that for once only a quartet would play while the work was shown, or even a recording of the great B minor Mass by Bach or Beethoven's in D major. The lack of opportunity and doubt as to how this would be received have prevented me from carrying this out. And yet I know that this combination of music and sculpture would be a wonderful experience.

ISAMU NOGUCHI

*Plates 57, 58*    In his preface to Isamu Noguchi's *A Sculptor's World*, R. Buckminster Fuller called him 'a scientist-artist: that is, he is one of the rare intuitive, original question askers and responders'. Noguchi (1905–) is no doubt the artist who knows how to give imaginative shape to conceptual realizations, to kinetic responses, to forms reflecting tomorrow's world.

His autobiography is written with a conscious tautness which makes his writing as much alive as his sculptures. He writes with the same simple precision and structural suggestiveness which his shapes convey. What greater plasticity can we demand from a single sentence in which he describes the meeting with his father in Japan in 1931 where he had returned against his father's will: 'My father would come to call on me, and we would hold long silent conversations'. His book tells us of the scope of his work. Besides sculpting he has designed furniture, dance and theatre sets as well as costumes; gardens,

[2](see page 341).                                                                          211

plazas and playgrounds. His sketches and brush drawings are little masterpieces.

Noguchi's work reveals a great deal of the man, and his writing enforces the impressions gained from his creations: the lonely self of a man trying to come as close to the feeling of earth as possible, searching for the irreducible in life that lies beyond sophistication and overcleverness, for the plasticity of form which breathes in its morphologic existence and implies imminent motion. He does not see with eyes that feed the mind with romanticized interpretations. Driving through the wide open spaces in the West he makes a point of denying cloud formations any symbolic meaning and insists on 'their own abstract beauty'. To him, each thing exists and speaks for itself in a non-symbolistic manner. To him, the meaning of a thing lies in its evocative essence which moves us, and throughout his book we sense his incessant search for meaning, as throughout his life he tried to make things more meaningful to himself.

His work breathes the poetry of a formula and the cleanliness of a poetic line which knows no adjectives. Fate – or rather his own will – could easily have driven him into any scientific discipline. As a matter of fact, he started to study medicine, and his first sculptures at the age of twenty showed a great feeling for anatomy. The determined spareness of his written, drawn, or sculpted lines is a part of his attitude toward life. He went to Paris to become Brancusi's student. When Brancusi refused, he became his stone-cutter.

As the son of a Bryn Mawr-educated mother and a Japanese poet, he inherited the sensibilities of two cultures ('Why do I continuously go back to Japan, except to renew my contact with the earth? . . . I go there like a beggar or a thief, seeking the last warmth of the earth.') The theatre offers Noguchi the fulfilment of a poetic reality which the reality of life still denies him: to give sculpture its place in the daily ritual ('There is joy in seeing sculpture come to life on the stage in its own world of timeless time. Then the very air becomes charged with meaning and emotion, and form plays its integral part in the re-enactment of a ritual.').

His sculptures are closest to the world of movement, and this is one reason for his harmonious collaboration with the dancer, Martha Graham. His set designs lend themselves to extensions of the dancer's anatomy and movements, they are as elusive as the dance itself and functional in their becoming a part of theatre magic, prop as well as visual image. Noguchi approaches his sculptures with a dancer's feelings, trying to be

XI   Egon Schiele NUDE

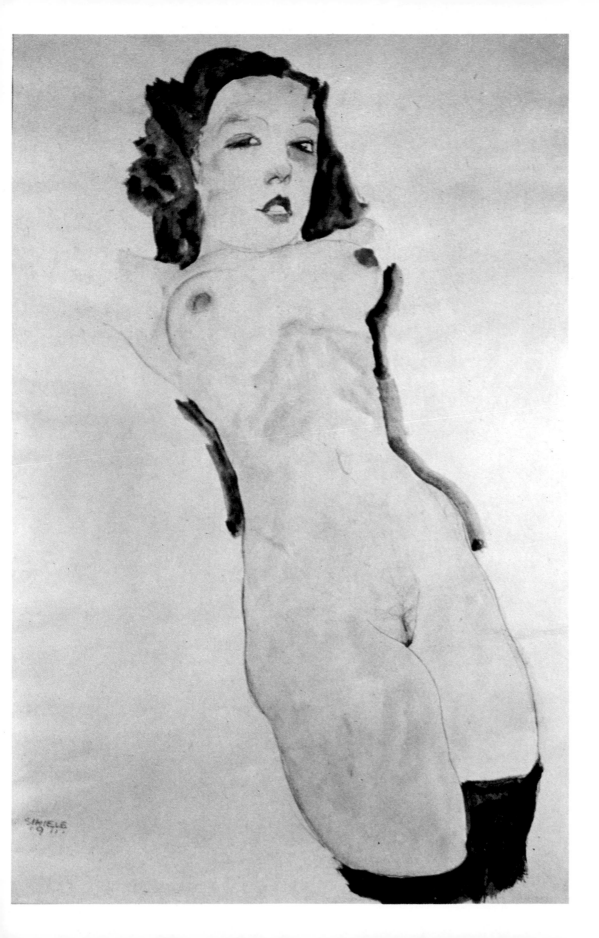

XII  Salvador Dali UNTITLED PAINTING

54 Ernst Barlach THE REUNION (CHRIST AND THOMAS)

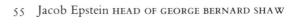

55 Jacob Epstein HEAD OF GEORGE BERNARD SHAW

56 Jean Arp CHESSMAN

57   Isamu Noguchi SET FOR MARTHA GRAHAM'S 'HERODIADE'

58   Isamu Noguchi MAN WITH FLUTE

free of the earth, and he says of one of his marble carvings, *Kouros:* 'It defies gravity, defies time in a sense. The very fragility gives a thrill; the danger excites. It's like life – you can lose it at any moment . . .'

To him, space is inconceivable if not defined by movement, light, and time itself. There is continuous growth in art as there is in nature, and growth is constant change attuned to life. Noguchi perceives space as 'the continuum of our existence', as a challenge to the sculptor to animate it, to bring order into it, to give it its ultimate meaning.

As the most scientifically oriented sculptor of our time, he asks questions and tries to answer them:

New concepts of the physical world and of psychology may give insight into knowledge, but the visible world, in human terms, is more than scientific truths. It enters our consciousness as emotion as well as knowledge; trees grow in vigour, flowers hang evanescent, and mountains lie somnolent – with meaning. The promise of sculpture is to project these inner presences into forms that can be recognized as important and meaningful in themselves. Our heritage is now the world. Art for the first time may be said to have a world consciousness.

## JEAN ARP

*Plate 56*

Jean or Hans Arp (1887–) was born in Strasbourg. Like most Alsatian people, he grew up in a bi-lingual atmosphere which accounts for some of his prose and poetry being written in French or German. After his early contacts with modern painting in Paris, he withdrew from the world in solitude in the Swiss mountains. He learned to converse with the silence of nature and tried to find an art delivered from enslaved imagination, divested of all imitative interpretation. In 1915 he became one of the driving spirits of the Dada movement in Zürich; later he also contributed to the exhibitions and periodicals of the surrealists.

If he is better known for his sculptural work than for his poetry and essayistic, and sometimes lyric, prose, it is due to the fact that most of the Dadaist writing remained confined to its time; it had helped destroy the bloated bogus of tradition but could not keep alive as literary imprint. And yet, next to Barlach, Jean Arp expressed himself with equal strength as visual and verbal artist.

In both media he reacted against a world fully mechanized but out of joint. ('Man has no longer anything to do that is essential, but he wants to do this nothing quickly and with superhuman noise.') Man appeared to Arp as 'a tiny button on a giant senseless machine', as he wrote in his *Notes From a Dada Diary* in 1932. To counteract the man-made madness of our time, he returned to nature. ('I love nature, but never nature's surrogate.') Arp wanted to 'produce', not reproduce, and produce 'directly and not through interpretation'. He was preoccupied with odd configurations, as he called them, trying to break up the entity of objects and beings into sundry parts, especially reducing man's haloed image of self-reflection to a simple, inanimate part of his surroundings.

We find a similar tendency in his poetry, in *Die Wolken-pumpe* (The Cloud Pump), *Muscheln und Schirme* (Shells and Umbrellas), *Der Pyramidenrock* (The Pyramid's Petticoat), or *Le Siège de l'air* (The Air Chair). Out of shreds of images and the sequences of non-sequiturs he creates a world of irrational freedom and paradoxical ties, a world in which the descriptive sentence, painting an idea or feeling in time, is as non-existent as a legible concept of space in his visual art. But through the deformation of meaning and the deflation of logic vested in speech he evokes images and sensations which are beautiful nevertheless, as such lines from his poetry indicate:

*at the edge of the fairy-tale the night knits roses . . .*
Or:
*the commas and full stops jump into the hats of kisses*
*and escape from the hair-raising springtime*

*But he can also mock with tantalizing absurdities and grotesquesqueries:*

*the three young lordships in bloom sway on their vanilla stem*
*the feather floats in the mirror with the navel of light laugh with your arms*
*three flowers present a nubile diamond to the celestial glove*

The structural growth which emanates from his sculptures conveys a feeling of innate movement and the realization of latent forces arrested in the material itself. There is a strong lyric quality in Arp which derives from his basic philosophy. He saw real life as a world of memories and dreams 'which flow together like mighty streams'. Arp wrote an essay, *The World of Memory and Dream*, in which he conjures up the image of his late wife and co-worker, Sophie Taeuber. It is a lyrically written account of a man's feelings for his deceased love:

Only fairy-tales of perfected beauty could reflect the splendour and light of her being . . . She painted the soul of the dream, the in-visible reality. She drew radiant, geometric messages . . . Most often

I meet Sophie under the olive trees of the Mediterranean . . . she offers me large grapes which are weeping eyes . . . Do I dream when I see Sophie blissfully alive? . . . The world of memory and dream is the real world. It is related to art which is shaped at the edge of earthly unreality.

To Jean Arp his poetic writings were as important as his visual art. Both presented themselves to him as organic entity and continuity. Some of his poetry was always with him. He would reread it, add new passages, give it new life of the life that is now.

### ERNST BARLACH

*Plate 54*

Ernst Barlach's (1870–1938) father, a physician, loved to draw for recreation, and almost all members of his family drew and painted for the pleasure of it. Being a man also interested in literature, his father accepted it in a matter-of-fact manner when his son began to paint and write verses in his early youth.

There can be no doubt that Barlach, the sculptor, overpowers Barlach, the writer, and, if we wish to categorize, we could say that Barlach, the draughtsman, who left us some stunning lithographs, drawings, and woodcuts, ranks next to the sculptor. In the beginning, Barlach thought of himself more as a writer, and it was not before his sixtieth year that he publicly admitted in his famous radio speech about the artist in his time – in January 1933, shortly before Hitler came to power – that he spoke as a sculptor and 'occasional' dramatist.

Barlach discovered his artistic identity rather late in life. He wrote his first play when he was 42 years of age. Six years previously when returning from a journey to Southern Russia he had found 'his own true self' and gave it sculptural expression. Returning from this trip in 1906 he wrote:

An unbelievable awareness dawned upon me: You may dare anything that is a part of you without timidity, the most outward and the most inward, gestures of piety and restrained fury, since there is an expression for everything, may it be hellish paradise or heavenly hell, as you find realized one of the two or both in Russia.

At this point of his life forces took hold of him which determined his creative awakening and growth, forces which can be described as a searching for God in the tortured face of man, a strange exaltation of mysticism, a return to the medieval image of the artisan. He spent most of his life as a recluse in the little town of Güstrow in the province of Mecklenburg, isolated from the noisy market life, from the intellectual

Babel of the big cities. In the solitude of his little workshop he struggled to find the image of human existence, and arrested the voice of God in man, in compact, angular forms, sculpted or drawn, which protest their lot of loneliness. These shapes are real people, sometimes static in appearance, but always expressing the drama of their lives. They are never naked. On the contrary, the garments accentuate a tragic heaviness, the burden of man's destiny. The garments imprison man in his own cloak as if he had to be ashamed of having been made in the image of God. There is a medieval monkishness in his attitude. There is also a medieval simplicity in his forms, devoid of ornaments and details, an aesthetic bareness more naked than nudity could ever be.

Most of his sculptures show single figures. When two figures find each other, it is out of fear or faith. ('I have to be able to feel pity . . . Man and his gesture tell enough.') Barlach is an artist deeply concerned with man's love and faith, terror and suffering. He does not recognize art for art's sake. He creates because he himself cannot help wrestling with the meaning of existence and because art is to him a moral justification of life. Once he wrote: 'Whosoever concerns himself with aesthetics for its own sake, does something much akin to a sin against the Holy Spirit'.

As in his sculptures and drawings we also find in his plays and prose reality spiritualized but still real in its recognizable vividness. Long before he became a sculptor his prose showed his passion for visual imagery. The look, the eyes, dominate his early descriptions. For instance, the eyes of a child gaze at the world: 'My stupid round peepholes were full of colour, full of the freshest colour of children's souls. Here were the heavenly blue and the gold of the sun, the red of the sunset and the northern lights, they all were there, and it was certainly impossible to find more beautiful colour pots . . .'

Neither his prose nor his plays were conventional. He tried to dramatize the finding of the higher values and spiritual essence of life, as already indicated in his first play, *Der Tote Tag* (The Dead Day) in which a mother tries to prevent her son from becoming a man and finding his estranged father who, at the end of the play, is revealed as the symbol of God or *the* spirit ('Strange that man does not want to know that his father is God'). The play's mystical connotations made its staging difficult. But Barlach felt that a voice deep within forced him to write plays and that, with regard to such urgency and importance of subject matter, it is irrelevant whether the plays are built according to rules in any book. An indescribable 'must' compelled him to write these plays, 'otherwise I might have taken to drinking or become mad', as he said in a letter published by Herbert Günther. 'The thought of escape into a far distance from where I would certainly never return, gnaws like a worm at my soul. I call this quite simply latent madness. The petit bourgeois as which I appear on the surface keeps me clear-headed, and so I am a sculptor and draughtsman and writer, and all three out of some blind rage . . .'

He was only interested in giving shape to the mystery of existence, whatever form it may take: 'I desire nothing', he said in an interview in 1932, 'except to be an artist, pure and simple. It is my belief that what cannot be expressed in words can, through plastic form, reach another man's soul. To be sure, it is the pleasure of my creative urge to hover again and again over such problems as the meaning of life and other mountain peaks in the realm of the spirit'.

Hitler had Barlach's war memorials and statues removed and his work declared 'degenerate art'. He was forbidden to exhibit and threatened with the *Verbot* to work as an artist. For quite some time Barlach, who had spoken and written against the danger of Fascism, resisted the advice of his friends to leave the country. He was afraid of uprooting himself from his country's past which had helped him to grow ('A man can be forced to flee, but I shudder when I contemplate that in exile one can also become exiled from one's self or wither away in homelessness'). Some time later he wrote his publisher, Reinhold Piper: '. . . The louder the "Heils" roar, instead of cheering and raising my arm in Roman fashion, the more I pull my hat down over my eyes . . .' When, in 1938, he was finally ready to emigrate ('I am selling my property', he wrote Piper. 'I shall go whenever it is possible to work for a few more years at an adequate level . . .'), it was too late. His broken spirit rallied once more to fight on. But his broken heart gave up.

Käthe Kollwitz, whose etchings and drawings are closest to Barlach's work, expressed more consciously than he did, through the choice of her subject matter and in her *Diaries and Letters*, a *Weltanschauung* which reflected Barlach's outlook on life. In her diary entries during World War I she said: 'Humanity's goal goes beyond the first stage of happiness – elimination of poverty, disease – also beyond the complete development of the forces within itself. The goal is to develop divinity, spirituality'.

She survived Ernst Barlach by seven years. Among the very

few artists who came to say goodbye to Barlach for the last time, was Käthe Kollwitz, then seventy-one years old, outlawed by the Nazis and still defying the inhumanity of humanity. She recorded her impressions of Barlach's funeral:

I entered through a side door and came upon his work table with its assemblage of tools, with some of his works standing against it. As I turned to one side, toward the studio room proper, I saw Barlach lying in the open coffin. The coffin stood in the middle of the room. His bier was solemnly and expensively decorated. He lay with head turned completely to one side, as though to conceal himself. The arms extended and the hands folded together, very small and thin. All around against the walls, his silent figures. Behind the coffin, a heap of pine boughs. Above the coffin, the mask of the Güstrow cathedral angel. His small dog kept running around the coffin and sniffing at it.

The ceremony was held over the closed coffin. Pastor Schwartzkopf, who spent eight years in Güstrow and was close to Barlach, delivered the sermon . . . Then passages from the Book of Job, passages from Barlach's letters and books. The struggle, the search, the cry for God . . .

# PART THREE: THE WRITER WHO PAINTS

## The Poetic Doodlers

Doodling is one of the many manifestations of our unconscious. What a wonderful feeling it is to criss-cross lines, to make dots and circles, to scrawl nonsense pictures in order to rid oneself of hostilities, tensions, or only of a surplus of fanciful images which most of the time have their own *raison d'être*! Those of us with artistic senses probably scribble designs and shapes or recognizable figures, sometimes less clearly defined than on other occasions.

In these cases the pen does not play the blind game of the unconscious. A sense of form directs eye and hand, an aesthetic feeling controls the line. The hand may start with a dot or circle, but soon a guiding idea takes hold and decides the literary concept of the drawing. This does not mean that any emotional significance is excluded or that the subconscious wishes are not expressed in a substitutive form.

Some drawings seem to express intent and purpose, even though their genesis was doodling. Many writers begin to draw in full awareness of their limited control. They expect to be overcome and directed by that unknown quantity within. As in everything else, the degree of unawareness varies with each writer and each drawing he tries to make.

I have permitted myself some latitude in lumping together a variety of writers under the generic title of *Poetic Doodlers*. Some have taken drawing very seriously and worked on it as any craftsman would, others have used it as a visual note made on the margin of a manuscript, or as a mental crutch to whatever degree and in whatever situation.

Gifted children initially display an ability to draw before they are quite able to rhyme. It is therefore understandable that many writers start by expressing themselves through drawing. As they feel increasingly on safe ground as poets, they may still go through years of ambivalence and vacillation, never quite sure which road to choose until, so very often, the road is decided for them. Some of these writers continue to draw all their lives. Some recall at the age of thirty or forty the joy drawing brought to them in their early youth.

Friedrich Schiller
Self-caricature

225

Henrik Ibsen (1828–1906), whose position in the world of drama is uncontested, worked with brush and pencil in his youth. It was far more than doodling with him. Even though he never reached any remarkable level, he went about trying to get instruction in painting in a rather systematic way. His drawings and paintings have a naive quality about them, one can sense the endeavour exerted, the perspiration creating little more than a conventional likeness of a landscape, be it a watercolour, an oil painting, or a pencil sketch. These visualizations recall clean, nice rhymes without poetry in them.

In a letter to his biographer, J. B. Halvorsen, he tells about the various schools he attended and the many painters he worked with and concludes: '. . . but in 1860 the preparations for *Love's Comedy* and *The Pretenders* gradually absorbed my interests, and from that time I put painting on the shelf.' His memory seems to be at fault, because some of his better paintings were done about 1862, but the fact is that as a painter Ibsen would have been a failure.

Franz Grillparzer (1781–1872), the Austrian dramatist, is often mentioned together with Goethe and Schiller, although he did not quite reach their stature and remained rather unknown outside the German language border. But his most romantic play, *The Dream, A Life*, influenced Maeterlinck and Gerhart Hauptmann, and his novella, *The Poor Minstrel*, is a most perfect example of its genre.

He called music his 'powerful rival of poetry' and thought that, while 'poetry intends to give body to the spirit, music spiritualizes the sensuous'. Grillparzer enjoyed letting his fantasy guide his hands on the piano keys and composed a few songs. A scurrilous scene is pictured in his autobiography. Instead of sheet music he put an engraving in front of himself and played the pictorialized scene on the piano as if it were a musical composition.

He never attempted to draw or paint in order to create a work of art. His drawings were exclusively related to his plays and supported his memory. To sketch a theme or scene made it easier to create the eventual stage image.

*Plate 61*

His relationship to music, however, was more intimate and had the tragic undertone of a lost chance or a lost child. At an advanced age, Grillparzer once wrote to Adalbert Stifter: 'I feel like a one-time rich man who has lost his fortune gambling on the stock exchange, for poetry has forsaken me as music did some time earlier'.

The relation of the poet to the painter was quite different

in Stifter's (1805–1868) case. From his earliest youth, he, who became one of the great *Erzähler* in German literature, wrote and painted. He strongly believed in himself as a painter because painting meant to him an accomplishment hard to achieve but an art in which he thought he would excel while 'as a writer I am only a dilettante'. Stifter was in his forties when a German encyclopedia listed him as a painter, also known as a man of *belles lettres*. But Nietzsche, one of the great stylists, considered him one of the few German tellers of tales whose style was immaculate.

The Germans have always thought of his novels and poetic tales of the Bohemian Forest as the best descriptions of nature in their language.

. . . in winter the two pinnacles called 'horns' are snow-white and on clear days stand out in the dusky atmosphere with blinding brilliance; all the alpine meadows at the base of the summits are white then, as well as their sloping shoulders; even the precipitous rock-faces or walls as the people call them, are coated with a white velvet nap of hoar-frost and glazed with ice-tissue, so the entire mass towers like an enchanted castle above the darkish weight of grey forest mantling the base. In summer as the sun and temperate winds melt the snow on the deep gradients, the horns soar up, as the mountain people say, black into the sky, their surface marked only by exquisite little flecks and snow-veins . . .

It is only lately that his landscape paintings have been claimed as fine examples of the nineteenth-century genre. It is easy to compare his poetic descriptions of nature with his gentle, atmospheric paintings. Stifter ought to belong with those in this book who gave equal time and talent to both writing and painting, if only his paintings were more daring and had less of the same romantic spirit, of that meticulous vision and bland beauty we find with many another German painter of Stifter's time. At one point he himself confessed: 'I must write, otherwise I would have to die'.

Close to Stifter is the Swiss novelist Gottfried Keller (1819–1890) whose realistic and purposeful fiction, particularly his educational novel *Der Grüne Heinrich* ranks him high among nineteenth-century writers. In his novel he describes the struggle between the painter and writer in him. In his youth, Keller desperately wanted the career of a professional painter and went through hunger and humiliation until he discovered his great gift for writing.

As a mature and recognized writer he admitted in a letter that his painting talent silently faded away in its early years

227

before it reached maturity. But as soon as he fully realized that he was not the great pioneering painter of his age, he could afford to do a few fine landscape pictures which have the very personal expression of the amateur, the genuine lover of the art. Some of his manuscript pages, but also the margin of the minutes kept during long hours of the *Regierungsrat* in the Swiss government, show doodled sketches of landscapes and people. Undoubtedly, drawing and painting made him find himself the poet whose visual ability gave his prose descriptive power and made it possible for him in moments of graphic mood to scribble or paint to his heart's desire.

Physicist and professor at the University of Göttingen, Georg Christoph Lichtenberg (1742–1799) belongs to the greatest wits of world literature. Behind his polished epigrams with their poisonous points directed at the heart of their target, hid a philosopher. This German Swift wrote:

One can live in this world on soothsaying but not on truthsaying. The great with their long arms often do less damage than their lackeys with short ones.
I regard reviews as a kind of infant's disease to which newborn books are exposed.

He attacked the *Sturm und Drang* writers for their uncontrolled emotionalism and satirized Lavater's theories on physiognomy for their pseudo-scientific ring. The title of his attack, *On Physiognomy versus the Physiognomists. For the Promotion of Love and Knowledge of Man* parodied Lavater's title: *Physiognomic Fragments. For the Promotion of a Knowledge of Man and of Love of Man.*

Lichtenberg also mastered the drawing of facial expressions as he showed in his physiognomic sketches in one of his letters in which he varied the expression of one and the same face with great skill. After all, it was he who wrote: 'I have made a sketch of him so that, on the Day of Judgment, he can the more easily find his body again.'

Georg Büchner (1813–1837) died at the age of twenty-four, unable to establish that he was one of the rare geniuses of dramatic literature. But the few works he left behind make us believe that his destiny deprived mankind. With his *Danton's Death* the first passive, existentialist hero was born, and with his *Wozzeck*, a brutal drama of mental aberration and obsession, he gave articulate testimony to his talent. He also wrote a delightful comedy, *Leonce and Lena*, in the commedia dell' arte style. In it he lays bare the futility of life among the idle rich, in which the realization of one's own absurdity and the

G. C. Lichtenberg
Physiognomic sketches

*Plate 63*

ability to love are the only moments of saving grace. He anticipated much that happened more than a century later.

We know that Georg Büchner scribbled strange characters on the margin of his *Wozzeck* script which seem to have little or no bearing on the dramatically powerful figures in the play. It looks as if his thoughts wanted to make a visual note of something unrelated or wished to stop and collect themselves, gathering strength for a new dramatic assault.

At the age of twenty, Thomas Mann (1875–1955) spent a year in Rome with his brother Heinrich. The only book on which they worked together was written and illustrated there. Its title was *Picture Book for Good Children*. The subtitle, probably the longest, most misleading and malicious of all subtitles in literary history was: 'Seventy-five artistic master-pieces, among them twenty-eight colour pictures and forty-seven engravings besides sixteen artful poems and many textual remarks of a morally enlightening and entertaining content, collected and published with great care and parti-cular regard for the moral thinking of the maturing German youth'.

While Heinrich Mann (1871–1950) had a great gift for painting and vacillated in his youth between painting and writing, Thomas had a remarkable hand for drawing the grotesque caricature. However, he never felt the desire to perfect his talent. As a matter of fact, after these first attempts, he never drew again.

The picture book in question was only issued in a single copy which was lost when Hitler came to power in 1933. Some of the drawings are extant, however, and were repro-duced in Viktor Mann's memoirs, *We Were Five*.

Thomas Mann's drawings are a revelation. Of all German writers he is the one who could pose with some justification as Goethe's heir. Some sections of his work and a few un-forgettable figures, such as Felix Krull, have a gentle, in-gratiating humour.

His early drawings present a picture diametrically opposed to the professorial profundity which speaks to us from his work. The humour of those early drawings has all the con-notations of vicious satire. At first sight it may be difficult to reconcile these drawings of youthful wantonness with Mann's later epic work. The drawings show disrespect, a touch of morbidity and a knifelike, analytic mind. Let us not forget that in the picture entitled *Laben* life puts out its phallic tongue. But also let us not forget that Mann's major themes were disease and death, the artist's position in a society of decay, and that Mann delighted in characterizing the weaknesses of weak men.

Paul Verlaine (1844–1896), this tragic and wretched poet, who produced subtle, haunting and magic verses, drew all his life. His drawings are in the truest sense poetic doodlings, revealing the honest and naive alter ego of a morbid, perverted, and untamable temperament. How much love went into the sketch of Arthur Rimbaud, his great passion, done with a few ink lines! He could be poisonous in his caricatures, or simply lyrical if he felt like it. When free from his evil moods, Verlaine could be full of fun with a flair for the grotesque and almost burlesque, which often escaped into his drawings, about which he said in his *Confessions:*

*Plate 68*

The day charmed me and, although I was afraid in the dark, the night attracted me, and driven by curiosity I tried to search in it for I don't know what kind of shades of white and grey. No doubt, it was this disposition for which I have to be grateful that I felt at an extremely early age a marked joy to smear each piece of paper of which I could get hold with ink, pencil, dissolved carmine lacquer, Prussian blue and gum, what is usually considered a talent for painting. I drew epileptic men in wild, glowing colours. Then there were mostly soldiers whose anatomy consisted of respect and who were put on elves; moreover, ladies with big flounces put together out of disconnected flourishes, the whole, without any purpose, to appear like a bang. Everything put down with a few lines with pen or pencil or a few strokes with the paint brush. I often used my fingers, if not my tongue, to wipe out mercilessly those 'designs' which did not satisfy me. From these 'attempts' I retained the mania to fill the margins of my manuscripts and my intimate letters with shapeless drawings which reprehensible flatterers pretended to find droll. Or perhaps could I have become a great painter instead of the poet I am?

The man, who gave sur-realism its name, was known as Guillaume Albert Wladimir Alexandre Apollinaire de Kostrowitzky (1880–1918), poet, short story writer, essayist, art critic, impresario, editor, journalist and bohemian. He was the inventor of the *calligrammes*, the typographical derangement of poems, and he did some watercolours in the last year of his life.

*Plate 69*

If there ever was an extroverted artist who could not help appearing in person and performing with his confrères at banquets, galleries, and cafés, it was Apollinaire. This French poet, born as an illegitimate child of Polish parentage in Rome, became the spokesman for the radical new movements during the first two decades of this century. He was a brilliant conversationalist of impressive appearance and a huge mental appetite. He sometimes erased the border lines between imitation and originality, but his arguments were always so convincing that it did not matter. He was an articulate advocate for cubism and won the case. Also, he was lucky. Time was on his side.

Like Baudelaire, he too was a poet rooted in the visual image. He used the word 'music' for those paintings which negated all likeness with reality. Apollinaire was also a mystic in a fashion who believed that 'mysticism verges very closely on eroticism'. He may have been influenced by Alfred Jarry when he wrote his sensational play, *The Breasts of Tiresias*. He subtitled it 'Drame Sur-réaliste' and thus introduced a new term for a 'New Spirit that . . . shall not fail to captivate the elite, and promises to transform arts and manners into universal joy . . .'

'A man is infinitely more complicated than his thoughts', said Paul Valéry, whose thoughts were infinitely complicated. Valéry began his career as a symbolist poet, but later turned to philosophy, mathematics, science, and economics. He became famous for his literary and philosophic essays which he simply called *Variety*.

He has said that he was attracted to writing poetry as a mental exercise only. He developed a mathematical metaphysic to guide him in philosophic speculations and in his essays on the arts. At one point of his life Valéry experienced a crisis which brought about a hiatus in his creative writing for about twenty years, a fact which – together with his dualism – made him appreciate the creative impulse or the process of the intellect more than its finished product. On the other hand, he demanded skill and perfection and demonstrated both in his poetry which, despite its emphasis on rigidity and technique, evokes tender and sensual impressions.

He was known for his personal aloofness and belief in an intellectual elite. He made a point of being considered a businessman rather than a bohemian and of publishing his works only in limited and distinctive editions. He recognized that the process of creativity oscillates between a pure, potential world in which everything is absolute and an impure world of the actual in which everything is relative.

*Plate 67*

It is not surprising at all that Paul Valéry was inclined to paint and draw. What is strange is that his drawings lack freedom and flight of imagination and are conventional in technique. The Apollonian control exerted in this area of his activity resulted in rigidity and reveals as impulse a literary

231

rather than visual conception. Drawing was probably little more to him than another mental exercise.

A phenomenon in our technological age was Frederico Garcia Lorca (1889–1936), poet, dramatist, prose writer, musician, draughtsman, folklorist, lecturer, director of the theatrical group 'La Barraca' under the Spanish Republican government, cofounder with La Argentina of the Ballet Madrid in 1932.

He had a genius for fusing the forces of life into a unified power. He had a poet's facility in identifying with nature, with the people and their folkloristic tradition. He was more realistic than any realist and more surrealistic than any surrealist. His was a spirit obsessed with primitive passion and the vision of death. His many plays whose lyricisms and prose passages are highly dramatic, testify to being rooted in Spanish folklore and in the poet's preoccupation with flaming flesh, ecstatic love and death.

In 1929 he visited New York. This city became a powerful symbol of the prison of man's mind, of man's unfulfilled dreams. *The Poet in New York* reflects Lorca's solitude in the man-made madness that surrounded him in this city with its 'extra-human architecture', its 'furious rhythm of geometry and anguish'. 'Among shapes turning serpents' Lorca finds himself lost in the loneliness that engulfs man in what to him was a strange world, in which everything loses its identity. He cannot find his own face, grown different with the passing of each day which is driven by a hidden dynamism of destruction. Lorca records his impressions and visions in dream-like symbols in the *Dawn in New York:*

*Plate 71*

> *Which signs of spring*
> *do you hold in your hand?*
> *A rose of blood and a white lily.*

Caught in the canyons of long avenues, he draws images forced upon him by the master blueprint of doom.

In 1936 Lorca reached his peak as a dramatist in his least stylized play, *The House of Bernarda Alba.* Shortly after he had finished it, he was executed by Generalissimo Franco's Falangist bands.

'Franz Kafka (1883–1924) was a gifted draughtsman', said Johannes Urzidil, a writer and artist, one of Kafka's friends in Prague in the years after World War I. 'Kafka was a genius who could have been a genius in any medium he tried'.

While Kafka studied at the German University in Prague his notebooks were full of drawings. Later, letters, diaries and

Fra Vestnas.

Tegnet af Henr. Ibsen. 1862.

59    Henrik Ibsen
DRAWING

60    Gottfried Keller
LANDSCAPE

61 Franz Grillparzer MANUSCRIPT PAGE

62 Friedrich Schiller DRAWING OF THE ARTIST'S HAND

XIII    Adalbert Stifter FABRIKSGARTEN IN SCHWADORF

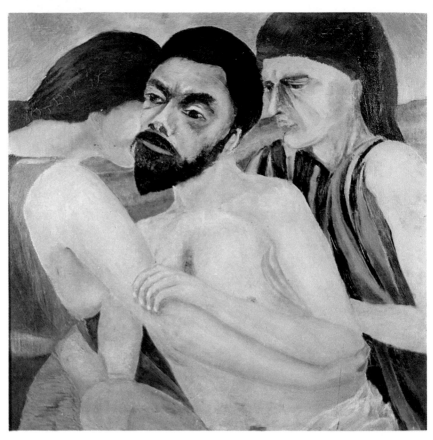

XIV  D. H. Lawrence RESURRECTION

XV  D. H. Lawrence FLIGHT WITH AN AMAZON

manuscripts prove that his sketches were born simultaneously with his ideas and, as Mr. Urzidil points out, 'may have helped him in forming his ideas'.

In his book, *There Goes Kafka*, Johannes Urzidil speaks of Kafka's desire to draw, but also refers to Kafka's contention that Jews were primarily narrators and not painters. The sketches so far known show Kafka's visualizations as being motivated by his search for truth. ('There is a goal but no way; what we call the way is mere wavering.') There was no wavering between writing and drawing in Kafka's life. He had taken art classes as a young man, but the greatest visual training seemed to have come from the beauty of Prague, from the sights during his travels and from the interest he took in painting. His inspiration to draw, however, came from his deep desire to express himself graphically.

Several writers found a complementing trend between his writings and drawings, a 'constant give and take between the plastic and literary arts' (Heinz Ladendorf in Wallraf-Richartz-Jahrbuch), 'the parallelism between his drawing and narrative visions can hardly be overlooked' (Max Brod in *Kafka's Belief and Doctrine*).

The clarity and precision of Kafka's prose can be recognized in the few drawings known to me. But there is less of the strange blending of nightmare and reality in the drawings, so prominent a characteristic in his prose. His drawings show a remarkable feeling for movement which, in many cases, is one of the unconscious means of relief from isolation, tension, and anxieties. Kafka's world is full of them, full of guilt, from which man tries in vain to escape and find salvation. Even where a drawing shows a position of withdrawal, the tortured gesture of an introvert, the movement itself is of surprising strength which insinuates at least a kinesthetic chance of escape. ('There are countless places of refuge, there is only one place of salvation; but the possibilities of salvation, again, are as numerous as all the places of refuge.')

It is a long way from all these aforementioned writers to Antoine de Saint-Exupéry (1900–1944), aviator, soldier, poet, prose writer, artist, philosopher, and moralist, a man who saw the world from above. Now that we try to bring the cosmos closer to the earth we should be listening to one who was close to the spheres, from which one sees life in a more philosophic way.

Like so many of those who of late have successfully challenged the creator with the flying machine, have found new beauty in living on earth, Saint-Exupéry gave it the most

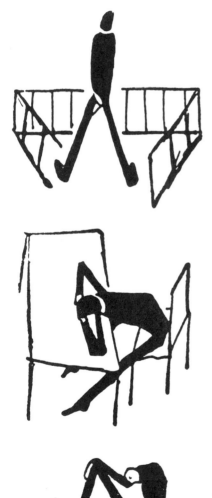

Franz Kafka
Sketches on MS of *The Trial*

237

poetic expression in his various books. He was very conscious of belonging to a new race of man and to a new world in which the 'living-together' assumes new moral aspects. ('Love does not consist in gazing at each other but in looking together in the same direction.') 'What am I if not a partici- pant?' cries the aviator in *Flight to Arras*. Saint-Exupéry was the first to realize during his night flights that however far man tries to get away from the earth, the closer he will come to it.

At the age of six he had drawn a boa constrictor which had swallowed an elephant. We can now see this drawing on one of the opening pages of *The Little Prince*. But when the six- year-old showed his drawing to the grown-ups they took it for the picture of a hat and told the boy that he had no talent for drawing or painting.

As an adult who loved to doodle and draw and who illustrated some of his books, he must have thought of how this moment of ridicule stifled his talent, though it did not kill it. In the case of *The Little Prince* the drawings came first and helped him create this classic children's story. Saint-Exupéry showed some of these drawings to his American publisher, who suggested that the writer continue to experiment:

*Plate 66*

He would call us up excitedly at different times to show us how the drawings were coming along. When we suggested colour, he started experimenting with that. I am quite sure the pictures and the book developed together in his mind and I am also sure they provided him with a new medium for expressing his own phil- osophy as well as a form of relaxation in this new departure for his work.

A defect in the engine of Saint-Exupéry's plane made an emergency landing in the desert necessary. Then and there he must have learned about the wisdom of the sands, and it was during these hours of loneliness that he had the vision of that little prince whose beautiful thoughts and feelings Saint- Exupéry copied from a few of the many pages written in the wind by the clumsy hand of eternity.

## The Writer's Visual Awareness

GOETHE, THE OLYMPIAN
When we call Johann Wolfgang von Goethe (1749–1832) the olympian we refer to a man thoroughly awe-inspiring. We can see him sitting on a high pedestal, monumental in his

pose, gracefully accepting the world's homage. And rightly so. He was the last great humanist of Renaissance stature, a universal genius.

No one would think of calling Leonardo olympian because he seems human, all too human to us; he is the eternal seeker, little interested in his own status. With Leonardo it is never the result that matters, but the road leading to it; with Goethe we have the feeling of accomplishment crowning the purpose of his existence, even though he stressed time and again that the process of constant work, the inner growth, decides the destiny of the artist. ('Everyone wants to *be* someone; nobody wants to grow.')

Goethe never created any character, any idea, any image that would not be based on his own experiences. He never tolerated his fantasy to elope with him, he never sent his imagination to seek the novel and to discover the unknown through which he himself could not move. With him we are on secure grounds, we have never the feeling of an adventure that may leave us floating on the endless sea. In whatever he did – and what did he not do? – we sense his strong feeling for the real, the living, and the concrete, expressed after long oscillation between his *logos* and intuition ('. . . little as one creates with conscious predetermination, conscious effort becomes necessary in the process of completing . . .').

To understand the uniqueness of Goethe as a world in himself within a world full of turbulent changes, we must remind ourselves that he was born at the very end of the Baroque period and that, when he died at the age of eighty-three, Romanticism had reached its climactic point. He participated in the *Sturm und Drang* period; his youthful *The Sorrows of Young Werther* (1774) ushered in Romanticism; his Italian journeys turned him into a classicist; and his great humanistic document, the second part of *Faust*, was the epitome of classic Romanticism.

Goethe's life is an amazing phenomenon because he exemplified his era while remaining above its currents. He foresaw the weakness and destructiveness in the future greatness of man, in his scientific genius, and yet he recognized progress as inescapable and man's dynamic quality as wholesome. ('I love him who strives for the impossible.') In his eyes, the true romantic, however alienated he may be from the world and isolated from himself, feels free to experiment and to move in all directions. This classic example of the eternal romantic – as Goethe must have seen himself – wonders about the uniqueness of the self as an unlimited source of ever-changing values.

239

('For a man to achieve all that is demanded of him he must regard himself as greater than he is.')

Goethe-Faust, the eternal seeker, begins with the realization: 'Es irrt der Mensch so lang er strebt' (man errs as long as he strives). Written about sixty years later, Faust ends with the pragmatic statement that 'only that which is fruitful is true', and that 'if you want to reach the infinite, traverse the finite to all sides'. In a symbolic way, this is what Goethe accomplished. There has never been another human being more interested and creatively involved in all phenomena of nature, in all areas of human activity, from politics to all art forms, than Goethe. From his own poems, plays, prose writings, from his letters and talks with Eckermann, it becomes obvious that there is no worldly area he would not have surveyed, nor any niche into which he would not have looked. ('Thinking is more interesting than knowing, but less interesting than looking.')

Stupendous about Goethe is his continuous effort to get to know everything, to be able to absorb it and coordinate the endless details of the world's knowledge and fuse them into one man's wisdom. Although his accomplishments in this direction seem unfathomable to us, he recognized the limitations of man and, despite his incessant drive to 'expand into the universe', he realized that, from time to time, one must be selective. But as one of the first universalists he felt encouraged to observe that what some eliminate others take up, and carry on. ('Then there arises the splendid feeling that true man is only humanity all together and that the individual can only be glad and happy if he has the courage to feel himself part of the whole.')

There were a few men in the twentieth century of encyclopedic knowledge. Aldous Huxley and Lord Russell, André Gide and Malraux come to mind. But they could not probe, experiment and test their knowledge in all spheres of interest as Goethe could. Theirs was, no doubt, a stupendous accumulation of knowledge, but Goethe thoroughly experienced what he knew. His will to penetrate existence in all its phases began at an early age. Still in Strasbourg he preferred to associate with medical men and attended medical lectures while studying jurisprudence. When he went to see the Cathedral, he studied it by making drawings and taking measurements.

His simultaneous activites are surprising. In the year 1790 when his play *Tasso* was issued and he sent to his publisher the first – fragmentary – version of *Faust* while finishing his

*Metamorphosis* of the plants, he began to work on his *Farbenlehre*. But that year he journeyed to Italy for the second time, staying there from March until June. There he wrote his Venetian epigrams and propounded his theory on the bone structure of the skull. In July he wrote to the Chamberlain at the Court of Weimar, von Knebel: 'My mind drives me more and more toward the natural sciences'. Shortly afterwards he participated in military manoeuvres in Silesia and could not resist viewing the first steam-engine on the continent. He also visited mines (he knew much about mining, agriculture, forestry, and horticulture). The last months of that year he devoted to scientific studies (optics, botany, anatomy) and began his osteologic investigations while writing poems and prose which never stopped flowing from him.

The year 1790, chosen at random, was characteristic of Goethe's life. Shortly before, he had been in Italy for a year and a half and had found himself 'in this lonesomeness . . . but as what? – as artist!' It was during that journey that he gave up the thought of becoming a painter, although he never stopped drawing. ('We should talk less and draw more. Personally, I would like to renounce speech altogether and, like organic nature, communicate everything I have to say in sketches'.) He even made scene designs during his twenty-six years as director of the ducal theatre in Weimar and theorized on their nature as well as on his conception of acting. ('An actor ought to become an apprentice of a sculptor and painter'.)

*Plate 72*

His plays are not as theatrical as they are poetic and thought-provoking. He admitted that he had 'written in opposition to the stage' and said to Eckermann: 'I could have written many a good play, but giving it a second thought, I do not regret not having done it. I have always seen all my work symbolically only, and, fundamentally, it was rather the same to me whether I made pots or dishes'. Goethe could not have expressed his idea of total integration of the artistic will, of unity in multiplicity more succinctly. He said the *Urphänomen* (the primordial phenomenon) was ideal as the ultimate recognizable; real as the recognized; symbolic because it embraces all possible cases; and identical with all cases.

In May 1815 Goethe sent what he called a 'general confession of faith' to the young son of the Mayor of Frankfurt, Christian Heinrich Schlosser, a little-known statement which is not even included in the most complete editions of Goethe's work of 140 volumes. In this confession he formulates a theory on the arts:

a.  Everything is found in nature that is in the subject matter.
y.  and a bit more of it.
b.  Everything is found in the subject matter that is in nature
z.  and a bit more of it.
b can recognize a, but y can only be surmised through z. Out of it emerges the balance of the world and the balance of the circle of life in which we are caught. That human being able to embrace all four in utmost clarity has always been called GOD by all people.

Whatever Goethe attempted to investigate – and it matters little today that some of his scientific studies are more or less obsolete – his starting point was nature which he explored from the viewpoint of a common origin of all living matter and discovered, as proof of evolution, the rudiment of the inter-maxillary bone in man. He did not anticipate Darwin's theory of natural selection, but his thoughts moved in the same direction. As is to be expected, his approach to science was one of intuition and sensuous experience. But because of his drawings and investigations of nature he was constantly forced to sharpen his sense of observation. ('Without my work in natural science I should never have known human beings as they really are. In no other activity can one come so close to direct perception and clear thought, or realize so fully the errors of the senses, the mistakes of the intellect, the weakness and greatness of human character.')

Intuition played a decisive part in his life and creativity. He thought that man's imagination is nature's equal and that, in the final analysis, the creative instinct in the artist has its own will. ('Of the truly creative no one is ever master; it must be left to go its own way.') Although he is not free of errors of judgment – for instance, by thinking too highly of the composer Zelter and too little of Schubert – his insight into the essence of art nevertheless shows an unerring intuition and proves his foresight in aesthetic definitions fully acceptable in the mid-twentieth-century:

The greatest works of art are plainly displeasing; they are ideals which can and should provide any approximate satisfaction.
Art matures a long time before it is beautiful, albeit art, that true and great, is often indeed truer and greater than beauty itself.
Art, another nature, just as mysterious, but more understandable, for it springs from the understanding.

Goethe's intuition sometimes bordered on the visionary. He tells us of a vision he once had. Leaving his beloved Fredericke he saw himself returning to her, riding a white horse, wrapped

242

in a white coat. Many years later and quite unexpectedly, he came back to her in the way he had visualized. The best proof of the intensity of both his physical and his psychic mind is another instance in which his seismographic sensitivity registered an earthquake that took place in Sicily, thousands of miles away from his home in Weimar. It took two weeks for the news about this terrible earthquake to reach Goethe, confirming his *Gefühl*.

Goethe, the epitome of the intellectual, was an accomplished horseman, swimmer and skater; he loved to dance; he acted and was an amateur cellist; he knew Hebrew, Greek and Latin, French, Italian and English; he translated Byron, Cellini, Voltaire, Diderot, and he was at home as much in Oriental as Western literature; he edited literary and scientific periodicals at times. There was no discipline, no activity alien to him, from archaeology to zoology.

Nature was as kind to him as to Sophocles. He was a handsome youth and imposing in his old age. He was sure of his own spiritual perfection, and a moderate excess in self-observation and self-admiration was not only justified but also a part of the insatiable urge in him to find the key to the world's secret while revealing himself to the world through his works and deeds.

When we speak of Goethe as the olympian we may very well mean that the gods were good to him, withholding nothing and bestowing profusely on him much of their many wonders. This, mankind has gratefully acknowledged. Even to his very last words, 'Light – more light!' expressing the simple desire of a dying man to have the shades pulled up, the world has attached the symbolic meaning of man's eternal struggle to fulfil the potentialities of life, to reach for the sun.

### E. T. A. HOFFMANN

The genius of the opera-bouffe, Jacques Offenbach, wrote his only serious opera shortly before he died. And it is because of this work, *The Tales of Hoffmann*, based on three stories by E. T. A. Hoffmann (1776–1822), that this most versatile talent of the Romantic era is known to the world.

Literary-minded people are well aware of his genius in writing fantasies in which everyday reality is confronted with the weird and supernatural. They know of the unique influence he had on some of the great writers of his own time, mainly in France on Balzac, Hugo, Gautier, and Musset, but also in England on Lord Byron, Scott, and Dickens, and on the

243

American poet Edgar Allan Poe as well as on the Russian Gogol. The Germans think of Hoffmann as one of their great writers of the Romantic era and have given him a special niche as the author of fantastic stories and weird tales full of grotesqueries, but particularly as the author of the demonic novel, *Die Elixiere des Teufels*.

Only the serious student of the opera may remember that Hoffmann's *Undine* was called 'one of the cleverest works' by Carl Maria von Weber, who under its influence, composed *Der Freischütz*, which, in turn, was one of the few operas to shape musical history. The dance-oriented person may be surprised to learn that the story of the classical ballet *Coppélia* is based on one of Hoffmann's stories and that Tchaikowsky's *The Nutcracker* ballet was inspired by Hoffmann's story *The Nutcracker and the King of Mice*. Only a theatre historian will know that, during the expressionist era, some of Hoffmann's tales – Prinzessin Brambilla (1920) and Signor Formica (1922) – were dramatized and produced by the Moscow Kamernyi Teatr and that one of the first silent movies of historic importance, *Das Kabinett des Dr. Caligari*, was an E. T. A. Hoffmann story.

Since versatility was one of the trademarks of Romanticism, it made Hoffmann less conspicuous than he may have deserved to be. Excesses of all kinds were not surprising, and the public made little of the fact that E. T. A. Hoffmann was a composer and story writer, a painter, draughtsman, caricaturist, and scene designer, a conductor and stage director, an essayist and critic. There were, in fact, very few artistic areas in which Hoffmann did not test his skill. At times he was also active as a music teacher and, as was customary among most of his colleagues, he took up various professional careers. He was a state official, archivist, and judge of the supreme court (*Kammergerichtsrat*) in Berlin.

*Plate 77*

The variety of Hoffmann's talents is unique and stupendous. They are so diversified that, beyond their mutually fructifying effects, they have had destructive implications, particularly in regard to Hoffmann's very complex psyche. His pathological *Seelenzustand* obviously found expression and relief through the writing of his stories, whose studies from a purely psychological viewpoint would make an enjoyable subject for psychoanalysis. Hoffmann's stories are not only highly entertaining, they are revealing confessions of a morbid mind. In contrast to the universal genius of his contemporary, Goethe, Hoffmann's versatility has an acrobatic quality, often frightening in its self-destructive challenge.

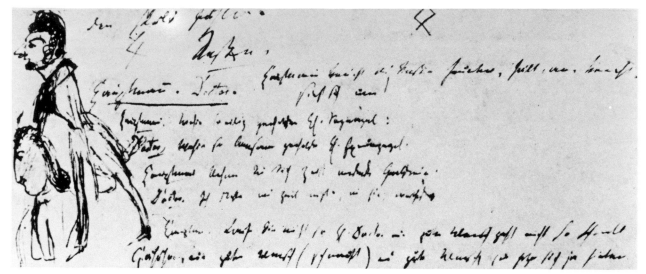

63   Georg Büchner MANUSCRIPT PAGE OF 'WOZZECK'

64   Thomas Mann LIFE

65   Thomas Mann MOTHER NATURE

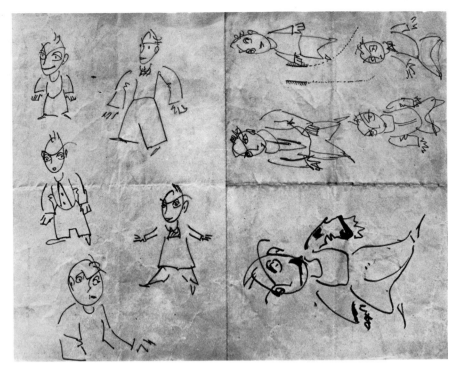

66   Antoine de Saint Exupéry SKETCHES

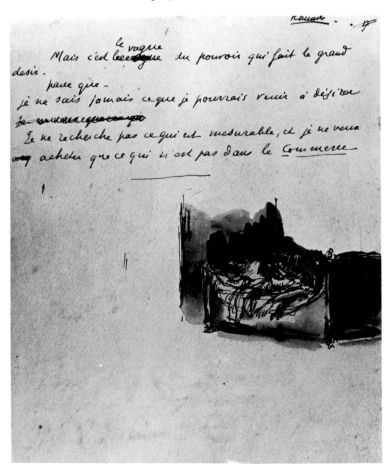

68   Paul Verlaine CHILD STANDING

67   Paul Valéry BED ON MANUSCRIPT FRAGMENT

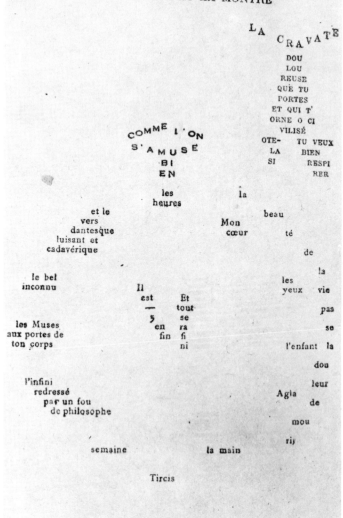

LA CRAVATE ET LA MONTRE

LA CRAVATE

DOU
LOU
REUSE
QUE TU
PORTES
ET QUI T'
ORNE O CI
VILISÉ
OTE- TU VEUX
LA BIEN
SI RESPI
RER

COMME L'ON
S'AMUSE
BI
EN

les                    la
heures

et le                         beau
vers              Mon
dantesque        cœur        té
luisant et
cadavérique                          de

                                        la
le bel                                 les
inconnu          Il      Et      yeux    vie
                 est    tout
                 —      se              pas
les Muses        5      ra
aux portes de    en     fi              se
ton corps        fin    ni
                        ni              l'enfant  la

                                                dou

l'infini                                        leur
redressé                           Agla        de
par un fou
de philosophe                                  mou

                                               rir

semaine              la main

           Tircis

71 · Federico Garcia Lorca SELF-PORTRAIT IN NEW YORK

While in his late twenties he had doubts as to the direction in which he felt pulled, and he asked himself whether he was 'born to be a painter or musician'. At the age of twenty-eight he wrote: 'A many-coloured world full of magic flickered and flared around me – it is as if something great would soon have to come of it – some work of art has to emerge from this chaos! – will it be a book, an opera, a painting – quod diis placibit'.

Despite his diversified abilities he never created what Richard Wagner, two decades after Hoffmann's death, achieved: a *Gesamtkunstwerk*. It was only after his initial attempts at writing libretti to his own operas, preceding Wagner in this endeavour, that he gave up this idea and rather concentrated on the composition. He expressed his serious doubts that any one person could produce a work in which text and music would be of equal excellence. Besides writing eight operas and two Singspiele, he also composed piano sonatas, a symphony, Lieder, choruses, ballet music and incidental pieces for plays.

Hoffmann must have realized the pitfalls that lie in mingling multiple talents indiscriminately. But although he never quite abandoned the practice of any of his gifts completely at any time in his life, we find a marked shift in emphasis in his creative output. At one point we find him conducting a festive concert at the Mniszek Palais in Warsaw in a hall embellished by his own frescoes.

When he was appointed *Musikdirektor* of the theatre in Bamberg (which to this day is called the E. T. A. Hoffmann-Theater), he could not help conducting operas and directing plays. Moreover, he designed a number of stage settings. During the years he stayed in Bamberg he was particularly creative as a composer, painter, and writer. Hoffmann was well-known for his cantankerous and morose disposition; but the Bamberg period was his happiest in that he had an emotionally gratifying relationship and composed – almost as proof of his inner peace – a great deal of sacred music. His rather conscious realization in those years that he should devote more time to creative writing is significant. Not that he would have ever stopped writing! But it was only during the last decade of his life that he gained recognition as a great story-teller, describing as he did the pathology of everyday life, finding the image of the unreality of bourgeois reality, the nightmarish symbol of man's hidden hostilities, desires, and guilt feelings – all entertainingly released through the invention of bizarre stories.

The painter in him inspired many novellas about painters, and the musician Hoffmann made the writer invent stories about musicians. His autobiographical *Lebensansichten des Kapellmeister Johannes Kreisler* shows 'the deepest conception of the German musician', as Oswald Spengler said, and, in a way, this work is the forerunner of Thomas Mann's study of the archetypal German musician in *Doktor Faustus*. Robert Schumann was so impressed by the creation of Hoffmann's musical *Doppelgänger* that he felt inspired to compose his *Kreisleriana*.

As a music critic Hoffmann showed a great understanding for Bach and Beethoven. (In his day Bach had to be rediscovered, and it was Hoffmann who brought Bach's importance to the music consciousness of the world.) In general, Hoffmann's observations on music exerted far greater influence on his contemporaries than his aesthetic critiques on the visual arts. There is no doubt that Hoffmann had sold his soul to music as a very young man, as evidenced by the fact that he changed the third of his Christian names from Wilhelm to Amadeus in deference to Mozart.

If we wish to search for the primary, spinal point of creativity in this talent-ridden artist, we can only find it in his creative writings in which painting and music are fully focalized and absorbed. True, he believed in himself as a painter and he never gave up drawing, and his passionate love belonged to music. But history, in its biased impartiality, records E. T. A. Hoffmann as a prolific and skilled teller of tales. Perhaps we should not lose sight of the demands of daily life which forced and tempted him time and again to take the one or the other of his talents out of his sleeve or pocket like a magician. In so doing he pleased the moment, but was tricked by posterity.

VICTOR HUGO AND THE DRAWINGS OF
FRENCH WRITERS

Undoubtedly, nations have their characteristics, and certain artistic inclinations have a great deal to do with surrounding temperament and climate, with a cultural past as conditioned by history. It is certainly remarkable that the French men of letters more than writers of any other nation have cultivated an enormous interest in the dance, from Gautier and Mallarmé to Valéry and Cocteau. Moreover, the French writers also surprise us with their desire to express themselves visually.

*Plate 86*

Their sheer number, let alone the quality of their drawings, is dazzling.

They took to drawing as if it had been hashish of which Théophile Gautier wrote in one of his feuilletons in *La Presse* in 1843:

My sense of hearing became particularly strong. I could hear the sound of colours. The green, red, blue, yellow reached me perfectly clear as if coming to me on waves.

*Plates 76, 67*
*Plates 73, 51*

The endless list of painting poets is almost all-inclusive, from Alexandre Dumas fils to Proust and Valéry, from Gautier and George Sand to Paul Claudel and André Malraux. They all have in common the visualization of an image as 'la forme optique de la pensée' (the optical form of the thought).[3]

In their varied degree of imperfection their drawings are self-revealing because they have a touch of the outsider, the iconoclast. They show the poet sometimes in a mood of self-irony or playfulness. Most betray how insecurity in a craft can have charm and daring. Most of these drawings need no comment.

*Plate 79*

Above all these poets, who have painted and drawn, towers one artist, who is also a titan as a writer: Victor Hugo (1802–1885). Dramatist, poet, novelist, satirist, draughtsman, politician, senator and professional exile, Hugo was Romanticism incarnate. Perhaps with a touch of flamboyancy, he made himself the spokesman of a new era in 1827. ('A poet is a world shut up within a man.') His productivity was as amazing as his versatility. He had an innate feeling for *les grandes passions*. To some of his critics he appeared too violent, virile, vain, and egotistical, but, by the same token, Hugo fought against poverty and for the poor, and remained all his life a forceful fighter for his ideas. ('Despotism violates the moral frontier, as invasion violates the geographical frontier.') No one can say that he did not live fully and consciously every minute of his day.

Almost all his drawings have a deeper meaning for Hugo himself than for the spectator to whom they may be stunning in their artistry, in their strange suggestive power. For him his drawings were commentaries upon his thoughts, illustrations of his poetic ideas which so often reveal the visualization of a design as their origin. I choose an example at random from *Les Misérables*: 'Animals are nothing but the forms of our virtues and vices, wandering before our eyes, the visible phantoms of our souls'.

Victor Hugo
'The Nonsense That I Wrote
Before I Was Born'

[3](see page 341).

In a letter to his publisher Hugo calls his drawings 'old scraps from the margin of manuscripts' and admits that they were put on paper 'clumsily by a literary man preoccupied by his work'. It is interesting that many of his sketches are made on the margin of his thoughts while writing and obviously reveal their function in the process of his creativity. As Hugo was accustomed to use any scrap of paper that was at hand to write down his thoughts, his drawings have the kind of immediacy of the unruly mind that seeks expression.

His fascination with medieval imagery, with the spirit of Gothic romanticism, is strongly reflected in his drawings of landscapes and castles. In many of his pictures the horrible and the graceful are strangely mixed, showing Hugo's delight in antithesis. ('We must rescue the hangman from his torture and the tyrant from his throne.') Dilapidated buildings often appear in his sketches. Rivers with their castles and ruins haunted him, conjuring up the cobwebs of memories that speak of a life long past. For some years it was his habit to send a watercolour or drawing to some of his more intimate friends for New Year's day. One he had sent to Saint Victor in 1868 pictured a burnt-down village, ravaged by war, stained with blood. To underline its Goyaesque quality of accusation and fury he drew an empty cradle in it with the inscription: 'Organisation Militaire'.

Hugo's infatuation with the medieval image can be related to his veneration of Albrecht Dürer, whom, among the old masters, he admired most ('O Dürer, master mine, painter old and pensive!'). But the interest in the Middle Ages was, moreover, a feature of his time. Théophile Gautier had hailed Hugo's manifesto of Romanticism as written down in the preface to Hugo's drama *Cromwell* with the words, 'It shines before our eyes like Moses when he came down from Mount Sinai with the ten commandments'. Neither did Gautier doubt Hugo's greatness as a painter of the romantic school:

Whenever he travels he makes sketches of everything that strikes his eye. The outline of a hill, a break in the horizon, an old belfry – any of these will suffice for the subject of a rough drawing, which the same evening will see worked up almost to the finish of an engraving, and the object of unbound surprise even to the most accomplished artists.

Hugo never had any systematic training in drawing, not more than anyone learns in school. He often used some doodling or an inkspot to give a stunning metamorphosis to an artistic

Victor Hugo
Caricature of a Classic

image. Amused, he once remarked: 'My inkstand is generally my palette; if I want a lighter shade, a glass of water is my only requisite, although a few drops of coffee are occasionally very useful'. When in exile he accompanied one of his drawings sent to a friend with the words: 'My drawings, or what are called so, are sometimes wild. If this one is too difficult for you to engrave, select another. In my undisciplined way, I use the feather of my pen as much as its point'.

There are very few indications that Victor Hugo loved to draw when he was of school age. The charming figure of a bird within an egg-shell is found in one of his exercise books which he had filled with unsatisfactory verses at the age of thirteen. In the boy's own handwriting the drawing is whimsically characterized as 'The nonsense that I wrote before I was born'. About his discovery of his drawing talent, which turned into a drawing fury at times, he wrote:

The first time I took a sketch from nature was after I had reached maturity. I was making an excursion near Paris, travelling with a lady in a carriage. In a village the vehicle stayed to change horses. I stepped down, and as we happened to be near the church I went inside and was so much struck by the graceful beauty of the apse that I made an attempt to copy some of the details. My hat served for an easel. I had only about ten minutes at my disposal, but when I was called back I had so far finished my sketch that it was a very fair souvenir of the place. Then for the first time I realized how beneficially copying from nature might be combined with my literary pursuits. The lady travelling with me asked me whether I intended to be an artist, and we laughed together at the suggestion . . .

### WILLIAM MAKEPEACE THACKERAY

'Time finds a withered leaf in every laurel', William Makepeace Thackeray (1811–1863) once wrote, and there are several such leaves in the laurels of the man, now mainly known for *Vanity Fair*.

Thackeray is a good example of a man of letters who could draw well and to whom drawing came as easily as writing. His satiric and parodistic talent was manifest in his drawings while he was still at school. There was a tremendous urge in the young Thackeray to sketch whenever there was an occasion, and he liked to burlesque Shakespearean characters as well as the most ordinary situations in life. Thus, Macbeth appeared to him as a butcher holding two blood-stained knives in his hands, with Lady Macbeth patting his shoulder encouragingly; or in one of his allegorical drawings, entitled

*Painting*, he would show us a boy blacking boots. At that time, he tried to emulate the great caricaturist George Cruikshank.

In 1833 he seriously thought of becoming a painter. He later reminisced about it in a letter to his mother: 'At twenty you know we all thought I was a genius at drawing'. But in those days, and particularly in Victorian England, an artist was considered a socially inferior person, and Thackeray assured his mother that he would embark on this profession as 'an independent man who is not obliged to look to his brush for his livelihood'. He went to Paris to escape the Victorian stigma. There he studied drawing and could live with the Parisian artists with the happy feeling of no longer having to live up to the position of an English gentleman of fortune. On the other hand, he avoided the Left Bank Bohemians. He could never quite rid himself of the attitude of the dandy with a touch of the Byronic hero. But he fell in with a group of fellow expatriates, who enjoyed their dolce vita, gambling and drinking to excess. In those days it became clear to Thackeray that he would never become a professional painter.

It cannot be said how much the environmental stigma of the artist was responsible for his reluctance to work hard on his paintings, or whether it was his lack of patience ('He had not the patience to be an artist with pencil and brush', George Cruikshank said). Thackeray's failure to live up to his talent as a draughtsman seemed to have been a case of 'character defeating genius'. He who gave us a gallery of portraits depicting all kinds of snobs, was one himself, as he candidly admitted in the title of his book, *The Snobs of England by One of Themselves*. He must have looked down on serious artistic work, on work per se, since he also wrote only under financial pressure and loathed the idea of having to make a living.

While appraising the Victorian upper- and middle-class society in England he tried to uphold a gentlemanlike attitude which he felt the middle-class should take over from the aristocracy. This explains Walter de la Mare's remark that Thackeray 'wrote for the most part books about gentlemen for gentlemen'. Thackeray could have risen to Swiftian satire because he had the gift of hitting the mark with poisonous arrows. But he preferred to eschew all radicalism and to write with good-humoured moderation, always being ready with a witty joke, never really intent on improving mankind. ('Society having ordained certain customs, men are bound to obey the laws of society, and conform to its harmless orders.')

*The Duality of Vision*

In his writings he satirized romantic sentiment vividly because he mistrusted and tried to escape the same quality in himself. He became *the* writer for the bourgeoisie because he called attention to shared faults. While criticizing the Victorian double standard, he could circumscribe his own attitude by saying: '. . . laugh honestly, hit no foul blow, and tell the truth when at his very broadest grin – never forgetting that if Fun is good, Truth is still better, and Love best of all'. Only *Vanity Fair* was intended to have a strongly unsettling effect ('What I want to make is a set of people living without God . . . greedy, pompous men, perfectly self-satisfied for the most part, and at ease about their superior virtue.').

When he fell on hard times, he did hack journalist work and added to his meagre income by illustrating the texts of other writers. He wrote for many publications, mainly for Fraser's Magazine and Punch. ('If it had not been for Punch I wonder where I should be.') Sporadically and always when driven by the need for money, he worked frantically in both media. 'I am in a ceaseless whirl and whizz from morning to night', he wrote his mother, 'now with the book, now with the drawings, now with articles . . .'

He wrote with apparent ease ('The wicked are wicked, no doubt, and they go astray and they fall, and they come by their deserts; but who can tell the mischief which the very virtuous do?'). His verbal wit weighed as lightly on his tongue as the humour in his drawings. He made sketches for almost all his books. His serious illustrations, mostly ordinary genre images characteristic of the academic approach of the nineteenth century, never reach beyond a mediocre level. It is only in his satiric drawings that his talent recalls the remarkable beginnings of his youth, full of promises which were later reduced to the easily achieved effect of the first stroke. As *Plate 74* example may serve here a page from his story of *The Rose and Ring*, which made their possessors attractive and lovable, a magic story that became a part of his *Christmas Books*, a Victorian best-seller.

THE EXCURSIONS OF HERMANN HESSE

*Plates XVII, XVIII*  Hermann Hesse (1877–1962), the German poet-novelist-painter, who received the Nobel Prize in 1946, lived in Switzerland most of his life. The choice of this island of isolation was symbolic of his innate desire to withdraw from life in a truly mystic fashion.

The two facts that impressed the young Hesse in his parental home and which were to become strong influences in his later life were the piety of his parents, who devoted day and night to missionary work, and his grandfather's closets full of books on Asia, of figures and images of Buddha. His parents wanted him to study theology, and he was placed in a monastery from which he ran away. He finally became an apprentice in a bookstore, a job which suited him.

When he was twenty-two, a collection of sketches appeared in print, *An Hour Behind Midnight*. One of his first reviewers wrote: 'It is worth while talking about a book which, inspired by awe and piousness, speaks to us in a dark, praying voice: for art is not far from this book. The beginning of art is piousness; piousness toward oneself, toward all experience, all things, toward a great image and one's own untested strength . . . Out of such feelings Hermann Hesse's book emerged'. The reviewer's name was Rainer Maria Rilke.

Hesse more than any other writer succumbed to the compulsion to document every step of his life; in fact, his literary work, his drawings and paintings exist only as a reflection of what he did, saw, and experienced.

A new poetic creation begins to arise for me at the moment when a figure becomes visible which, for a while, can be symbol and bearer of my experiences, my thoughts, my problems. The emergence of such a mythical person is the creative moment from which everything issues. Almost all my writings in prose are 'soul' biographies, none of them really deals with stories, plots, and suspense. Basically, they are all monologues in which a single person – this mythical figure – is explored in relationship to the world and his own self.

His works have often been put on the shelf under Romanticism. True, he always prided himself on being a traditionalist. 'I never strived for the new form, for being an avant-gardist and pace-maker. It may have hurt some of my works, but may have been useful to others, and I gladly stand by it.' His brand of romanticism can best be described as an inward search and not as a backward flight, as a step-by-step penetration of his self and not as the exaltation of his ego. In keeping with this viewpoint, he early recognized the significance of the unmasking of our inner world (in Jungian rather than Freudian terms), and felt very close to Kafka's mystic symbolism and exploration of man's isolation.

His romanticism opposed a civilization caught in a web of slogans, with its beauty price-tagged, its dreams on clearance sale. His kind of romanticism was also reflected in his protagonists, who range through the various layers of their subconscious longing to free themselves from their inner

256

72  Johann Wolfgang Goethe DRAWING MADE AT BILIN

73  George Sand LANDSCAPE

And now I daresay you are anxious to
see a likeness of Prince GIGLIO, and
guess at once that this is he. If he is not
very handsome in your estimation, be
sure he is very good looking in his own
I have seen uglier men (and women too)
perfectly well satisfied with their looks.
It has been already stated in page 1, that
as long as he has a smart coat to wear, a
good horse to ride (Cigars were not invented yet or depend on it, Master Giglio
would have liked them too )-as long as
he had
money in his pocket - or rather to
take out of his pocket for he was very good
natured, my young prince did not care
for the loss of his crown and sceptre, being a thoughtless youth not much inclined to politics or any kind of learning.
So his tutor the Reverend Mr Muff
Of Oxford had a sinecure. Giglio would

74    William Makepeace Thackeray THE ROSE AND THE RING

75    E. T. A. Hoffmann SCORE OF E FLAT-MAJOR SYMPHONY

76　Alexandre Dumas fils STATUE OF A BULL

77　E. T. A. Hoffmann TWO HORSEBACK RIDERS

78 Alfred de Vigny DANTE AND FRIEND

*Le révérend Laquemin Hérode*

79 Victor Hugo THE REVEREND LAQUEMIN HERODE

chaos and to find a oneness with fate, a oneness of all being. In his entire work – in many variations and forms – he painted 'the plight of lonely men with the problem of existence and with the yearning after a new orientation for an age that has lost its bearings'. Hesse always counteracted the exuberant and puerile facets of romanticism with knowing rationality and an overactive consciousness.

He was fully aware of the interrelation and interdependence of expressive means, even though he knew that writing was the focal point of his creative will. He said: 'From my thirteenth year on one thing was clear to me. I wanted to become a poet or nothing at all'.

In his novel *Gertrude* he let his hero speak of his early realization that 'of all invisible powers music was destined to have the strongest hold on me and to rule me'. That there was music in the world, that we could be moved by music always meant to him 'deep comfort and the justification of existence'. Hesse was so obsessed with music as a means of escape into ecstatic feelings that he recognized the danger: one cannot tear it out of one's heart without bleeding to death. For the romantic, as Hesse saw it, music was light-years away from reality, the final illusion, the beloved who made him drunk without offering relief and redemption, it remained the unattainable which possessed him. In the last analysis, *Gertrude* exemplifies, through the tragic struggle of the musician Muoth, the struggle of the lonesome artist with himself. The feeling of aloneness and alienation which Hesse acutely felt around 1910 found its expression in this novel as much as in the novel following shortly thereafter, *Rosshalde*.

From his early youth Hesse loved music. He played the violin, his wife the piano. He even wrote an opera libretto for one of his composer friends. 'The desire for pure melody is perhaps finally more important to me as a poet than the penetration of a significant subject matter', he once wrote in one of his letters. Music and musicians appear and reappear in many of his works.

In *Steppenwolf* the spirit of Mozart dominates Harry Haller's thoughts. ('. . . I was reminded of the eternal, of Mozart, of the stars.') When Harry faces Goethe's spirit, the conversation is about Mozart. Goethe says, '*The Magic Flute* presents life to us as a wondrous song. It honours our feelings, transient as they are, as something eternal and divine . . . It preaches optimism and faith'. Whereupon Hesse-Haller cries out in a rage: '. . . God knows why you hit of all things on the *Magic Flute* that is dearer to me than anything else in the world

. . .' In another discussion Haller remarks that 'there is the immortal music that lives on even when it is not actually being played'. In *Steppenwolf* Hesse pictures the German intellectual constantly rebelling against the word, the logos, while courting music. 'And so the German spirit, carousing in music, in wonderful creations of sound, and wonderful beauties of feeling and mood that were never pressed home to reality, has left the greater part of its practical gifts to decay. None of us intellectuals is at home in reality.' And *Steppenwolf* ends with the words that Mozart is waiting for him.

Hesse was thirty-seven when he recreated himself in the figure of the painter Veraguth in *Rosshalde*. It was as if he knew that he would have to paint one day. But the character of his painter exists in the same spiritual isolation as his musician Muoth. He described the painter who finds refuge from life in his work only: 'He suffered, he bore heavy pain, and he was starved like a wolf from loneliness. This sufferer had tried to exist with pride and aloneness and could not take it, he lay in ambush for a human being, for a warm glance and a touch of understanding, and he was ready to throw himself away for it'. Hesse shaped the character of a lonely man whose loneliness was brought about by his being an artist. He painted the tragedy of the poet in the artist – no matter whether he is a musician or painter – of the man who compulsively lives a life of withinness and cries out for the hand to save him from drowning in his spiritual isolation.

Hesse was attuned to the Zen spirit of eternal loneliness as no other European writer. He apparently knew he could only grow in his magnificent aloneness, even though something else in him wanted desperately to escape it.

In his prose works Hesse always tried to find the simplest expression and give it the most complex content. It seems that painting watercolours helped him restore a balance between the simplicity of emotion and the complexity of intellect. His aquarelles, of which he must have made a few hundred, are like diary entries, his visual impressions from day to day. In these pictorial notes – colour images most of the time, written like annotations on the margin of his daily existence – he put down the simple ways of nature as he saw them. These pictures have the same disarming simplicity as most of his poems. It seems that many of his surface feelings have easily found their way into verse, and his aquarelles reflect an immediate sense reaction to the nature surrounding him. He wrote:

> . . . .
> *And in the beginning fall*
> *Of my life I sit alone,*
> *Look into the beautiful, cruel eye of the world,*
> *Choose colours of love and paint her,*
> *Who so often deceived me,*
> *Whom I still love, always and always . . .*

His romantic feelings are emptied into such lines which would be inconsequential were it not for the fact that they show us how much Hesse equated painting with being, eternal longing with love, his inner being with the outside world. Somewhere else he said: '. . . When I paint, the trees have faces and the houses laugh or dance or cry, but most of the time one cannot recognize whether the tree is a pear-tree or a chestnut tree.' In painting he was an unconscious realist, and it was through painting that he strengthened his feeling for form.

That he saw with the eyes of a painter may be one of the reasons why so much in his work is visual and richly descriptive. His *Siddartha* – the result of a trip to India – is full of word-dissolved colour and its language uses imagery which is visual in its effect. But while we see the painter mixing the colours on his palette, we hear the music that fills his ears. His language moves in lovely cadences, sometimes in rhythmic cascades:

But he, Siddartha, created no joy for himself, nor did he find pleasures. Walking along the rosy paths in the garden full of figs, sitting in the blueish shadow of the grove of contemplation, washing his limbs in the daily bath of atonement, sacrificing in the dark shadows of the mango woods, his gestures were proper and perfect, he was loved by everyone, and, in spite of all joy around him, there was no joy in his heart. Dreams and restless thoughts came to him out of the river's water, out of the glistening stars of the night, out of the melting rays of the sun; dreams and restlessness of the soul came to him out of sacrificial smoke, emanated from the verses of the Rig-Veda, trickled from the teachings of the old Brahmans.

Hesse was constantly preoccupied with the struggle between the painter and musician in himself, and this struggle found its way into several books. It is strongest in his novelette *Klingsor's Last Summer*. We can sense how the music should liberate Klingsor from the naturalism of colour, while the colours should help chain the burst of music. Klingsor is again one of those mythical figures which come right out of Hesse's gallery of self-portraits.

Painting had its redeeming effects for Hesse to which he
alluded when he wrote: '. . . One day I discovered a totally
new joy. I was already forty years old when I started to paint.
Not that I thought of myself as a painter or that I wanted to
become one. But to paint is wonderful, it makes me gayer
and more tolerant. One has red and blue fingers afterwards
and not black fingers as from writing . . .'

When he finally took up painting many of his friends were
dismayed and annoyed with him. They probably thought
that his new occupation would steal time from his writing.
They did not realize that this was 'something very necessary,
fortunate, and beautiful' for him. The people, he complained,
'would like us to stay the way we were, they would like us
not to change our face. But my face refuses to comply, it
needs to change often'. And, on another occasion, he explained
himself in more general terms: 'The life of a human being and
the work of a poet grows from a hundred and thousand roots
and, as long as it is not finished, absorbs a hundred and thous-
and new relationships and connections . . .'. Such life and work
are so complex, he felt, that, if a life were really notated from
beginning to end with all its roots and ramifications, its
story would be an epos, as rich as the whole history of mankind.

To Hesse, there was no formula for life. As he saw it, life
not only oscillates between two poles, such as body and
spirit, saint and sinner, but between a thousand poles. With
his protagonist in *Steppenwolf* Hesse discovered that man is
nothing else than the narrow and perilous bridge between
nature and spirit; he seems to tell us that we must overcome
'the sickness of the times themselves', as reflected in our self, by
walking from step to step through fulfilment and frustration
to constantly new dimensions of our consciousness.

Hesse was a constant seeker of inner harmony and tried to
live with music, colour, and the word by letting the music
influence the verbal flow and give it that sense of form which
the strokes of his brush taught him. He was a nonconformist,
a prober of human depth, a soothsayer of the inner truth, a
philosopher who had the stubbornness of his conviction and
the strength to escape into his 'self' in order to free himself
from its confinement.

THE PAINTING GENIUS OF STRINDBERG
When Ibsen said about Johann August Strindberg (1849–1912),
'He will be greater than I', he thought of course of the writer
and not the painter Strindberg. Eric Bentley, in an essay on

264

Strindberg, questioned 'how a major modern writer can be so little known' as Strindberg is, and he answered his own question, 'I do not know, but that is certainly the case'. I can only continue to wonder why it is so little known what a powerful painter and draughtsman Strindberg was.

This tormented, anguished, searching man, this explosive, undisciplined, brilliant dramatist, poet, novelist, and essayist whose work ranges from naturalism to symbolism to mysticism can be better understood when we see his tortures transmitted to cancas. He called himself 'a wild man', 'a scoffer', and he became famous for wanting to force all Noras back into their *Doll's Houses*. But he was one of the first to master the dramatization of psychological conflicts, and his characters, mostly exceptional creatures in difficult situations, were as much in conflict with themselves as their creator was with himself.

All his life he wrote with flaming words against the injustice suffered by man from the hands of the female and society. He became a pessimist out of too much love for mankind. His passion, his overwrought mind, made the silence of his solitude articulate. Paraphrasing Lytton Strachey's comment about an English poet, we could say that Strindberg lost his faith in woman, the life-giver, as a young man and then spent the rest of his life feverishly looking for it.

He once gave advice to a young artist saying that painting 'sharpens the eye for description'. But Strindberg's interest in painting, drawing, and sculpting went beyond the obvious. He often felt the need to escape the ordinary, the daily routine, his writing chores, and, driven to find the secret door to what was hidden from him, he sought it in painting. Only occasionally did he think of his gift for the visual arts as a means of livelihood.

As a young man he studied and copied nature. But then in his autobiographical book, *The Son of a Servant Woman*, he says:

One should paint what one feels inside and not go out and draw logs and stones, which certainly in themselves are insignificant, and only in passing through the sensibilities of the subject can one get any form. Johan always painted the sea, with the coast in the foreground; crossed pines, some bare rocks farther out, and a sea-marker and a buoy. The sky was mostly overcast with a weak or strong opening of light on the horizon; the setting of the sun, or moonlight; or clear daylight.

Strindberg began to paint when he began to write. But he only painted intermittently as if going through phases

265

synchronized with his growth as a writer. His painting periods were between 1872 and 1875 and from 1892 to 1895 when he stayed most of the time in Austria and France. Finally, as a symbolist, he created his best paintings in Stockholm between 1900 and 1907. But he never gave up drawing; he even worked as an illustrator since he thought he was a fine sketcher.

*Plates XVI, 80*

His paintings were shown in 1894 and 1895 at the Konstnärsförbundet's (Artists' Guild) exhibit and then, as late as 1911, in Hallin's shop in Stockholm. After the Gummeson exhibition in 1924 Strindberg was more generally recognized as a painter, and with the showing of his works in Paris and other European cities on the occasion of the fiftieth anniversary of his death the art world took greater interest in his painting genius. Armed with critical hindsight, some of the critics then discovered him as a forerunner of abstract painting.

In the years when Strindberg did not paint, he worked as an art critic for two major Stockholm newspapers. His contributions in this area were important at the time and for the Scandinavian countries, even though this passionately articulate man seemed confused about the new art movements and some of its practitioners because the painter in Strindberg collided with the critic, and because his own visualizations were daring but with a difference.

He reported on French Impressionism when it was still new:

Impressionism is what a photograph becomes when the poser does not sit still, or, when one sees trees photographed during windy weather. – This is certainly jest! – Yes, it certainly is! – But there is a certain nature in it! . . . – Which is to say, that they mean one should paint the impressions and not nature itself.

Strindberg realized that the modern painter should see 'nature in its entirety such as it seems, not as it is in reality'. His comprehension of painting was closely oriented to the style of Turner, to his dramatic boldness in composition, to his stress on light and space, to the abstraction rather than the surface impression of nature.

In the 1880s he went through a period in which he rejected visual art per se, as we can deduce from a letter he wrote in 1883: 'Will you please loan me Rousseau, that part that deals with the harm the arts and sciences have on mankind'. And a year later: 'My distaste for art, as being fake, has a kind of fantastic religious character'.

His interest in painting became very strong again in the 1890s, probably due to his personal contact with some of the great French painters of that time, especially with Gauguin, and the encouragement he received from them. Strindberg was certainly an iconoclast in many ways, but his refusal of Gauguin's request to preface the sale catalogue for his exhibit before his final departure to Tahiti in 1895, has puzzled the art world ever since. Did Strindberg feel too uncertain of himself as a painter and critic so that he withdrew into a kind of literary subterfuge? Two 'congeneric minds', to borrow Baudelaire's phrase, collided, two rebellious titans. Strindberg explained his hesitation and retreat with almost pathetic frankness:

I cannot grasp your art, and I cannot love it. I know that this avowal will neither astonish nor wound you, because you seem to be only strengthened by the hatred of others . . . I saw on the walls of your studio an uproar of sunlit pictures, which pursued me in my sleep . . . A sea which pours forth from a volcano, a sky in which no God can live – Sir, said I in my dream, you have created a new heaven and earth, but I am not delighted in the midst of your creation. It is too sunny for me. I prefer more chiaroscuro. And in your paradise there lives an Eve who is not my ideal . . . Gauguin, the savage who hates a wearisome civilization . . . Bon Voyage, Master: but come back here to me. I shall by that time perhaps have learned to understand your art better, which will permit me to make a true preface for a new catalogue of a new sale, since I am beginning to feel an immense need for becoming savage and creating a new world.

Gauguin's reply which he printed together with Strindberg's letter shows his contempt for the society he tried to escape and for the weakness of his comrade:

I had the idea of asking you for a preface, when I saw you the other day in my studio playing the guitar and singing, your blue northern eyes gazing attentively at the pictures on the walls. I had then the presentiment of a revolt, of a shock between your civilization and my barbarism. You suffer from your civilization. My barbarism is to me a renewal of youth.

A year before this incident Strindberg exclaimed in a letter: 'I am the first to paint genuine symbolism!' It was the period in which his entire thinking became keyed to symbolism. Also that year he wrote one of his most significant essays on himself as a painter.

The main theme of his nearly one hundred canvases has always been nature in her restless moments; the threatening clouds, the agitated sea whipped against rocks, a buoy amidst the stormy sea, a river in flood. There is the frenzied exis-

August Strindberg
Self-caricature

tence of life which corresponds with the inner turmoil and impulses of the writer. Even a solitary thistle, a flower on the deserted beach completes the image of this man. His most often used colours were a dark grey, blue, black and white, insinuating the drama of nature through the colour schemes.

In his essay *Of the New Arts! or Chance in Artistic Creation* he speaks of his method:

. . . the hand manipulates the palette knife/which Strindberg used instead of a paint brush/at random, yet retaining the pattern of nature without wanting to copy it, the whole revealing itself as the charming confusion of the unconscious and conscious. It's natural art where the artist works like capricious nature and without a determined goal.

He goes one step forward challenging chance. He had the idea of moulding in clay a young man worshipping. But the figure displeased him and, 'In a fit of despair I let my hand fall on the head of the unfortunate boy. There you have it! A metamorphosis of which Ovid would not have dreamed'. Under the blow, head, face, neck, shoulders and arms changed and the whole was 'transformed into a nine-year-old boy crying and hiding his tears with his hands. With a bit of retouching the little statue was perfect'. This was the hour when automatic art, action sculpting and painting was born.

He devised a new art form which he called *L'art fortuit*. Paintings 'result as a combination of half chance and half the painter's intentions'. He claimed that he only painted in 'his hours of leisure'. It must be questioned whether the creative person ever has a moment of leisure, whether such an hour borrowed from his life is not an intrinsic part of his creative process. In Strindberg's case – as in many other cases – hours destined for silence and meditation are sidetracked into the creation of a soundless language of colours and shapes.

Strindberg also admits that he tries to finish a painting in two or three hours, as long as his disposition lasts, and that when he starts painting he is prompted by vague intentions only. He thinks of art as only coming into being in order 'to go like all the rest'. And what is his last word of advice? 'Imitate nature as close as you can; and even better, imitate the manner in which nature creates!'

## THE BURNING COLOURS OF D. H. LAWRENCE
D. H. Lawrence (1885–1930) was a passionate writer, who cared about the truth of human values and genuine feelings. He wanted to create new myths of sexuality in which eroticism

XVII   Hermann Hesse KLEINER GESANG

XVIII   Hermann Hesse TICINO LANDSCAPE

XIX   Henry Miller UNTITLED

XX   Henry Miller VAL'S BIRTHDAY GIFT

XXI   Ludwig Bemelmans HARBOUR

XXII   Robert Rauschenberg STUDY

XXIII   Robert Rauschenberg WINTER POOL

would reign supreme, divorced from the cliché images of love. Despite his visions of virile paroxysms he strongly believed in the virginal spirit. In his search for truth he decapitated the sophisticated lies of modern man and laid bare the primitive powers which are still very much alive in us.

*Plates XV, XVI* Only in this light can we understand and enjoy Lawrence's paintings. He was as passionate about them as about anything else. Knowing them helps one to realize the inner torments and outer explosions of this writer. One can justifiably agree with Herbert Read that 'the primary interest of the paintings of D. H. Lawrence is that they were painted by a genius whose natural medium of expression was the written word'. But the theme of this book is to confront the many secondary artistic outlets with the one craft the artist masters, from the playful doodle to the almost equal power of expression.

In Lawrence's paintings the lack of craftsmanship is obvious. But we also realize that we face in him a great human being and important writer, who finds personal delight and an essential outlet in painting. He tells us that 'suddenly at the age of forty I begin to paint myself and am fascinated'. He admits that he could never draw properly at school because he was supposed to draw what he stared at. But 'the only thing one can look into, stare into, and see only vision, is the vision itself: the visionary image'.

One day in Florence when Maria Huxley brought him a few canvases he discovered that he could not only copy old masters but that, facing a blank canvas, he could fill it with shapes and colours. When he had 'the real courage to try . . . it became an orgy, making pictures'.

He could not stare at models and paint, he could not work from nature which became 'more or less a plaster cast to me'. And when he tried, the results were disastrous. Because of such failures he had often declared he could not paint. 'Perhaps', he thought, 'I can't. But I verily believe I can make pictures which is to me all that matters in this respect. The art of painting consists of making pictures, and so many artists accomplish canvases without coming within miles of painting a picture'.

His inability to paint from nature would not in itself be a sign of poor artistry. Daumier could not draw from nature, and Corot confessed 'one never feels sure what one does outdoors', and he usually finished his pictures in the studio. Malraux commented on it: '. . . while some of Corot's pictures, even the fluid, give an impression of being extraordinarily "true to nature", though no doubt the picture resembles the landscape it depicts, the landscape does not resemble the picture'.

Even Heinrich Heine comes to Lawrence's defence:

In artistic matters I am a supernaturalist. I believe that the artist cannot find all his forms in nature, but that the most remarkable are revealed to him in his soul, like the innate symbology of innate ideas, and at the same instant.

Lawrence echoes Heine's idea:

The pictures must all come out of the artist's inside, awareness of forms and figures. We can call it memory, but it is more than memory. It is the image as it lives in the consciousness, alive like a bird, but unknown . . . To me, a picture has delight in it, or it isn't a picture.

When Lawrence paints he seems to conjure up the dark gods. 'We know so much, we feel so little!' he cries out and rejects this excessively conscious age of ours. He does not mind theorizing per se, but when one stands in front of the easel, he recommends one to 'shut your theoretic eye and go for it with instinct and intuition'.

He tries to recreate unashamedly the inner vision of what his naked eye sees because he believes in 'the poetry of that which is at hand: the immediate present. In the immediate present there is no perfection, no consummation, nothing finished. The strands are all flying, quivering, intermingling into the web, the waters shaking the moon'.

Lawrence is given to excesses as a man and artist. He quite consciously delights in painting flesh in fleshier tones than flesh can be, and blood, in the most vivid red he can muster even if it is out of key with the rest of the picture. 'I delighted so in painting that bloodstream', he confesses. 'I could not resist the urge to make it real red–red, only I couldn't get it bloody enough, the warm, slightly steaming, liquid red blood. I wanted to experience the lust of killing in that picture. Killing is natural to man, you know. It is just as natural as lying with a woman. I often feel I could kill and enjoy it.'

In such excesses he reveals how literary his approach to painting was, just as his writings betray his visual mind. In his prose and poetry he achieves a sensual quality of a heightened poetic sensibility which is so many shades cruder in his paintings because of lack of craftsmanship. But the feelings and intentions are the same in his arrested sense of the pictorial when painting with words, as they are in the liberated sense of the literary when writing with colours and shapes. His explanation of the writer-painter in himself reads:

All my life I have from time to time gone back to paint, because it gave me a form of delight that words can never give. Perhaps the joy in words goes deeper and is for that reason more unconscious. The conscious delight is certainly stronger in paint . . .

HENRY MILLER, ICONOCLAST

To paint is to love again. It's only when we look with eyes of love that we see as the painter sees. His is a love, moreover, which is free of possessiveness. What the painter sees he is duty bound to share. Usually he makes us see and feel what ordinarily we ignore or are immune to. His manner of approaching the world tells us, in effect, that nothing is vile or hideous, nothing is stale, flat and unpalatable unless it be our own power of vision. To see is not only to look. One must look-see. See into and around.

This is probably the key paragraph in Henry Miller's book, *To Paint Is to Love Again*, and the key to understanding Henry Miller, the painter. He discovered the use of pencil, brush, and colours in 1928, when he was thirty-seven. At that time he still struggled to find himself and, what is often more difficult, to remain true to himself. He succeeded in keeping himself isolated from the traumatic pressures of a society which hourly surrenders to its own air-conditioned nightmares, and in creating a life of his own making, which is convincingly reflected in his writings.

Beginning with *Tropic of Cancer* in 1935, he wrote a series of novels, stories and essays which show a fantastic wit and a mystical emphasis on sex. His preoccupation with the prime forces of man in their brutal nakedness never becomes vulgar for vulgarity's sake. Miller cannot help recognizing Eros being as much the god of our daily life as Mammon, and the vivid vitality of some of his salacious descriptions is a part of his blind belief in joy, exuberance, love – notions which, in his private Thesaurus, are synonyms for life. A case could be made for his writings having a surrealistic quality, with the erotic overtones in the imagery of a dreamlike reality and the uncontrolled release of psychic automatism. But his literary output, his verbal expression, has little, or almost nothing, in common with his approach to painting. Neither the potent sensuousness nor the imaginative scope of his prose works would let us surmise the quality of his watercolours.

There seems, however, one fragile bridge leading from Miller's writings to his watercolours: the pillars of this bridge rest in Arthur Rimbaud's symbolism and use of surrealistic images. Through Rimbaud – to whom Miller is very much attuned and about whom he wrote a book – we learn to see colours with different eyes. Rimbaud not only invented the colours of the vowels ('A black, E white, I red, O blue, U green'), he flattered himself that he 'was inventing a poetic language accessible . . . to all the senses'. In both Rimbaud's and Miller's writings, though on different planes, we get a sense of prophetic revelation through the vision of colour. Miller has always tried to attack all the senses and has come to be obsessed with colours, their intimate and endless interrelation. Speaking of his painter friend Emil Schnellock, he wrote:

In moments of enthusiasm over the juicy colours he was squeezing on to his palette he would declare that he loved them, the colors, so much he could eat them right out of the tube. It was he who introduced me to cadmium red *light*. I never liked the cadmium reds, still don't, but cadmium red *light* sends me. I'm crazy about yellow ochre too. And gamboge and Indian yellow – dangerous colors to play with, I am told. Crimson alizarin is another 'dangerous' favourite. As for chromium oxide and veridian, they leave me cold. Give me rose madder, scarlet lake or Rose Tyrien, and I'm in heaven . . . I make mention of these various colors only by way of saying that it was thus we often passed a wonderful evening – merely reeling off the names of the colors and expatiating on their qualities. It was a drunken, sentimental kind of talk, thoroughly euphoric.

He also tells us that on days when he 'can't draw at all, even a rectangle', he begins to mix colours and plays with their fascinating combinations through the colour wheel.

Miller's notion that 'to paint is to love again' is disarming as much as it is revealing. Miller 'wasn't hepped on becoming a painter. Not at all'. He came to it, carried on the wings of a naive enthusiasm, and he kept the saving grace of the child who is overwhelmed by the forms and colours he sees and gives them the *Gestalt* of his own inner world. What blessing is such uninhibited recreation, still unspoiled by the knowledge of the great masters, by the pressures of one's own ambition!

Henry Miller preserved this feeling of utter naiveté, although he knew of the masters and their achievements. There were some who exerted quite a considerable influence on his eye and mind: Paul Klee, George Grosz, and, above all, the Japanese painters. But Miller frankly concedes, 'the one thing I never learned from them, and it is truly disgraceful to admit, is discipline'. He has been learning by trial and error, by groping, stumbling, questioning. By his own admission he paints with the joy of a child-like man for whom 'the paintings of children belong side by side with the works of the masters'.

He gives his watercolours the same feeling of abandon in his spontaneous approach to them as a child will. The man in the child-in-man knows that it is not enough to be in love with what one does, 'one must also know how to make love. In love self is obliterated. Only the beloved counts. Whether the beloved be a bowl of fruit, a pastoral scene, or the interior of a bawdy house makes no difference. One must be in it and of it wholly'.

*Plates XX, XXI* He is totally engrossed in his watercolours, which convey the feeling of perfection left imperfect. Miller's own feeling about watercolours is that they neither can nor should capture substance, that they are at their best when they have a certain flavour and perfume ('*Ambiance*, that is what the watercolour renders par excellence'). In his book on painting he elucidates this point by saying that only the essence of a subject should be given, 'the skyness of a sky, the treeness of a tree, the housiness of a house . . . it evokes, elicits, excites. Because of all that has been so artfully omitted, drowned or forgotten one is left free to roam, free to invent, free to imagine'.

His paintings can far more easily do justice to this concept than his prose which, even in its most sophisticated elusiveness, verbalizes too much. But basically Miller is a writer. He is wedded to writing. For him, to paint is to steal away to his mistress. With her he feels free, without responsibility, unafraid of making a mistake. At the crack of dawn he would get up to look at the watercolours he did the day before. It is, in his own words, 'like stealing a look at the beloved while she sleeps'. When he is tired or has reached an impasse in writing, he would leave his desk and sneak into his studio to paint. He feels that doing this, he empties his mind for writing. There is almost a therapeutic purpose in changing from one medium to another.

As a matter of fact, he thinks that if he had not discovered this outlet in 1928 he would have gone insane. Not that his mind would ever have stopped being active while doing his watercolours. But the switch in focus to painting caused him to see everything in a new light, different from the way the mind of the writer in him works ('the impression I had was of painting with some other part of my being'). Also, the effort invested in the work was of another nature. Writing demands a total surrender of the mind to a piece of blank paper that has to be filled with words. But painting, having become the love affair of his life, did not raise the same demands. It was play. ('While I played, for I never looked on it as work, I whistled, hummed, danced on one foot, then the other, and talked to myself.')

Lacking technique, having no sense of perspective, being unable to draw an animal correctly, actually doing everything the wrong way never mattered to him. Occasionally, he turned out watercolours *en masse*. He offered them to anyone who liked them for a song, for a meal or an umbrella, for painting material to be able to go on painting. Even if there is a touch of Dufy or a trace of Klee in his paintings, they always carry Henry Miller's trademark: a poetic sensuousness that lies in his colours, a joy of being that is an essential part of his subject matter. His landscapes are from no place in particular, his faces are of the clowns in the face of all of us. There is sun, the magic of an imaginary world, the atmosphere of the daily carnival of life. But whatever the painting may try to be – and it will be many things to many people – its childlike enthusiasm will speak for its creator. ('A painting must perspire with ecstasy.') And sometimes, intoxicated with whatever modest success his watercolours may seem to him, he is able to abandon his writing and to go on painting for days – 'but sooner or later the writing drags me back to my desk'.

His books are no longer *verbotene Literatur*, sold under the counter. He no longer lives in self-styled exile. He now hides in his house on a quiet street in a suburb of Los Angeles. He is surrounded by his watercolours and books. The latter would not have been written without the help of the former. There – in the world of his 'housiness' – he has remained an exile in his native land:

To paint is to love again, and to love is to live to the fullest. But what kind of love, what sort of life can one hope to find in a vacuum cluttered with every conceivable gadget, every conceivable money maker, every last comfort, every useless luxury? To live and love, and to give expression to it in paint, one must also be a true believer. There must be something to worship. Where in this broad land is the Holy of Holies hidden?

A STUDY IN CONTRASTS: MEHRING AND TRAKL

I have known Walter Mehring's poems since my earliest youth. He had written a revolutionary play, *The Merchant of Berlin*, which was produced by Erwin Piscator in his politically oriented theatre in 1929. Mehring also wrote novels and novellas. As a young Bohemian he was a part of the Dada existence of the Berlin artists in the twenties. He was a daily guest in the studios of the then yet unknown and now famous painters, he sat with them in the cafés in Berlin, Vienna, Munich and Paris.

*Plate 83*

Mehring is an interesting draughtsman and art critic. 'In thirty or forty years today's opponents of the new art will decorate their shop windows with Picassos', was one of his prophetic passages in an essay written in 1916 when he was only twenty years old. Rainer Maria Rilke wrote him in the autumn of 1917: 'Wanda Landowska recommended you to me as a special connoisseur of the new art movement. If it is not annoying to you I would be pleased to see such an exhibition with you some time in order to become initiated in the secrets of this artistic approach . . .'

Walter Mehring was one of the early contributors to *Sturm*, the first German avant-garde art magazine, founded by Herwarth Walden in 1910. Walden began his career as a pianist, then became a pamphleteer and art dealer before starting the magazine that discovered and furthered such artists as Paul Klee and Marc Chagall. Walden fought for and defended the German expressionists, the Italian futurists, and the French cubists. Mehring, who was one of his more important spokesmen, says of Walden that in spite of his fanatic attitude toward the avant-garde he felt that neither artists nor new art form should be narrowed by definitions. 'Every definition is unimportant', was his motto. 'What is important is to see.'

In 1959 a collection of Mehring's poems with some of his drawings appeared under the title of *Morning Song of a Porter*. Instead of a preface he wrote a kind of prologue in the third person. In it he dedicated the book to Hans Christian Andersen – whom he had revered since his childhood – and to Andersen's masterpiece: *Picture Book Without Pictures*. Then he wrote: 'Similar to the great Dane Andersen he/Mehring/has roamed around a great deal, at first in his native city Berlin . . . in many ports like Hamburg . . . Marseille, Le Havre, New York . . .; and gone into exile, he was a guest in small hotels, in flops and night asylums; as refugee in concentration camps . . . But wherever he was he took up the pen, his only weapon, and when his lips were silenced, he escaped to his drawing pen . . .'

To express himself in poems and chansons was Walter Mehring's forte. Whatever he sings about, sailors and their ports, his flight through France, or the Cathedral of Chartres, about the tragedy of the coloured people or moon and love over the big cities – there is a whipping rhythm in his lyric power. His hard-hitting language bristles with an imagery that aims from close range at its target. His poems give the impression of coming from a dynamic personality of towering strength, whoring and drinking and, always feeling challenged by the world, throwing its challenge back at it with protean fury. As an example I quote one of the poems he wrote in his Manhattan exile, in a dingy, book-cluttered room where his reminiscences, *The Lost Library*, were also born:

### THE WHITE MAN'S INN

*The demons laughed and had their fiendish fun.*
  *The man, dead drunk, stepped out and left the inn.*
    *Last sou, you'll bring me luck! he bellowed with a grin.*
      *I'll make a thousand dollars out of one . . .*
        *I'll buy those whores with the angelic air –*
      *Remove all poverty! – What do I care –*
    *The world is mine! I'll give the world no rest . . .*
  *Drunk, Manitou? Get out of here, you pest!*
*The demons laughed and had their fiendish fun . . .*

*Still in the starlit sky their laughter dwelt.*
  *What's all the fun about? The drunkard yelled.*
    *As for the tip, I'll throw myself between your jaws . . .*
      *We'll gamble eye for eye – the die is cast:*
        *Eternity for but a godlike second – fast!*
      *The loser pays for the next round – such are the laws –*
    *I do not give a damn for it, poor sinner . . .*
  *Yes, Manitou, let's see who is the winner!*
*The crescent of the moon with laughter swelled . . .*

*He lost his drunkenness in sleep and found*
  *At dawn the laughing morning in the gutter.*
    *He grabbed the gutter-gold and then began to count*
      *His value at the present dollar rate –*
        *And tottered to the tavern – through its shutter –*
      *And drank away his soul, sun, moon and stars, and drank it*
                                              *straight,*
    *Drank to all drunkards: It's on me – to you!*
  *Glass after glass – Your health, friend Manitou!*
*The sun laughed down on misery and clutter.*

80   August Strindberg SAILING-MARK

81   Georg Trakl SELF-PORTRAIT

82   Max Jacob MOTHER AND CHILD WALKING

83   Walter Mehring AN ITALIAN VILLAGE

84  Max Jacob DOUARNENEZ,
FINISTÈRE LANDSCAPE

85  Alfred de Musset MALE FIGURE AND ANGEL

86  Théophile Gautier PORTRAIT OF CARLOTTA GRISI

*Demonic giggles waited everywhere*
  *To follow his zigzag, to see him fall*
    *And fight, as if he – now or never – had to bear*
      *The brunt of bitter battles – then they heard him call*
        *And wondered that, from death, he dared to take*
      *A bottle of elixir – to forsake*
    *The world. He babbled dying: Death, to you!*
  *And then his skull was filled by Manitou*
*Who grinned, while all the demons cried with laughter . . .*

In the days when he was writing this poem I met him in his room on the upper West Side of Manhattan. He is a rather short, sloppily slender person, with the slight stoop of the introverted intellectual, who likes to escape within with a sarcastic remark. How far removed seemed his outer shape from the powerful lines of his poems, which would better have fitted a reckless Irish sailor with the lilt of poetry. But when Walter Mehring showed me his drawings I could clearly see the two different halves of his face. The wish face of his poetry, and the gentle, sophisticated face with its dreamlike look. Even though his drawings had the imprint of the tumultuous expressionistic era, they appeared remote from the tempest of his verbal rage. They have a story-telling, fairytale-like quality reflecting the inner world of the author's visualization. They are closest to the writer Mehring when he turns into the easy-going feuilletonist and raconteur in print who can enchant the reader with his reminiscences of the great things past.

One could easily say that Walter Mehring is a minor artist because he outlived the promise of genius in his youth. Mehring's work and life may well reflect the disintegrating forces which, from one cataclysmic event to the next, played foul with the creativity of a man of *belles lettres*, a man whose sensibilities do not bring forth the necessary strength to overcome the hurdles thrown into his path by history. The energy needed for the mere survival of the day can erode the creative power of an artist whose original destiny was that of Bohemian ease and felicity.

Georg Trakl, who died at the age of twenty-seven, remained a minor artist because life denied him the opportunity to prove the contrary. Trakl's work is a tantalizing and haunting fragment because his life, tortured from within and without, remained a fragment. Born in Salzburg in 1887, he lived his formative years in the first decade of this century. As a child he showed no particular signs of alienation or melancholy.

At that time he was very much attached to one of his sisters, with whom he shared his love of music. He played the piano with great skill. Music seems to have been anchor and refuge and, in those early years of his life, still strong enough to stabilize his mental state. He could write such simple lyricism as *Transfigured Autumn*:

> *Thus powerfully ends the year*
> *With golden wine and fruit again.*
> *How silent are the forests here,*
> *Those mates of all the lonely men.*
>
> *The farmer says: It's done, all's well.*
> *The vesper chimes sing long and low,*
> *And of good cheer they toll and tell.*
> *Migrating birds greetings bestow.*
>
> *Love's gentle time is always so.*
> *Downstream it is an interlude*
> *Of landscape pictures in a row.*
> *And all fades into quietude.*

But this period of inner calm was of short duration. Soon negative feelings broke through his idyllic visualizations. His images with their many-splendoured adjectives took on a more compulsive realization of man's unabsolved guilt. He himself saw his poems as an expression of 'an imperfect penance'. He abhorred the idea of having to live in an age of spiritual corruption and decadence. He wrote in a letter, 'already I feel very nearly beyond this world', and when he said shortly before his death that he was 'half born', it was the expression of fear of 'completing his birth' by becoming more deeply involved in the life as he saw it. Trakl must have felt as though he were carrying the curse of the world's cancer within him, a feeling which finally led to his desire for self-destruction.

It was only in his later adolescent years that the foreboding of his and the world's doom frightened him into poetic images which continued Hölderlin's brooding imagination and Baudelaire's deep despair. It was then that he began to reach a frightening state of guilt feelings and that his work telescoped the anxieties of the twentieth century. Lines like 'Oh, the bitter hour of decline/when we gaze at a stony face in dark waters' were a Cassandra cry which he feared would not be heard.

From a literary viewpoint Trakl belonged with the first expressionistic writers. His language of which Martin Heidegger said that it spoke out of an 'ambiguous ambiguity', became heightened to colourful symbolism. At points his symbolic designs are as impenetrable or wide open to interpretation as some of the poems of Rainer Maria Rilke who was greatly influenced by Trakl. Rilke accepted the generally pessimistic and despairing undercurrent in Trakl's work in an affirmative sense, seeing in lament a kind of praise of the limitations of human life as much as of its greatness. He wrote:

Trakl's poetry is to me an object of sublime existence . . . It occurs to me that this whole work has a parallel in the aspiration of a Li-Tai-Pe: in both, falling is the pretext for the most continuous ascension. In the history of the poem Trakl's books are important contributions to the liberation of the poetic image. They seem to me to have mapped out a new dimension of the spirit and to have disproved that prejudice which judges all poetry only in terms of feeling and content, as if in the direction of lament there were only lament – but here too there is world again.

But Trakl's world, his existential being in the world, was beset by the world's daily horrors. To survive the day he began to drink. He also became addicted to drugs. He failed as a student, and his final choice to take up the career of a dispensing chemist may have been prompted by his desire to have easy access to potent drugs. When the First World War started, Trakl was attached to the medical corps of the Austrian Army and, at the Galician front in 1914, he could not face the cruelties of man-made madness. One day he took an overdose of cocaine, deliberately or misjudging its potency.

The prose and poetry he wrote in the days before his death lay bare the despair of a lonely man caught in the chaos of his time. 'Coming down the rocky path, madness got hold of me', he wrote in his prose poem *Revelation and Decline*. 'And I cried out loud into the night; and while I bent over the silent waters with my silver fingers, I saw that my face had left me. And the white voice spoke to me: Kill yourself! With a sigh, a boy's shadow rose within me and looked at me radiantly that, weeping, I fell down under the trees, under the huge vault of the stars.'

In these lines, expressed through words of searing symbolism, we can recognize the schizophrenic temper of the time as seen through Trakl's own state of being. Whenever reading Georg Trakl, I cannot help visualizing the flaming soul of a poet standing at the gates of twentieth-century purgatory. I see his face in its Christlike torture, the frontal view of a peasant's face, poetic in its symbolic primitivity, the way he painted himself during one night of revelation and prophetic doom. A few wild brush strokes of dark green and reddish brown give his head the obsessed quality of the tormented seer.

A very short time later he wrote his last poems. The last but one he called *Lament*. In it he saw the greatness and beauty of man swallowed by the merciless waves of the time. He saw the boat of existence battered and shattered as it ran against the reef of life. This poem reflects the physical and mental pain with which his self-portrait speaks to us:

> *Sleep and death, the eerie eagles,*
> *Whirr around this head all night:*
> *The icy wave of eternity*
> *Would devour the golden image*
> *Of man. The purple body*
> *Breaks against the deadly reefs.*
> *And the dark voice laments*
> *Over the sea.*
> *Sister of stormy sadness;*
> *Look, how the fearful boat is sinking*
> *Under the stars,*
> *The silent face of night.*

## Equal Time for Equal Talent

WILLIAM BLAKE, VISIONARY

Neither a madman nor a crank could have written such a simple and, in its simplicity, eternally valid thought:

> *To see the world in a grain of sand*
> *And a heaven in a wild flower,*
> *Hold infinity in the palm of your hand*
> *And eternity in an hour.*

But William Blake (1757–1827) was not taken seriously by the Age of Reason in spite of the lucidity of his thoughts. For his contemporaries and for many people to this day – including such artists as Dante Gabriel Rossetti and such critics as T. S. Eliot – Blake's independent spirit has seemed to be an outgrowth of an untutored man whose little Latin and less Greek forced him into the role of a visionary. Yet, even though he was self-taught and not a savant, he possessed the knowledge of the generally educated person of his time.

His unique gift, however, was to see with an inner eye. His work is therefore less sophisticated and polished than it is

*Plate 87*

intuitively inspired, and has the hallmark of an artist of Dantesque sublimity. His archaic forms may have appeared crude in the time of the Baroque and even more so later in the era of revived classicism. But from his drawings and writings issues an unbroken spiritual intensity, an imaginative directness, original and artistically strong, although more often than not uncomfortable to the eye and ear.

True, Blake was an uncomfortable man. He undoubtedly enjoyed suffering his visions which, in their apocalyptic connotations, were uttered with prophetic power. He diagnosed the growing ills of the world as the symptoms that fully broke out as the malaise which tortures twentieth-century man. He foresaw the approaching darkness of money-minded industrialization, brightened by false promises. He was an avowed republican and called himself a faithful 'Son of Liberty'. It was Blake who saved Tom Paine's life by helping him to escape to France. Blake himself was once tried for high treason, having been accused of making seditious remarks, which he undoubtedly made. But he was acquitted. Records tell us that several times he was invited to soirées of that society which, for its own amusement, always tolerates a fool who says the truth. Such invitations, however, became less frequent until they stopped altogether, because his opinions, diametrically opposed to current thoughts, were expressed with vehement firmness and in an alienating spirit. ('Always be ready to speak your mind, and a base man will avoid you.')

Blake was a blazing spirit of total innocence, embracing the mystic and creative powers of life wherever he found them. In an age of polished superficialities in the arts and in mores and manners, the spirit of the past became his daily companion. He had a deep feeling for the austere spirit of the Gothic which he never lost and which was in keeping with his conviction that his visionary faculty was nothing unusual. He believed that, if cultivated, anyone would be able to see visions. He was strongly influenced by the movement of pietism which inundated his age.

Emanuel Swedenborg's *Divine Love* prompted Blake to compose his own epigrammatic thoughts in *The Marriage of Heaven and Hell*. Johann Kaspar Lavater's *Aphorisms* was also a well-worn and fully annotated volume in Blake's small library. Lavater believed in miracles and in the possibility of activating spiritual powers. Blake was impressed by the noble mind and the supersensual faculties of this man. When Lavater wrote: '. . . he only who has enjoyed immortal moments can reproduce them', Blake made the marginal note: 'O that men would seek immortal moments! O that men would converse with God!'

All his life Blake would seek and try to converse with God. To understand Blake's drawings and poems, which both emerged from the same inner strength and belief, we must see his psychotic state with his own eyes of innocence; we see him walk on the edge of sanity, but being blessed and led by the hand of God in whom he believed as the one and only mysterious universal power, we do not see him fall into the dark of mental night. On the contrary, it seems that having been impelled to dare and challenge the impossible, inner light and lightness carry him along in safety.

When he was a boy of eight he had his first visions and from then on he lived in a world of his own which was more real to him than reality. He could imagine himself being any famous character of history and particularly of Biblical times and he could say with the conviction of a madman but with a knowing smile: 'I am Moses . . .', or: 'The other day I heard Milton say to me . . .'. It was a fantasy world in which he acted with the same artless gusto as a child would in his own world of make-believe. Blake's wife was simple and utterly devoted to him. She not only took such utterances as seriously as he wanted them to be taken, but she also worked actively with him on his engraving and printing jobs. In her eyes he was the one and only genius. Unknowingly, she may have played the role of catalyst at times, and always was his stabilizing support.

Blake extolled energy as eternal delight with an almost Nietzschean exaltation and believed in the man restored to a totality of being ('. . . the poetic genius is the true man . . .'). His works reflect his reliance on impulse. ('I tell you, no virtue can exist without breaking these ten commandments. Jesus was all virtue, and acted from impulse and not from rules.')

Blake praised the fundamental innocence of man's senses and thought that sex could raise man to visionary insight. He was possessed by the kind of religious ecstasy that made King David dance nakedly around the Ark, that infused the Hassidim and Shakers with an ecstatic feeling of joy in their communication with God through song and movement. Blake wanted to open all channels to let the vital energies of man break loose. In his eyes, God could have created the world only in a moment of ecstasy.

To *see* is all that matters to Blake. ('If the doors of perception were cleansed, everything would appear to man as it is, infinite.') To see is to know and to know is the way by which man's vision can reach the ultimate, but this demands the oneness of the whole being, body, emotions, and intellect. Out of this oneness come William Blake's drawings and poems. Both flow from the power of innocence and the skill of inartificiality. When, as a child, he could first hold a pencil he began to scrawl the crude likeness of man and beast, and never stopped drawing. Between the age of eleven and twelve his first irregular verses showed his original mind. He saw in his poems greater accomplishments than in his designs, which rarely treated the same subjects. They may be independent creations, but they are of kindred conceptions.

At the age of twenty-seven reports tell us of gatherings in the houses of Blake's friends where the poet-painter would read and sing several of his verses to which he composed his own melodies. When the Author & Printer William Blake published his now famous *Songs of Innocence* in 1789, Blake wrote, designed, printed, engraved the book, as a matter of fact he did everything except manufacture the paper. Together with his wife he made the coloured inks for it.

Blake had a touch of the Biblical prophets. He could see into the depths of his being. The visual and literary images formed there and combined to express his heightened sense of mystery, (the creation as an act of mercy, as he said). Like every visionary he was real enough to see the world in its nakedness and strong enough to believe in himself. He had no doubts about his genius when he wrote:

> *If the Sun & Moon should doubt*
> *They'd immediately go out.*

DANTE GABRIEL ROSSETTI'S HOUSE OF LIFE
A revival of William Blake would have fitted into the movements of dissenters of our own age, the hippies and yippies, even better than the interest they took in *art nouveau*, which gave the lost struggle of the Pre-Raphaelites a new direction and a new decorative image, commercially exploitable.

One of the reactions to the growing Industrial Revolution in the latter half of the nineteenth century was the longing of many artists for a new feeling for and a new simplification of design and ornament. These artists took their inspiration from the Japanese prints, then *en vogue*. They realized that William Morris's[4] (1834–1896) hope for a regeneration of art by a return to the late Middle Ages had failed.

[4](see page 341).

The aesthetics of William Morris, one of the leaders of the Pre-Raphaelites, rejected the realities of industrial Victorian England. He not only strived for a reform of the arts but also of the crafts. He foresaw the danger of cheap mass-production and wanted to stem the tide with more meaningful handiwork. Recalling the image of the medieval artisan, he wanted to revive the taste for genuine simplicity.

Since there are no isolated phenomena in history, the Pre-Raphaelites' sympathy with a 'neo-Medievalism' coincided with religion's reconquering of some of the territory lost to materialism and science. The Pre-Raphaelite Brotherhood was founded in 1848; six years later the Pope announced the dogma of the immaculate conception. This religious trend was foreshadowed by the Nazarenes, a group of German painters, founded in Rome in 1810. However, their attempt to turn the artistic clock back to early Christian art failed because their work was naive, uninspired and uninspiring.

The brotherhood of English painters and poets, like the Nazarenes, withdrew from their century and sought their inspiration in works preceding Raphael, whom they reproached for having initiated the tradition of the grand manner, idealizing nature and achieving beauty at the expense of deep human feelings and reality. In attaching themselves to older schools of thought for their source material, they imitated the intent of those early painters rather than their technique. The essential idea was to become craftsmen again, 'honest to God', to strive for morality, the unconventional but strongly religious truth, the sincerity which lies in simplicity. The problem with this and other artistic groups of this kind is that it is impossible to become a new primitive in a sophisticated and industrialized society.

Dante Gabriel Rossetti (1828–1882) was most representative of the artistic will of the Pre-Raphaelites, both in painting and poetry. He skilfully combined both media as no other artist before or after him, being lyrical and graphic at the very same time and about the very same subjects. His poetry was abstract in thought with much use of pictorial, descriptive detail, highly sensuous and colourful images, although obscured by mysterious symbolism. A predilection for the supernatural and the morbid is characteristic of the poetry of the Pre-Raphaelites, and Rossetti in particular. The initial letters of Life, Love, Death, and Fate are all as if capitalized and painted on medieval illuminated pages.

There are many paradoxes in Rossetti's work and life. Although one can feel his deep personal involvement in his

*Plate 88*

poetry, especially in *The House of Life*, and in his paintings, his is an art for art's sake. Despite having been an Italian he out-Britished all Englishmen. Images of nature dominate his poetry, but he disliked the country. No one can reproach him for not having been steeped in mysticism, for having put 'material conditions above spiritual aspirations' or for having stressed fleshliness 'to the ignoring or overshadowing of spiritual beauty', as he said in his defence. Nevertheless, he became the symbolic target of 'The Fleshly School of Poetry' in Robert Buchanan's famous attack on the Pre-Raphaelites, whom he charged with having formed 'a solemn league and covenant to extol fleshliness as the distinct and supreme end of poetic and pictorial art'.

Rossetti wrote sonnets on various subjects, moods and experiences. As his brother William Michael indicated, Dante Gabriel felt drawn to astrology and saw in the title, *The House of Life*, a heightened zodiacal image indicative of Love, Change, and Fate, symbols for the triple forces ruling man's existence. To Rossetti

> *A Sonnet is a moment's monument,*
> *Memorial from the Soul's eternity*
> *To one dead deathless hour.*

In this introductory and explanatory poem to *The House of Life* Rossetti compares the work of a sonneteer with that of a carver working in ivory or ebony, depending on whether his subject emerges from light or dark.

There is the visual artist in the poet as much as the poet speaking to us through his paintings. Standing at the easel Rossetti was not so much interested in recreating the impression of his eye as in the subject matter itself, in its religious and mystical meaning and message. Thus, he sacrificed the pictorial for the literary, as indicated by the choice of titles for his paintings: *The Salutation of Beatrice, Dante's Dream, The Magdalene at the Door of Simon the Pharisee.*

Rossetti wrote in a letter about a small oil painting, entitled *Water-willow* that the female figure in this painting is, 'as it were, speaking to you, and embodying in her expression the penetrating sweetness of the scene and season'. When he sent one of his canvases to its buyer, he wrote: 'I have somewhat extended my idea of the picture, and have written a sonnet (which I subjoin and shall have put on the frame) to embody the conception – that of *Beauty the Palm-Giver*, i.e. the *Principle of Beauty*, which draws all high-toned men to itself

whether with the aim of embodying it in art, or only of
attaining its enjoyment in life'. A pen-and-ink drawing,
*The Sonnet*, was done for the eightieth birthday of Rossetti's
mother. In it, he tried to visualize the same idea expressed in a
sonnet which accompanied the picture.

Inner need turned into obsession or mannerism turned into
a need made him write sonnets for and with his paintings,
usually working on both simultaneously. For his first picture,
*The Girlhood of Mary Virgin* he wrote two sonnets; one of
them begins:

> *This is that blessed Mary, pre-elect*
> *God's Virgin . . .*

His *Ecce Ancilla Domini*, better known as *The Annunciation*,
was sent to be exhibited with two sonnets around its frame.

Reading William Michael Rossetti's account of his brother
as designer and writer, I was puzzled to see the many excerpts
from letters which show so much stress on self-reliance that it
almost strikes one as a feeling of insecurity to be overcome.
About *The Roman Widow*: 'I really think it looks well, its
fair luminous colour seems to melt into the gold frame . . .
like a part of it'. Of the watercolour *Joan of Arc* he wrote,
'Neither in expression, colour, nor design, did I ever do a
better thing'. Or: 'I have pleased myself with the *Proserpine*,
having begun an entirely new one, which I feel sure is the
best picture I have painted'. When he made a crayon drawing
of Mrs Morris, 'which I am sure', he wrote, according to his
brother, 'is the best thing I ever did'. Etc. etc.

Perhaps, for all we know, writing may have come more
easily to him than painting. For some time his influence as a
painter was considerable. Kandinsky believed that Rossetti
sought the 'inner' by way of the 'external'. And William
Butler Yeats said of himself as a young man: 'I was in all
things Pre-Raphaelite'. But the twentieth century has been
rather contemptuous of the work of the Pre-Raphaelites and
thinks of Dante Gabriel Rossetti that he was full of good
intentions which were paved with too much heavenly stuff.

## JEAN COCTEAU, PROTEAN PRESTIDIGITATEUR

If ever versatility danced on a tightrope and performed tricks
worthy of a master prestidigitator, it was that of Jean Cocteau
(1891–1963). His protean personality with its built-in fountain
of exuberance bewildered and mystified many people.
Brilliant and playful as he was, he struck many a quixotic note.

*Plates 89, 90*

294

While the world rushed from the experience of one cataclysmic event to the anxieties of the next, he could confess 'the unpardonable and the scandalous, in an age which scorns happiness, I am a happy man. And I am going to tell you the secret of my happiness. It is quite simple. I love mankind. I love love. I hate hate. I try to understand and to accept. Every episode provides a dock from which I can set sail and discover something new . . . I am pessimistic with optimism, with the conviction that all is better than it seems, with a totally mad desire for harmony'.

On other occasions he said that he was neither happy nor sad, but that he could be excessively one or the other. And he often deluded everyone, including himself, about anything he really felt and thought by the ease with which he could articulate. He expressed himself with equal facility as poet, novelist, essayist, draftsman, muralist, costume and scene designer, actor, mythologist, playwright, film director, librettist, and conversationalist. He was at home in the ballet world in the role of a scenarist and choreographer. He was manager for the Negro boxer, Al Brown, and played the role of a producer for clowns, dancers, and acrobats.

Sometimes one cannot help feeling that he enjoyed being thought of as an artistic snob who made fun of his public, as wearing masks to entertain by entertaining himself. At times he appeared like a magician who let the public in on his tricks to fool them into believing that everything was easy. But only the magician knows how much sweat lies behind the bluff and pretence of his work. Caught off-guard, Cocteau, the magician, admitted once, 'it is said that everything is easy for me. That is not true'. Then, remembering the part he played to please himself and confuse the others, he continued: 'It is precisely my lack of talent which fascinates me in one piece of work and blinds me to all others. That is why my work is so diverse and so abundant, why I cannot understand where or why I created it'.

But behind all the facility and exhibitionism worked a probing mind; and behind the seemingly constant inconstancy was self-discipline and the desire for inner homogeneity. Now, looking back on the fulfilled life of Jean Cocteau, one finds the paradox manifested in his work no longer as puzzling as it was. His total output shows method in its madness and little excess in its surprises. Cocteau's philosophy brought him close to Nietzsche's ideal of being like 'a dancer in the battle', a dancer who could proudly say of himself, 'I am a lie that always says the truth'.

Like his Orpheus, he insisted on having the right to be different. But the central theme of his work was in no way different from any other important artist of any time: the probing and recreating of man. He felt that 'every man is a night, and the artist's task is to bring this night into daylight'.

In his sentence: 'To be reborn one must burn oneself alive', lies the key to understanding his genius. And his thought of rising like a phoenix from one's own ashes was echoed in a later statement: 'My discipline consists in not letting myself be enslaved by obsolete formulae'. Cocteau learned how to break with the cliché and became a pioneer in transferring the reflection of everyday life onto the printed page, onto the stage and screen. What we have come to accept as avant-garde in film and dance in the fifties and sixties has, in more ways than one, been built on Jean Cocteau's graphic daring and tangible imagination, on his living and dying, and living again.

In his formative years Cocteau, surrounded by actors, writers and critics, was understandably susceptible to praise which never stopped fanning his vanity since the day the actor Edouard de Max arranged for his young protegé a reading of his poems at the Théâtre Fémina. The critic Catulle Mendès was among those who constantly predicted a great future for Cocteau and thus nourished his innately narcissistic trend. Mendès was an aesthete, a relic of the nineteenth century, who cast a spell upon many of the younger men of letters during the first decade of the twentieth century. This was the environment that forced upon Cocteau the role of the literatus as much as the dandy.

Cocteau was twenty years old in 1909, an age in which a writer, if he were ever going to rebel, ought to rebel and seek new forms and new ways of expression. Cocteau embraced aesthetic values that were threadbare. At that time his favourite author was Oscar Wilde. He paid no attention to the fact that the world of arts was in a state of growing ferment. It was then and there that a joy in being playful seized him. Much later, with an astounding objectivity toward himself, he wrote: 'I played an absurd figure at that time, I was not myself. Some celebrated me out of foolishness, others credited my youth for many things. I became ridiculous, loquacious, wasteful, and took my loquacity and lavishness for articulateness and generosity'.

By then his first three volumes of poetry had been published of which he said later on he wished they had never been written. But at that time he plunged himself into the world of art, without knowing that it was more or less shallow water, into the ecstasy of a dilettantism which took itself seriously. He was the witty, worldly poet, who roamed through life with wide-open eyes, adoring and being adored. He believed himself to be *au courant*. For another three years, until 1912, he remained in this world of enthusiastic superficialities.

The turning point occurred one night when he came with Serge Diaghilev and Vaslav Nijinsky from supper after a performance of the Ballets Russes. 'Nijinsky was sulking as usual', Cocteau tells us. 'He was walking ahead of us. Diaghilev was amused at my behaviour. When I questioned him on his reserve (I was used to praise), he stopped, adjusted his monocle, and said to me: "Surprise me!" The idea of surprise, so entrancing in Apollinaire, had never occurred to me'. Etonne-moi! These now legendary words, thrown by Diaghilev at Cocteau as a personal challenge, have meanwhile assumed universal importance. Cocteau went into hiding, fleeing himself to find himself. He emerged with his ballet scenario *Parade* in 1917 to become the catalyst for the many experimentations and -isms of the twentieth century. Ever-changing surprise has been the most expressive feature of his search for artistic expression ever since. Cocteau gave 'newness' life and set it into motion. The cry for 'Surprise-Me' has survived him.

More often than not, the formative years are decisive for the artist in the shaping of the creative process. Although later on Cocteau went many ways and enjoyed all his detours, he never quite lost a certain touch of superficiality, he never quite overcame the flourish of his youth, a stigma which remained fastened upon his life and work.

With the necessarily changing attitudes toward creative minds in the world of the arts, it may well be recognized soon that the blemish of superficiality was actually Cocteau's forte, that he could never have achieved his all-embracing versatility if it had not been for this weakness. We easily accept that an artist seeks to express himself in another medium than the one in which he is an incontestable master. But we are highly suspicious when the fount of creativity spills over in all possible directions. We admire the fanatic drive in an artist, his need to be active, to create one work after the other, or to see him occupied with two or three books, canvases, statues, or even with a book or two while painting. But we do not expect to find him feverishly active in the most varied fields and with the apparent ease that seemed to be Cocteau's trademark. Our image of Leonardo is one of Renaissance complexity and grandeur, Goethe's universality has an olympian halo. The integrity of these men seems unquestionable in our mind, we do not doubt their seriousness which we associate with the dignity of their personality (even though their personal weaknesses are well known to us). What Cocteau lacks is the gesture of greatness as a person. That he always enjoyed playing the role of the *enfant terrible* creates a diminutive image in our mind. We read a personality trait into his work and neglect to see how serious an artist he was. It is always difficult for us to separate the man from his work. Cocteau, with his ostentatious brio and playfulness, with his showmanship, made such separation almost impossible. After all, it was he who once wrote: 'I want to be recognized by my ideas, or better, by my bearing'. And his detractors have always loved to take him at his word.

Cocteau was blamed by many of his critics, among them Kenneth Tynan, for his attitude of being '*trop occupé pour être engagé*', for being too busy to care. André Gide often expressed his doubts about Cocteau, the writer and thinker, who seemed to him to be too flippant, too lightweight. Eric Bentley considered Cocteau to be dead as an artist because in one of his early works, *Les Mariés sur la Tour Eiffel*, he protested against bourgeois solemnity, but in his later works, wooing a philistine audience, resigned himself to its solemnity, without giving up his own vacuousness. Others have maintained that, in his frantic search for beauty, love, and acceptance, Cocteau adopted the opinions, mannerisms, almost the *personae* of some of the great idols of his life, actually trying to *be* the various objects of his loves. Thus, branded as an impersonator of some of the most outstanding figures in twentieth-century art, music, and literature, he was blamed for being always just a step behind.

He would have been a bad magician, had he really limped behind his time. The fact is that, after a hesitant beginning, Cocteau's genius understood how to become a virtual focus of everything that was new, how to play the rallying point for tomorrow's revolution. He played it with an instinct which was uncanny. True, Cocteau was not a giant. He was not that kind of genius who, in proverbial loneliness, had to go his own way, searching and probing, finding and finally triumphing over the ultimately new. The twentieth century may not know such giants because its aim has been less definite and defined, its schedule has been one of greater haste than in any previous century. Picasso or Stravinsky – to mention two whose stature is somewhat bigger than that of many who left their imprint on the contemporary scene – have always created in complete awareness of having to be at least one, if not several steps ahead of everyone else. They were among Cocteau's teachers.

Stravinsky taught him to 'insult habit' – for only in that way can art be kept from becoming sterile. Picasso taught him 'to run faster than beauty'. ('If you keep step with her, your product will be photographic *kitsch*. If you run behind her, you accomplish only the mediocre'.) Erik Satie taught him to liberate art from adornment. And from his young poet-friend, Raymond Radiguet, Cocteau learned to rely on no premise and to distrust what is new for newness' sake. Above all, he gained from all four of his teachers the confidence he needed to find freedom for himself, he gained perspective and stamina for his life and his love affair with the arts.

There were contradictions in him. In his early comedy-ballets he achieved the triumph of the commonplace by rejuvenating it. He reduced the action to an almost embarrassing simplicity and clarity; in fact, what he wrote was so simple and legible that it gave the impression of hiding more than revealing. Having been a symbol of sophistication he could warn mankind that the greatest danger of our sophisticated age was our overcleverness. What Cocteau called 'poetry of the theatre' in contrast to 'poetry in the theatre' – poetry visualized rather than verbalized was the fulfilment of a theatrical magic in which the Greek chorus was fused with music-hall atmosphere in a final triumph of surprise and shock. It was an honest attempt to create a new theatrical spectacle in which classic simplicity is wedded to contemporary reality. But to heighten the theatre experience he searched for a bigger dimension and by giving his characters a super-human image he opened the doors to their dehumanization.

He said, 'I attach no importance to what people call style'. But then, probing the problems of art and the aesthetics, he came up with his famous definition of style as 'a simple way of saying complex things'.

Essentially, Cocteau was a poet, and we must see a poetic realization in whatever he did. When he turned to movie making, he created cinematic poetry. Wallace Fowlie pointed out that, for instance in *Blood of a Poet*, he did not intend to 'make a poetic film, but to allow the film itself to be the poem . . . He had always looked upon the "poetic" as really anti-poetic'.

Cocteau seemed to have had the least chance among France's eminent writers to be accepted by the French Academy and to become one of the forty 'immortals'. He stunned the literary world when he announced he would run for the chair of Jérôme Tharaud. He was elected in 1955 and in his carefully-worded speech, which was full of wit and paradoxes, he suggested that, since *he* had been admitted, the Academy should open its doors to the 'sublime race of bad subjects'. He conjured up the ghost of François Villon, probably meaning such artists as Jean Genet, and challenged the Academicians with the question of whether they would vote for Villon if he were alive. As a final note in this casual enumeration of Cocteau's contradictions it can be said that of all the great men of letters admitted to the Academy, Cocteau's name, associated with the flamboyant gesture of the man, is better known all over the world than his actual work.

When we agree with Martin Heidegger's concept that every poet *has* but one poem within him and writes variations on a leitmotif, then we might say that Cocteau had one basic talent, that of a poet, and whatever else he did emerged from it. He himself described the artist as a kind of prison from which works of art escape. In other words, every form of artistic expression is a psychic release from a dark, enigmatic prison cell. Most of his works, escaping into an unknown freedom from his most inner being, remain an enigma to himself, and 'it is the same with most of my actions. But our actions are joined to one another by a scarlet thread which we can neither stretch nor shorten'.

The oneness of his artistic creation can be seen in his description of the cinema as 'a form of graphic art. Through its mediation *I write in pictures*, and secure for my own ideology a power of actual fact'. The intrinsic oneness of the creative process is most strongly expressed in his preface to his ballet-comedy, *Les Mariés de la Tour Eiffel:*

A theatrical piece ought to be written, presented, costumed, furnished with musical accompaniment, played and danced by a single individual. This universal athlete does not exist. It is therefore important to replace the individual by what resembles an individual most: a friendly group.

To know that there is a central source or prison from which all creativity emerges did not mislead him into mixing his media. It was a rare experience for him to draw and write at the same time. An exception was *Portraits-Souvenir:* 'The articles were published in *Le Figaro* and that kind of article

87  William Blake PLUTUS

88  Dante Gabriel Rossetti DANTE'S AMOR

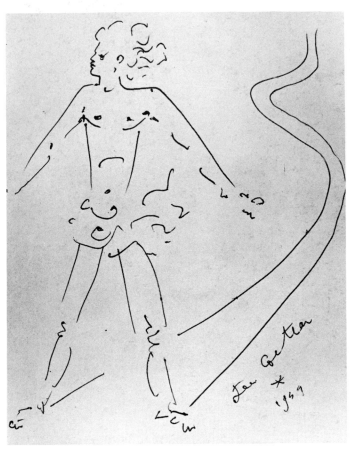

89   Jean Cocteau MALE FIGURE

90   Jean Cocteau PORTRAIT OF SERGE LIFAR

and drawing could be done with the same ink'. But he pointed out that it was rather unusual for him to draw in the margins of a page of writing, as, for instance, Michelangelo did. In this respect he was a strict disciplinarian because he knew the traps in mixing media. In shooting a film, for example, he may have been motivated by the poet in him and, though he saw through the camera eye with the eyes of a painter, he felt that he *wrote in pictures*. But 'if my activity is split up, the main thing is not to mix my efforts. I never decide on one of my branches without cutting off others'. Cocteau was very much aware of the problems caused by versatility being rather evenly divided between many divergent creative efforts, particularly if these efforts seemed to be achieved in a rather effortless way. He mentioned his versatility in his many books, defending himself, trying to explain himself, and attacking for being attacked. Since there can be no doubt about Cocteau's articulateness and his insight into the problems created by his multiple talents, there can be no better way in doing justice to him and to this book than by letting him explain himself in his own words, taken from different sources:

My hair has always grown in every direction and my teeth also and the bristles of my beard. My nerves and my soul must be planted in the same way. That is what makes me insoluble to people who develop in one direction. It is bewildering to those who might rid me of this mythological leprosy. They do not know how to begin explaining me.

My organic disorder is a protection because it scares away the inattentive. Thus I derive some advantage from it. It provides me with diversity, contrast, a speed in bending now in one direction and now in another, depending on the appeal of this or that object, and in allowing me to catch my balance at the end.

To subdue a gift should be the study of the man who finds he has it . . . the gifts of talent marry the first form they encounter and this form risks becoming permanent. My safeguard was to lose myself so deliberately that I could not preserve the slightest doubt.

After one piece of work, I escape. I look for new land. I fear the softness of habit. I want to be free of techniques, of experiment – awkward. I want to be a man of velleity, a traitor, an acrobat, an experimenter. A kind word would be: a magician.
A wave of the wand and books are written, the camera grinds, the pen draws, the actors play. It is very simple. Magician. That word facilitates everything. It is useless to analyse our own work. It was put together without effort.

Incapable of following one course, I proceed impulsively. I cannot follow one idea for long. I let it escape just when I should draw near and seize it. My whole life long I have hunted in that way, but I cannot do otherwise. This deceives those people who interpret my luck as skill, my mistakes as strategy . . . The legends about me turn away the fools. The very intelligent are suspicious of me. Who remain after these two categories? The wanderers who resemble me, who change their address more often than their shirt, and who pay with an exhibition for the right of staying where they are. This is why my solitude never seems silent. I appear only at the moment of the act and the parade . . .

Why do you write plays? the novelist asks me. Why do you write novels? the dramatist asks me. Why do you make films? the poet asks me. Why do you draw? the critic asks me. Why do you write? the artist asks me. Yes, why? I wonder myself. So that my seed will fly in every direction. I do not know too well the breath that is in me, but it is not tender. It makes fun of the sick. It does not know fatigue. It profits from my aptitude. It tries to give its form to trumpets. It moves against me from all sides, I mean, not breathing in but breathing out. This breath comes from a zone of man where man cannot descend, even if Virgil were to lead him, for Virgil himself would not go down there.
What is my business with genius? It is trying to turn me into an accomplice. What it wants is a pretext to carry out its low deeds.


## Jest, Satire, Irony and Deeper Meaning

'This is a strange business', Molière said, 'this business of making gentlefolk laugh'. Mark Twain no longer shook his head wondering about the strangeness of this business. He recognized that humour is a component of the tragic submerged like the bulk of an iceberg. We only see the top of the iceberg in the glittering sun, sparkling in its luminosity and deceptive lightness. Mark Twain looked beneath the surface and made us understand that 'the secret source of humour itself is not joy but sorrow. There is no humour in heaven'.

The clown's sadness behind his laughing mask has become cliché as much as the notion that it is the greatest art to be able to make people laugh. Clichés have a built-in resistance of truth. Undoubtedly, it must be a particular gift to have a sense of humour since this fortunate feature is always stressed in describing a person, whereas no one in his right, if not humorous, mind has ever said about someone that he has a sense of the tragic. Everyone has a different threshold of pain, and the same holds true for the threshold of laughter. What one person finds humorous may not make another move a muscle in his face.

What makes us laugh most of the time is the sudden recognition of the discrepancies in life, of how ludicrous and incongruous certain aspects of existence are. But we must always be aware that the comedy of something is not comic in itself, it is our reaction only that proves its comic aspects. Shakespeare said in *Love's Labour's Lost:* 'A jest's prosperity lies in the ear of him that hears it, never in the tongue of him that makes it'.

Our confrontation with visual humour is more immediate, our exposure to the experienced incongruities more instantaneous than to any verbal humour. Our mind with all its habitual manners of working through certain channels must tune in to the humour of a thing by finding the appropriate link between the accepted norm and the ridicule of whatever it may be. The mind must quickly summon commonsense logic to perceive the absurdity of the presented irrationalism. Our mind must have at its command sound affinities when puns or parodies are offered, it must know how to associate the logic with the illogic of contradiction and discontinuity. Often our mind has to work on two different planes in order to get the point.

The mechanism of humour may involuntarily translate the verbalized image into a visual image as in the following story: A young Austrian officer in the good old days when Arthur Schnitzler wrote *La Ronde* tried to obtain the favours of a high-class courtesan who knew that he was penniless. To get rid of this unwanted suitor, she told him that her heart was not free at the moment. The officer replied politely: 'But, gnädiges Fräulein, I never aimed as high as that!'

The humour in this story is achieved through the sharpened clash between the verbal simile and the physical image which we cannot help visualizing. We may tell or print the story with success, but we cannot draw it. There are areas of humour which do not lend themselves to any pictorialization. By the same token, there are those which cannot be told but must be shown.

The visual image is more quickly absorbed and assimilated by the eye than any verbal image, as it presupposes far less and provides us with a more familiar framework. In the visualization of humour the point made is conveyed in an epic manner rather than in a dramatic way. Our eyes rest on the drawing as a whole from the very first minute, they are not led in stages to a climactic point as in a verbal presentation. The flow of associations is quicker through visualizations in our age because film, television, and the illustrated book have trained us to respond vividly to the implication and suggestiveness of the visual. The whole world, from politics to culture, has been stripped to the comic.

The limitations and potentialities of language are obvious in the area of humour. The finesse of the language in wit, pun, and nonsense humour cannot easily be transferred onto the visual level. But any other form belonging to the category of humour, such as farce, clowning, parody, caricature, and satire can be expressed through the picture as well as the word, with visual caricature having a cutting edge over its verbal counterpart.

Verbal humour is at great disadvantage when facing the problem of translation. Language not only expresses thoughts, they also emerge from it, as we know. A great deal of humour is tied to idiomatic use of its language. All puns defy translation, and so does any deft phrase. The subtlety of wit stumbles with a stammer into another idiom. Most humour shows the cultural background of a nation and its peculiar characteristics which cannot easily step across geographic boundaries. The visual image is easily accepted internationally.

The caustic drawing hitting its goal with precision, like the drawings of Daumier, does not need any explanation. Nor does the good humorous story ask for pictorialization. But while the story may often gain by the complementary adding of a drawing or two, the cartoon may easily lose through words trying to explain the visually obvious. Some cartoonists, however, and all comic strip designers have made a practice of combining word and picture.

Generally, it can be assumed that there are drawings which need words as there are words which read better when illustrated by the author. What makes a humorist express himself in both areas is of course decided primarily by his talent for both art forms. But it often happens that the draughtsman receives his stimulation from the writer as much as the writer may sometimes feel inspired by his visual expression. In most cases we know what came first with a humorist, writing or drawing. But later on, when both art forms are accomplished, the humorist would have difficulty deciding whether he is a writer first and a draughtsman second. They all are humorists first, and writers and draughtsmen out of sheer necessity of having to free themselves from a curious blend of sadness and aggression through word and picture.

It was a strange, perhaps therapeutic, but certainly balancing, need for Mark Twain to draw. Wilhelm Busch was primarily a painter whose deep-bedded pessimism made him invent the sermonizing cartoon and hide an often cruel, hard-hitting satire behind a playful mask. James Thurber knew how to draw before he wrote, but became the master of irony and the bitter jest with deeper meaning in both art forms. Sir Max Beerbohm, who could write with the same nonchalance with which he drew, exemplifies the urbane caricaturist at a time when the Victorian age was making its frantic exit, a period which for lack of any other name was called by what it actually was: the *fin de siècle*. And finally, there is Ludwig Bemelmans, whose candid naiveté in his drawings blends *gemütlich* with the laughter of a man whose heart nor pen knew any evil and who wanted to let everyone live the good life he himself loved more than anything else.

These five are only examples of many different ways along which the writing and drawing pen can work together and make us realize how much fun there is in life, if we can take it seriously enough without taking ourselves too seriously.

### MARK TWAIN, HUMORIST AS A PAINTER

Mark Twain's (1835–1910) claim to immortality does not lie in the visual arts, even though he exhibited one of his drawings in the Paris Salon of 1879. This was the time when he stayed in Europe to gather material for his book, *A Tramp Abroad*. He went to Germany with his friend, the Reverend Joseph Twichell, with whom he intended to hike through Central Europe. But their walking tour finally turned into a trip by rail, carriage, and boat. They took a ride on the road to Heidelberg in Götz von Berlichingen's cab drawn by one horse. Twain made a sketch of it which he called *Leaving Heilbronn*. This sketch, anticipating the twentieth-century cartoons by several decades, has Twain's humour and gains more humour when viewed with his own comment:

*Plate 95*

The sketch has several blemishes in it. For instance, the wagon is not travelling as fast as the horse is. This is wrong. Again, the person trying to get out of the way is too small. He is out of perspective, as we say. The two upper lines are not the horse's back, they are the reins. There seems to be a wheel missing.

Twain was too serious a man to dabble in any of the arts. Even when he made two minor inventions he was eager to have them patented. While in Germany experiencing and researching whatever could be used for his new book which

Mark Twain
Joy

he loathed to write, he lost one of his notebooks. He felt, as he conceded, relieved and glad, hoping to have an excuse not to write the book. 'I was getting an idea that I had lost my faculty of writing sketches of travel', he wrote Twichell from Munich. But the notebook was found and *A Tramp Abroad* was written. It was while in Germany that Twain studied drawing and painting with some of the best teachers. He was a very diligent student, and wherever he stayed, in Munich, Geneva, or Rome, he took life classes and worked on human likeness.

His interest in art began much earlier in his career when he became addicted to doodling. He used pictographs more often than verbal notes for his lectures. Sketchy drawings inspired him more than any words could have done.

Twain was probably at his sarcastic best when doing portraits. The idea of doing portraits came to him after having been irritated and annoyed by the many mediocre portraits, including his own, that were published in *The Galaxy* magazine. When he faced his own un-likeness in this magazine he burst out: 'If I had been in my grave a thousand years when that appeared, I would have got up and visited the artist'. Although, at that time, he had no art training whatsoever and depended on his 'own crude standards' in judging what is a good or bad painting, he knew exactly what he did not like. His satiric sense was aroused, and he began to see in drawing and painting a means to issue some of his venom without incriminating himself through words. 'I can never look at those periodical portraits without feeling a wild, tempestuous ambition to be an artist.'

He came close to the fulfilment of this ambition after having taken lessons in painting for about six months. Like a child discovering that it can walk he began to run and to turn out dozens of portraits of all the great historic people whom he longed to reduce to their size of nonentities. That he included some of his pet hates of his own time is understandable. Now he was ready to execute such drawings as the king and duke in *Huckleberry Finn* or the royalties in *A Connecticut Yankee*. He did a satiric pen portrait of William III, King of Prussia. It combined a child's imagination with the devastating sarcasm of a satirist. This was one of his much admired portraits. 'It has received unbounded praise from all classes of the community, but that which gratifies me most is the frequent and cordial verdict that it resembles the Galaxy portraits', he said with biting irony. 'Those were my first love, my earliest admiration, the original source and incentive of my art ambition. Whatever I am in Art today, I owe to those portraits.'

It was very much a Mark Twain idea – I do not know of any other cartoonist who could have thought of it – to visualize a royal subject with his head on one canvas and the bust on another. Or Twain would skilfully mingle the recognizable features of one person with the characteristic expression of another and then call the portrait Howells & Laffan. Twain amused himself in telling us about his working method. 'First, I throw off a study – just a mere study, a few apparently random lines – and to look at it you could hardly ever suspect who it was going to be. Even I cannot tell myself' For his essay, *How to Make History Dates Stick*, Twain devised a series of portraits of English monarchs capturing an essential or symbolic feature of their reign in a naively funny manner. Thus, name and date become memorable.

As we so often encounter, writers who – more or less as a surprise to themselves – discover painting at a later period of their lives feel as if a new dimension has been added to their artistic expressiveness which gives their existence more meaning. Mark Twain was no exception: 'I am living a new and exalted life of late. It steeps me in a sacred rapture to see a portrait develop and take soul under my hand'.

He regarded his drawing and painting efforts with great seriousness but without ever forgetting to add a brush stroke of irony to his self-estimation as an artist. C. Merton Babcock refers in his *Mark Twain's Adventures in Art* to the satirist's study of *Joy* which Twain 'advised viewing . . . from the south to the southwest in order to ensure the best possible high-lighting as well as to reduce distortion to a minimum. The creation was prepared for exhibition at the Paris Salon and was to compete for the Prix de Rome. The author's only fear was that people might mistake it for a Botticelli, which would, of course, constitute a sacrifice of his reputation'.

Mark Twain also did a few self-portraits in which he proceeded against himself with the same merciless irony that he used against his other subjects, most of them victims. Psychoanalysis would probably delight in Mark Twain's candid admission that he, the great humorist and splendid lecturer, could not draw a good mouth and therefore left it out on most of his portraits. On one of his famous lecture tours in 1902, Mark Twain stopped at the Museum of Fine Arts at St Louis, where he spoke on *Principles of Art* and, on this occasion, received a Doctor of Arts degree. The humorist as a painter, *honoris causa*.

In an essay, *The Icon and the Portrait*, W. H. Auden refers to
the competitive existence of iconography and portraiture in
the visual arts. The separation of these two concepts occurred
after the middle of the sixteenth century when symbolism
gave way to the realistic detail which, in recent history, has
again surrendered to the iconographic, i.e. non-representa-
tional image. Auden speaking about the cartoon, mentions
Edward Lear (1812–1888) as the father of the tradition in
comic art. Lear, who started as drawing master to Queen
Victoria, was a painter of landscapes and birds. His fame,
however, is founded on his illustrated limericks and nonsense
songs in which his jests and jibes at sense and pathos show a
liberating gaiety. Sir W. S. Gilbert (1836–1911) followed his
compatriot with his attempts at drawing which show humour
but have not the bite of so many of his lyrics.

*Plate 96*

There is no doubt that the nineteenth century gave birth to
the cartoon. Lear was not the first to introduce the comic
picture story nor was his influence on its development as
immediate and strong as that of Wilhelm Busch, his junior by
twenty years (1832–1908). The first picture stories, highly
humorous and richly imaginative, enjoyed a great success in
the twenties and thirties of last century. Neither Lear nor
Busch could have accomplished what they did without
Rodolphe Töpffer (1799–1846), a native of Geneva and a
professor at the university of that city. Töpffer not only
wrote novels, but he also liked to draw and told the adventure
stories of Mr Vieuxbois and Mr Cryptogame in picture
sequences whose originality was highly praised even by such
a classic mind as Goethe. Another of his famous picture novels
in which he captured satire, mood, and movement with
Daumierlike intensity is *Master Paintbrush, the Journeys and
Adventures of Dr Festus*. For the first time in history the
narrative was basically pictorial, accompanied by a short text.
The impact of this caricaturist lies in the sequence of his
pictures rather than in the satiric skill of one image. Töpffer
is the first to use the apparently naive and loose line in his
drawings, the almost puerile sketch of the foolish grimace
of a wicked child's imagination, a method which some of the
twentieth-century cartoonists have perfected.

Rodolphe Töpffer
'Master Paintbrush'

There is a direct line from Töpffer to Busch. When Wilhelm
Busch created his illustrated poems, satirical and moralizing in
their content, the picture story was already in vogue in
Germany. Perhaps inspired by the success which the satirical
weekly, *Punch*, had enjoyed since 1841, but certainly as a

*Plate 92*

reaction to the political situation in Germany after the revolution in 1848, a magazine under the name of *Fliegende Blätter* (Flying Leaves) came into being. Even though the magazine avoided heated political polemics in view of the ruling reactionary elements, the need was felt to create a kind of humour and caricature which can hit the target, amuse while attacking and yet always escape the censor. The magazine *Fliegende Blätter* was the German counterpart to *La Caricature*, founded in Paris one revolution earlier, in 1830, and boasting such giants of the caricature as Daumier and Gavarni.

The editor of the *Fliegende Blätter*, Kaspar Braun, looked for contributors who could create that kind of diverting gaiety which is mostly non-political, sharp in its moral, and, if possible, inventing a new figure or type which could be used more often than once. He found the man he looked for in Wilhelm Busch.

*Plate 91*

Busch was a painter, who studied in Holland and Italy, but was very much indebted to the Dutch school of painting. He painted small oil canvases to the very end of his life, landscapes, peasants, genre scenes in the tradition of the Dutch masters but in a somewhat romantic and pre-impressionistic style. In the historic development of painting, however, Busch plays the role of a minor, though competent, artist. Some of his stories and many of his letters have a touch of the poet. His poems collected by himself in a volume, called *Critique of the Heart*, would long be forgotten had someone else authored them (and, as a matter of fact, they are only of interest to a literary historian). It is as the creator of cartoons, the skilful blending of easily memorable rhymes and pictures, that his work is of great importance.

He accepted the invitation of the *Fliegende Blätter* because he needed the money and, as he thought, the job was not too difficult. In the beginning he was given the theme for his drawings, but later he was at liberty to choose his own topics and to write the text for his drawings – although he never thought of himself as a writer, much less a poet. But he felt that the text under such drawings would be more fun in rhymes than in plain prose. And so he rhymed. In 1886 he wrote an autobiographical sketch *Von mir über mich* (About Me Written By Myself) in which he said:

To laugh is an expression of relative comfort . . . It may have been in 1859 that, for the first time, *Die Fliegenden Blätter* printed a drawing of mine with the text: two men walking on ice and one losing his head. Perhaps, as it became necessary, I illustrated the texts of others beside my own. But soon I thought I should do both myself. The situation began to crystallize and to be grouped in little picture stories followed by longer ones.

He threw, so he continued, his products on the market and let them jump around as boys do, with little concern whether they stepped on anyone's toes or not. But all this came about by mere chance and a new form developed with ease and with no thought of posterity. All he did was to create what was in demand.

There were two sides to Wilhelm Busch. In his paintings and prose he was a post-romantic, echoing the spirit of the 1830s. But in his cartoons he poured out his disillusionment and anti-romantic feelings about the world. He saw it as a world of unfulfilled wants and full of Weltschmerz. He detested humanity. Busch grew up with Kant and Schopenhauer at his bedside. Schopenhauer, known for his misogyny, struck a sympathetic chord in Wilhelm Busch who was an inveterate bachelor and said about himself:

Nor did he ever marry. On occasion he thinks to introduce a tax for all married men who cannot prove that they only married to please the fatherland. He who has a pretty and clever wife, who also treats her servants decently, ought to pay double the amount. The incoming money should go to the old bachelors to give them some joy too.

Much criticism took him rightly to task for the dark and often sinister incidents in his picture stories. This approach undoubtedly stems from his pessimistic outlook on life. At the risk of indulging in generalizations, we can visualize a mingling of a few very Germanic characteristics: The romantic seeker of the 'blue flower', who, at the moment of disillusionment, feels pulled down by a deep-bedded pessimism and finds solace and sublimation in the creation of cruel fantasies. *Max and Moritz*, those two boys full of practical jokes, of malicious pranks, are finally ground to powder in a mill. A similar story tells of *Fipp, the Ape* and a similar fate is in store for him. He is shot at the end for playing nasty and cruel tricks on people. And *The Pious Helen* burns to death after instigating a few ingenious incidents such as tying a burning paper bag on a dog's tail. The fun of course always ends with a funny, moralizing sermon.

When all this has been said, the fact of the purely technical achievement in perfecting a new trend of a combined literary

312

and artistic persuasion remains impressive. The creation of a type endowed with individual features was a novelty at that time; so was the simultaneous creation of an idea through drawings and a rhyme technique consisting mainly of two or four lines and forcing everyday banalities into a meaningful form. The scurrilous obviousness of the language, its succinct precision, its easy memorability were the reasons for the quick popularity of Wilhelm Busch and this new form which points unmistakably into the twentieth century, into an era which has come to rely on the digested presentation of the literary word and even more so on the visualization of life and art with a brief caption.

Thomas T. Heine, the founder of *Simplicissimus*, a satiric magazine which fulfilled the promise of the *Fliegende Blätter* by combining the homespun humour of *Punch* with the sophistication of *The New Yorker*, once spoke of Wilhelm Busch as 'the real inventor of the stenography of drawing'.

### SIR MAX AND THE NINETIES

'My gifts are small', Max Beerbohm said with mock modesty when he was knighted in 1939, 'I've used them very well and discreetly, never straining them, and the result is that I have made a charming little reputation'.

As a matter of fact, he had built such a magnificent reputation quite early in his life that it was difficult to live up to it. When history moved rapidly and drastically away from the image he helped to create and that created him, he kept the world at a distance and lived with the reflection of his own past greatness. After 1910 when he went to live in Italy in self-styled exile, he continued to defend a bastion which had already fallen.

While still studying at Merton College, Oxford, he was known as a brilliant wit, essayist, and caricaturist. At eighteen he was a recognized near-genius. His contributions to the famous Yellow Book were then savoured by the intelligentsia. At twenty-eight, in 1898, he succeeded George Bernard Shaw as drama critic of the *Saturday Review*. Stark Young called his essays 'grace and leisure themselves', and the lightness with which his wit sparkled in a manner of urbane maliciousness was startling. He delighted London's *fin de siècle* with his epigrammatic lightning, and he never stopped turning out aphoristic thoughts with surprising felicity: 'Most women are not so young as they are painted.' – 'The Socratic manner is not a game at which two can play.' – 'To say that a man is vain means merely that he is pleased with the

313

effect he produces on other people. A conceited man is satisfied with the effect he produces on himself.' – 'I maintain that though you would often in the fifteenth century have heard some snobbish Roman say, in a would-be-off-hand tone, "I am dining with the Borgias tonight", no Roman was ever able to say, "I dined last night with the Borgias".' – When Max Beerbohm once said about Aubrey Beardsley that he 'achieved masterpieces at an age when normal genius has as yet done little of which it will not be heartily ashamed thereafter', he could have been describing his own career in the Nineties.

There are certain images of the Nineties which come immediately to mind and, even though they may only vaguely be connected with Sir Max, they have symbolic meaning for the atmosphere in which he felt at home: women with wasplike waists sweeping the city streets with their froufrou ruffles; women on bicycles and men with monocles; over-stuffed rooms with bric-à-brac from the Orient and poetry being recited in cosy Turkish corners with the divan half-hidden behind a bead portiere; the air filled with the effervescence of champagne and the echo of cancans from dancing halls. It is perhaps most characteristic for Max that he was an ardent admirer and personal friend of Beardsley, 'a devotee of the Pre-Raphaelites', as Osbert Lancaster tells us, and it is probably most telling that Max confessed on his seventieth birthday in the course of a speech that his 'earliest ambition had been to be a painter in the style of Burne-Jones'.

But instead Max continued the eighteenth-century tradition of the single portrait caricature, and any student bent on learning the physiognomy of the Victorian age must leaf through the caricature books of Sir Max. These caricatures, first signed H. Maxwell Beerbohm, were later reduced to a simple Max when Max had come to mean the epitome of the sophisticated wit with which his seemingly careless drawings showed the nakedness of man, though fully dressed.

Max knew everybody who was somebody and caricatured him. He was also one of the world's best parodists, who liked to embarrass the better-known writers of his time with his sympathetic ridicule. Literary knowledge and finesse in the turning of a barbed phrase were Max's forte. In *Fifty Caricatures* a caption reads:

*Plates 93, 94*

> *A swear-word in a rustic slum*
> *A simple swear-word is to some,*
> *To Masefield something more.*

He is probably alluding to such lines as those in Masefield's *The Everlasting Mercy*:

> '*I'm climber Joe who climbed the spire!*'
> '*You're bloody Joe, the bloody liar!*'

At the same time he is parodying a famous passage from Wordsworth's *Peter Bell* in which Wordsworth says of the insensitive Peter:

> *A primrose by a river's brim*
> *A yellow primrose was to him,*
> *And it was nothing more.*

In *The Works of Max Beebohm* he wrote four lines under the title of *Autobiography:*

> *The one quality that Max*
> *Conspicuously lacks*
> *Is a certain High Seriousness, which may be met*
> *In* The Pall Mall Gazette.

Although trying to lampoon a newspaper, he made light of his own weakness in a disarming manner. Max's brilliance lacks seriousness in his writings and drawings, and he was well aware of it. This did not keep him from writing one of the most charming and amusing novels in 1911, *Zuleika Dobson*, which became a classic of its genre. It pictures Oxford of the late nineteenth century which was so very familiar to Max. In satirically grotesque exaggeration Oxford is stirred by the appearance of a fatal charmer ('Zuleika, on a desert island, would have spent most of her time in looking for a man's footprint'), and Max caught in this novel the picture of an entire period with deft irony. ('The dullard's envy of brilliant men is always assuaged by the suspicion that they will come to a bad end', he wrote in *Zuleika Dobson*, with the image of the brilliant man – and rightly so – being never too far from his own mirror reflection.)

Max had his little prejudices which were growing with the quickly changing times. He hardened in his dislike for parties which his wit failed to dominate, and he never took too much to women writers. In fairness to them I let Rebecca West describe Max as looking 'extraordinarily like a little Chinese dragon in white porcelain . . . Like them he has a perfectly round forehead and blue eyes that press forward in their eagerness; and his small hands and feet have the neat compactness of paws'.

Once Max said, 'I have known no man of genius who had not to pay, in some affliction or defect either physical or spiritual, for what the gods had given him'. Sir Max paid for his own genius heavily. As the symbol of a brilliant decade which frivolously tried to run away from itself, cushioning its fears with plush and covering the uncertainties of reality with the eccentricities of dandyism, Max saw time passing him by. As the honorary citizen of that one decade, he got his passport extended from time to time, but he no longer felt at home in the decades that followed the First World War. When he had burst upon the Nineties as one of its very bright young men, Oscar Wilde said of him, 'The gods have bestowed on Max the gift of eternal old age'. Max never became younger with the changing world. He once illuminated our civilization 'with suffused lighting', as Christopher Morley expressed it. But when the pioneering artists turned their searchlights on the world, Sir Max covered his eyes. He could not tolerate the growing vulgarity of artistic expression and became its outspoken critic. However, the voice of the urbane, discriminating aesthete in him was heard only as a faint echo from the past.

That he escaped to Italy and lived in Rapallo most of the time after 1910 is significant. It is even more significant that his intimate friends and neighbours there were two other refugees from our civilization, Gordon Craig and later Ezra Pound. *Plate 15* Sir Max had ten one-man exhibitions in London, but he did not revisit his native city until 1936 and then lamented its commercialization. After the Second World War he returned to Italy where he spent a few more years recollecting the past in that undisturbed tranquillity, polite wickedness and sophistication for which he had been crowned with such epithets as the irrepressible, the inimitable, and the impertinent long before he was knighted. When Sir Max died in 1956 he had reached his eighty-third year and the conclusion that 'There is always something rather absurd about the past', a statement he had made when, in his early career, writing about the 1880s.

## THE WORLD OF JAMES THURBER

If James Thurber (1894–1961) had written nothing else but *The Secret Life of Walter Mitty*, he would have secured for himself a safe niche in twentieth-century literature for having created a contemporary figure of classic dimensions. If he had not drawn any other cartoons than those of his resigned dogs, frightened men and frightened women, he would have been

recognized as one of the great satirists of the mid-century. But
he was also a successful essayist, parodist, muralist, an illustrator, dramatist, and amateur actor.

*The Secret Life of Walter Mitty* is not only the realization
of the little man's dreams of greatness; his life reflects more
than the triumph over the inadequacies of our daily existence,
over senseless entanglements with such trivia as shaving,
putting on overshoes, or manipulating the mysterious engine
of an automobile; Walter Mitty's adventurous daydreams are
not only escapades of a frustrated husband fleeing his nagging
wife. His story is representative of all this and of the compete-
tive pressures of our society in which man is reduced to being
a numbered cog in a faultily functioning machine of whose
purpose he remains ignorant. Walter Mitty is an existentialist
figure who flees the absurdities of reality to find solace in the
absurdities of fictitious deeds. On the one hand, he is the
Don Quixote of our middle-class existence; on the other, he
is superman capable of whatever man can dream of. Walter
Mitty, like the famous knight-errant, symbolizes the wish
dream of modern man while parodying himself.

This story is most representative of everything Thurber
wrote, symbolically and technically. In spite of the complexity
of its stream-of-consciousness form, it is written with clarity
and simplicity. Thurber's precision was achieved through
relentless rewriting. He could make ten and fifteen drafts of a
story, and he spent two years on a short book. He never
stopped polishing his prose until every word seemed right and
effective to him. The final passages of the Walter Mitty story
exemplify the succinctness of his style:

. . . It was two blocks to the parking lot. At the drug-store on the
corner she said, 'Wait here for me. I forgot something. I won't be
a minute'. She was more than a minute. Walter Mitty lighted a
cigarette. It began to rain, rain with sleet in it. He stood up against
the wall of the drugstore, smoking . . . He put his shoulders back
and heels together. 'To hell with the handerkerchief', said Walter
Mitty scornfully. He took one last drag on his cigarette and snapped
it away. Then, with that faint, fleeting smile playing about his lips,
he faced the firing squad; erect and motionless, proud and disdainful,
Walter Mitty the Undefeated, inscrutable to the last.

Symbolically, this story is significant for Thurber's entire
*oeuvre* because it shows his critical attitude toward our social
and human conditions. The story also demonstrates his strong
belief in fantasy. He once wrote: 'Fantasy is the food for the
mind, not facts'. He comes back to this notion in one of his

cartoons in which we see a social gathering and in the centre of the drawing the figure of a scholarly looking man in the attitude of the Thinker. Behind his back one woman explains to another: 'He doesn't know anything except facts'.

Thurber combines romanticism and satire with great skill. He attacks the excesses of scientists and psychologists whose unwitting efforts to direct or control man's imagination he loves to unmask. He is suspicious of efficiency achieved by the machine as much as he mistrusts the probing and analysing of the mystery that is the inner being with his dreams and fantasies. He finds 'the undisciplined mind . . . far better adapted to the confused world in which we live today than the streamlined mind'. Thurber fears and fights conformity, the pressures of habit, the narrows of man's mind. He likes to give his imagination free rein and to keep his mind open: 'I show any and all thoughts to their seats whether they have tickets or not. They can be under-age and without their parents, or they can be completely cockeyed; or they can show up without a stitch on: I let them in and show them to the best seats in my mind . . .'

Thurber's characters in his stories and drawings are baffled by the mysteries of the machine and humiliated by all kinds of inanimate things. In other words, he finds man bewildered and trapped by reality. Only the stoics who shoulder their share of burden, and the fighting dreamers who do not surrender to nihilism and cynicism prevail in Thurber's world. But man is divided into two sexes, and incompatibilities and matrimonial battles are helped along by the matriarchal myth, the mystery surrounding the woman as an object of romantic idealism, and the famous generalizations, 'Oh, well, you know how women are', and 'Isn't that just like a man?' Thurber once wrote: 'Marriage, as an instrument, is a well-nigh perfect thing. The trouble is that it cannot be successfully applied to the present-day emotional relationships of men and women. It could much more exactly be applied to something else, possibly professional tennis'.

Man is the dreamer and builder, woman the life-giver, the realist who keeps the house in order and the family intact. Most of Thurber's stories and drawings show the woman so strong and domineering because the man is so unrealistic and weak. In *The Owl in the Attic* Mrs Monroe is unpleasantly competent, mothering the helpless and frustrated Mr Monroe. This was how the battle of the sexes looked to Thurber in the beginning of his career. When he remarried, the aggressive menace of the women in his cartoons gave way to the realiza-

91  Wilhelm Busch THE BROKEN JUG

Schnupdiwup! da wird nach oben
Schon ein Huhn herauf gehoben.

92  Wilhelm Busch MAX AND MORITZ

93   Max Beerbohm
THE PRE–RAPHAELITE BROTHERHOOD —
OSCAR WILDE LECTURING

94   Max Beerbohm MR BERNARD SHAW

tion that the fault lay equally with both sexes. Their characteristics did not change in Thurber's creations, he merely adopted a more impartial attitude. There was nothing Strindbergian about Thurber: 'Men are more interesting than women'. he said, 'but women are indubitably more fascinating and possibly more amusing'.

He was neither a misogynist nor a misanthrope, but his fantasy often escapes with him into the animal kingdom. His menagerie is all-inclusive, but he has such favourites as penguins, seals, dolphins, bears, and, above all, dogs. The dog, in its innocent nobility, became his most faithful companion in his cartoons. The first dog appeared in one of his drawings merely for the purpose of symmetry. But, 'although at first he was a device, I gradually worked him in as a sound creature in a crazy world'.

In contrast to his mad and fierce-looking women and intimidated men, his dogs are creatures which always appear composed and happy. His dogs have a pensive, puzzled look in a ponderous head which belongs most of the time to the body of a bloodhound with the short legs of a basset. His drawings are marked by fortuitous spareness. Men, women, and dogs look very much the same, in all drawings, and it is the situation and position in which we find them that makes all the difference. His drawings seem to move and to be alive. Thurber was especially skilful in catching the image of several people at a party, or of masses of people moving. 'If the drawings have any merit', Thurber once said, 'it was that they were – some of them – funny. And that's what they were intended to be. They weren't intended to be a special form of art over which I struggled'. When his sight weakened, and he had more and more difficulties with drawing, he said: 'You mustn't think I grieve about not being able to draw. If I couldn't write, I couldn't live, but drawing to me is a little bit more than tossing cards in a hat'.

Thurber began to draw long before he began to write. He continued to draw as a journalist in Ohio, in Paris, and in New York where E. B. White recognized his talent. He introduced Thurber to Harold Ross, editor of *The New Yorker*, and Thurber worked for this magazine from 1927 until his death.

It is their casual character, their spontaneity, which gives his drawings the inescapable power of immediacy. Robert M. Coates wrote about Thurber that 'he regards himself primarily as a writer and is at once a little jealous of the Artist-Thurber and suspicious of anyone who admires the one

James Thurber
Dog

in preference to the other'. Thurber spent a long time building up his skill as a writer and used to slave over his work, whereas a drawing usually emerged from a doodling effort and became what he wanted it to be. In case it did not turn out satisfactorily, it was quickly discarded, and the doodling process began anew. 'My drawings sometimes seem to have reached completion by some other route than the common one of intent. They have been described as pre-intentionalist, meaning that they were finished before the ideas for them had occurred to me. I shall not argue the point.'

But Thurber, the writer, cannot be appreciated fully without giving Thurber, the artist, due credit. Even though he wanted to minimize his drawing efforts by saying that he drew mainly for relaxation and that drawing was a relief from writings, these none-efforts of doodled sketches are nevertheless an unconscious expression of Thurber's creative power. The drawings, in their casual simplicity, are unorganized revelations of his mind, while his writing, in its laboured simplicity, is its organized counterpart.

There are very few drawings of his without captions, which most of the time add the humour to the visual image by highlighting its fun or by stressing the casualness of life's incongruities. The writer often improves on the draughtsman's enigmatic notions by giving the jest its deeper meaning. When a Thurber dinosaur is insulted by a proud, arrogant-looking human, the beast replies, 'There are worse things than being extinct, and one of them is being you'.

Thurber's world is not without love, even though love causes misunderstandings and frictions. He is concerned about man and human dignity which, as he believes, 'is not only silly but a little sad. So are dreams and conventions and illusions. The fine brave fragile stuff that men live by. They look so swell, and go to pieces so easily'. But Thurber holds on desperately to dreams and illusions because they are the stuff that may not necessarily bring man to fulfilment but that remains the alter ego of life.

In his fable *The Moth and the Star* Thurber tells of a young and impressionable moth which wanted to reach a certain star. His parents chided him for being an idle dreamer instead of being as realistic as his brothers and sisters, who all had been singed badly flying around street and house lamps. But our moth

went right on trying to reach the star, which was four and one-third light years, or twenty-five trillion miles, away . . . He never did reach the star, but he went right on trying, night after night, and when he was a very, very old moth he began to think that he really had reached the star and he went around saying so. This gave him a deep and lasting pleasure, and he lived to a great old age. His parents and his brothers and his sisters had all been burned to death when they were quite young.

*Moral: Who flies afar from the sphere of our sorrow is here today and here tomorrow.*

Thurber also said about a year before he died: 'Let the meek inherit the earth – they have it coming to them'.

### LUDWIG BEMELMANS AND DIE GEMÜTLICHKEIT

When a boy gave his parents trouble in the good old days in Europe, he was sent to America. Ludwig Bemelmans (1898–1962) was such a boy. He may also be cited as a case for the importance of heredity. His Belgian father was a painter, a drop-out from society, and his genes were the sole paternal gift he found time to give his child. Ludwig was raised by his Bavarian mother. He was a rebellious boy who had to be transferred from the Lyceum in Regensburg to a private academy at Rothenburg, both in Bavaria. Finally, he had to be taken out of school entirely and apprenticed to his uncle, who owned a string of resort hotels in the Tyrolean mountains.

This was Bemelmans' first acquaintance with the restaurant and hotel business which was to play a great part in his future life. His apprenticeship, however, was apparently difficult and of short duration. Young Bemelmans was given the choice of going to reform school or to America. Naturally he preferred the adventures of freedom to virtual prison.

In December 1914 I was sixteen years old and came to America. The quality of my mind and its information at that time was such that, on sailing for America from the port of Rotterdam, I bought two pistols and much ammunition. With these I intended to protect myself against and fight the Indians.
. . . .
My second idea was that the elevated railroad of New York ran over the housetops, adapting itself to the height of the buildings in the manner of a roller coaster.

*My War With the United States Army* was the first literary reflection of his existence in the new world, a casual recounting of his life in the army. The various chapters of this book were translated from the pages of his diary, at that time still written in German and published much later when Bemelmans became recognized as an artist and writer.

First, he had to accept a minor position serving in the dining room of what he called in his autobiographical book the *Hotel Splendide*. From the position of a busboy he rose to the prominence of a waiter. In this three-year period he drew constantly. He was quite serious about his unserious drawings, took a few art lessons but soon realized that he could gain nothing from them. Schooling of any sort did not seem to agree with Bemelmans, and he was afraid of losing his spontaneity, the natural charm that was hidden in the naiveté of his approach to drawing things the way they looked to him.

Since so much of his daily life was raw material for his books, one could almost tell his life story with his own words and pictures. But there were very few turning points in his life, dramatic, exciting, or otherwise, except, in the mid-thirties, the recognition of him as a writer and painter with a flavour all his own. He became only slowly known, and first as an artist. It may have helped him to have decorated the studio of the famous violinist Jascha Heifetz. Then Bemelmans received a few assignments to illustrate books. For a short while he did a comic strip with verses for the *New York World*, but Bemelmans' humour was of such a special kind that his comic strip failed to attract the public eye. The humour of his drawings had a foreign touch which eluded the average American newspaper reader.

In 1933 Bemelmans opened his own restaurant which he kept going for a few years. He did the settings for a Broadway play in 1935, the year in which he also married. The nation-wide magazines discovered him about that time, *The New Yorker*, *Holiday*, *Vogue*, *Harper's Bazaar*, *Town & Country*. He received rather well-paid assignments which made it possible for him to live the way he always dreamt of living. Now with his headquarters in New York where he kept his silver-plated typewriter, he could indulge in his favourite pastime, which was travelling and which took up most of his time. It was said that he had an apartment of six rooms, one of which was in New York, the second in Paris, the others in London, Rome and Capri, the last being somewhere in a mountain village in the Tyrol.

Bemelmans claimed that he took to writing because he had insomnia and that if he could sleep well he would never have written a line. He also claimed that his mind worked best when immersed in hot water in his bath-tub at home and in bath-tubs all over Europe and South America. If so, insomnia and hot water are to be praised for being the cause of more than twenty books written by Ludwig Bemelmans.

His first books were made of pictures and verses for children, of which *Hansi* was the greatest success. It is characteristic for him that his children's books are greatly enjoyed by adults too, or by the child in man, because it is the child in us that feels so very much akin to Bemelmans' drawings and, to some extent, to his writing, no matter whether he addresses himself to the young or old.

Bemelmans' disarming naiveté lies in his style rather than in the content of his stories. His duality of vision not only embraces two art forms, it makes him see with the uninhibited and unaffected freshness and freedom of a child, while compelling him to comment with the grown-up wisdom of common sense. In one of his best stories, *Sacre du Printemps*, which he himself chose for inclusion in an omnibus called *This Is My Best*, he retained his usual humour of the sly understatement. But in picturing the macabre scene of Hitler's Germany, he injected a biting irony into his description of the life and death of one Emil Kratzig, who 'lived apart and sat alone', the last nonconformist.

When all the citizens were out in the Spring, Emil Kratzig sat at home with his curtains drawn and read forbidden books, and again when all were snug at home in the Winter, singing the songs of the 'Oven', 'Grand-father's clock, Tick, tock, tick, tock', or '*Ich bin so gern, so gern daheim, daheim in meiner stillen Klause*' he ran around outside in the snow and whistled. There was a long official report under K. Kratzig Emil. But while the Political Police shadowed him, they nevertheless left him alone. They did not disturb him. 'We must save him', said the Minister of Justice. 'He is the last one; we may need him as an example'. Besides, Emil Kratzig was an old man, and a foreigner; his maternal great grandfather had been a Frenchman.

In most of his other tales Bemelmans is a chronicler of daily life and the commonplace event, which he describes in a quasi-feuilletonistic manner. The German and French scene is closest to him, and he loves to mingle a few German or French phrases into his adopted English, which lends his style a vivid colouring. Language, Bemelmans demonstrates, is not necessarily something you are born with, but into which you can also grow. It is a way of life with him, something as personal as his drawings and paintings, which have the surprise of innocence and show the unschooled hand of a master who had *Plate XXI*   been apprenticed to life.

When, after World War II, he made another voyage to Europe to see what Europe was like, he 'set out to write a happy book . . .' He called it *The Best of Times*.

'I don't believe there is such a thing as a "bad people". There are in my opinion only misguided people and rotten governments . . . My faith is in the plain people . . . I wanted to go then and report the patient's recovery – of which I was, and am, certain. I wanted to stop wherever the flame of hope burned, and write of it, and even wherever the smallest flower of happiness grew, bend down to it, and carefully note its design and colour. However, outside the crystal-lit salons of palace hotels, and a few choice fun places . . . there was little gaiety . . . The original plan, then, was changed, and the reader must be warned that in spite of its gay pictures this did not turn out to be an altogether happy book . . . Man had fallen into the zeros, and he was at the mercy of politicians and bureaucrats, of whom his world is deadly sick.'

But even Bemelmans' sadness never loses sight of the humour that inhabits life, and if his words are not too happy, his drawings which usually accompany them – have a lightness and determination at the same time, telling us that, after all, this is the best of all worlds. The reason for this is probably that he was an innately happy man and that painting or drawing came first with him, writing as an intellectual afterthought, even though he may have written more than he painted.

Most of his stories, but more so his paintings, also betray Ludwig Bemelmans' deep-seated nostalgia – not for Europe, not for America, not for any city, nor for any home, but for life everywhere which, he feels, could be beautiful, and perhaps is.

# Envoy

## Omissions and Admissions

I did not set out to write an encyclopedic book on versatility. This is not said as an apology but as an explanation. It is also an admission of the frustration I felt while writing this book, in trying to keep it from growing beyond the originally visualized contours.

In investigating the sources and reasons for versatility with all their hereditary, sociological and psychological ramifications, one cannot help illustrating them with the artists themselves. In most cases the choice was so obvious that omission would have been inexcusable. In other cases the chosen artists were spokesmen for a movement, a trend, or were representatives of a vital generation. Only a few of them seemed to be the personification of lone figures, important by themselves but standing outside the trend of their time. Artists were also included because of the significant role they play in their own field and the interest they necessarily arouse by being creative in another field.

No artist, great or important in his principal area of activity, was judged as to his perfection in his secondary choice of creativity. The circumstances that led to this divergence, the meaning it had for the artist himself was the major criterion. What is perfection, anyhow? Is it not judged by different people and at different times differently? Does not the greatness of any artistic accomplishment lie in its intrinsic value and in the harmonious chord it strikes in you, the reader or spectator? I confess to a predilection for the not yet fully achieved perfection, for the fragmentary, the torso – in other words, for the highest accomplishment in incompleteness. It provides me with so much stimulation that I can creatively continue the dream the artist must have had while doing his work. And this is all an artist can wish for.

It was a great revelation to me while working on this book how intense is the need of so many artists to free themselves from onesidedness, to embrace as much of human experience and creative expression as is feasible. When I reflect for a moment and think of the many omissions of which I am aware I am tempted to throw a few more names into the ring, names that come immediately to my mind. Sherwood Anderson, E. E. Cummings, John Dos Passos, Kenneth Patchen, and C. P. Snow, they all were addicted to painting at times. Then there is Ivan Albright, the maverick painter, who, pre-occupied with the ugly physical detail of a Pinterlike life, wrote verse as 'a rest or reaction from painting' and who, in an autobiographical poem about a painter, said: 'And the sky is not blue to him . . . And the river is not held within its banks . . . And a tree is not a tree to him . . . And colours are not just colours to him'.

Albright seems to twist life to give it a new meaning, and there is humour in the cruel grotesqueries he creates to interpret what he sees. This reminds me of some sardonic humourists who have remained unmentioned. Jules Feiffer, who, in his cartoons, has given our time the disturbing face it tries to hide, and who has written a couple of satiric plays, revealing the terrifying *Little Murders* in the heart of man. The era of the first World War brought forth Joachim Ringelnatz (1883–1934), who drew, painted, and wrote from early childhood on and who kept up his talents in his Ringel-natzian manner, adding to them the gifts of actor and cabaret-ist. His whimsical fantasy places him between Lewis Carroll and Christian Morgenstern. He was one of the rare painter-poets, who was purely visual when he painted, sometimes serious, at other times playful, and literary when he wrote with his facile, scurrilous wit.

I can think of several writers who started as painters or draughtsmen, as Friedrich Dürrenmatt did, who gave it up as Robert Browning before him, who was also a gifted musician in his early years. And there are writers who have continued to work as visual artists: Peter Weiss, for instance, and Günter Grass. The versatility and dynamic force of Günter Grass takes my breath away, and I must stop for a moment to say that he choreographs and cooks, that he has been heard as a jazz drummer and politician ('It is not enough just to feel guilty about the past!') and has been seen as a painter, draughts-man and sculptor. Jean Anouilh used to draw for an advertis-ing agency and, later in life, did some watercolours. 'For me,' he once said, 'colour and shape are more agreeable than paper for bringing my demon to life. It is, anyhow, a less sombre and happier activity.'

The Czech brothers Karel and Josef Čapek were writers and painters, Karel (1890–1938) a writer, who did some drawings,

*Plate 99*

*Plate 102*

*Plate 104*

Karel Čapek
From *Dashenka, or the Life of a Puppy*

328

95　Mark Twain LEAVING HEILBRONN

There was an Old Man with a beard, who said, " It is just as I feared !—
　　Two Owls and a Hen, four Larks and a Wren,
　　　Have all built their nests in my beard !"

96　Edward Lear ILLUSTRATED LIMERICK

97　Ludwig Bemelmans ROBERT AT THE 'SPLENDIDE'

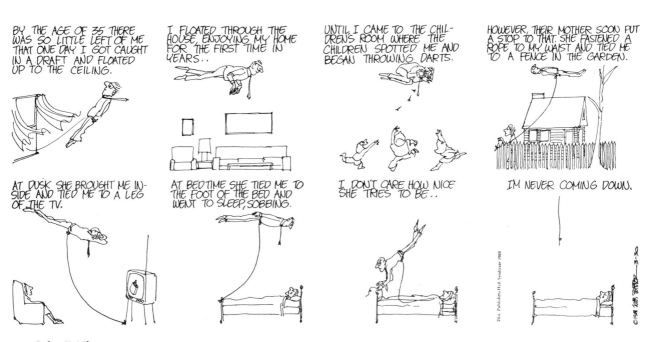

BY THE AGE OF 35 THERE WAS SO LITTLE LEFT OF ME THAT ONE DAY I GOT CAUGHT IN A DRAFT AND FLOATED UP TO THE CEILING.

I FLOATED THROUGH THE HOUSE, ENJOYING MY HOME FOR THE FIRST TIME IN YEARS..

UNTIL I CAME TO THE CHILDREN'S ROOM WHERE THE CHILDREN SPOTTED ME AND BEGAN THROWING DARTS.

HOWEVER, THEIR MOTHER SOON PUT A STOP TO THAT. SHE FASTENED A ROPE TO MY WAIST AND TIED ME TO A FENCE IN THE GARDEN.

AT DUSK SHE BROUGHT ME INSIDE AND TIED ME TO A LEG OF THE TV.

AT BEDTIME SHE TIED ME TO THE FOOT OF THE BED AND WENT TO SLEEP, SOBBING.

I DON'T CARE HOW NICE SHE TRIES TO BE..

I'M NEVER COMING DOWN.

100 Samuel F. B. Morse EXHIBITION GALLERY AT THE LOUVRE

101 Robert Fulton SELF-PORTRAIT

102  Joachim Ringelnatz ORPHANS

103  Josef Čapek WINTER

104  Günter Grass BOOK JACKET DESIGNS

and Josef (1887–1945) a painter, who also wrote. Karel is best known for his brilliant satirical play, *R.U.R.*, which anticipated Aldous Huxley's *Brave New World* and George Orwell's *1984*. He wrote other plays, travel sketches, novels, fanciful romances, essays, and three volumes of conversations with Thomas G. Masaryk. Together the two brothers wrote the allegorical satire, *The Insect Comedy*, in which butterflies, beetles, and ants behave as stupidly as man. Josef illustrated some of his brother's books, wrote a play of his own, *The Land of Many Names*, but he is better known for his drawings, lithographs, and paintings in which he developed a style of artless simplicity. A victim of Nazi terror, he died in the notorious concentration camp of Sachsenhausen-Oranienburg, where he wrote his moving *Poems from a Concentration Camp*.

*Plate 103*

Only to prove how little man profits from his self-inflicted horrors and how quickly time turns its other tragic cheek, we have a generation later Miroslav Holub (1923–), a medical man, microbiologist, essayist and sensitive poet (*Where the Blood Flows*, *The So-Called Heart*), who immortalized the immolation of Jan Palach against the suppression of liberalization in his country in the poem

> THE PRAGUE OF JAN PALACH
> *And here stomp Picasso's bulls.*
> *And here march Dali's elephants on spidery legs.*
> *And here beat Schönberg's drums.*
> *And here rides Señor de la Mancha.*
> *And here the Karamazovs are carrying Hamlet.*
> *And here is the nucleus of the atom.*
> *And here is the cosmodrome of the Moon.*
> *And here stands a statue without the torch.*
> *And here runs a torch without the statue.*
> *And it's all so simple. Where*
> *Man ends, the flame begins –*
> *And in the ensuing silence can be heard the crumbling*
> *Of ash worms. For*
> *All those millions of people, taken by and large,*
> *Are keeping their traps shut.*

Looking back into history I must conjure up the spirit of Pierre Augustin Caron de Beaumarchais, whose versatility has always intrigued me because of the sinister side of his fame as a litigant, pamphleteer, secret agent and international gun runner. This watchmaker by trade became one of the important French dramatists. ('We drink without being thirsty and make love at any time; that is all that distinguishes us from other animals', says his Figaro). To boot, Beaumarchais wrote the music to his *The Barber of Seville*, which, originally, was a comic opera interspersed with songs. He skilfully based his music on some of the Spanish airs he remembered from a journey to Madrid. ('That which is not worth speaking, they can sing.')

I have tried to be fair to the musicians and performing artists, to the writers, painters, and sculptors, but I have neglected the architects and inventors.

The prototypes of those combining professional painting with scientific inventions can only be found in the New World and particularly towards the end of the eighteenth and at the beginning of the nineteenth centuries when the artisans practised the applied sciences, hardly discriminating in their work between using brush and canvas or pliers and metal. Robert Fulton (1765–1815) mentioned that no mechanical invention could be complete until 'the artist knows the necessary proportions'. Artistry was in the skilled hands of those whose inventive minds were needed to solve the practical problems which grew from day to day with the continent.

During the days of the American Revolution Fulton was an expert gunsmith, but already in his late teens he painted landscapes and portraits. He was very skilled in both. History, *Plate 101* however, records him as the inventor of the steam boat, even though steam boats had been constructed before he launched his famous *Clermont* in 1807. But it was the first steam boat to be utilized commercially. Fulton also worked on water torpedoes and submarines as well as on other mechanical devices, while painting with a gentle hand.

The greater artist of the two painter-inventors in America was Samuel F. B. Morse (1791–1872), whose interest in electricity began in his college days. It was superseded by his desire to paint. There are many sides to Morse as a painter. *Plate 100* From his anatomic sketches one can notice his scientific approach to art. His landscapes are highly intellectualized. On the other hand, there are many examples showing a touch of sentimentality reflecting the Germanic influence so very strong in America at that time, and also a distinct satiric humour. Morse invented a fire engine in 1816, but he was as old as forty-one when he started work on his electric telegraph. That year he had put his hopes on his large canvas, *Exhibition Gallery of the Louvre*, containing small copies of thirty-seven masterpieces. It attracted little attention. Was it mere coincidence or related to his disappointment that he had the idea for the telegraph at that time? But the Morse code failed to signal to the world Morse's importance as a painter. He is now

334

recognized as one of the great nineteenth-century painters of America, which, however, at that time only boasted of the impressive John Singleton Copley and the rather jejune Benjamin West.

The archetype of the versatile architect is no doubt Christopher Wren (1632–1723), the builder of St Paul's and Greenwich, who was also President of the Royal Society, astronomer, biologist, botanist, geometrist, mathematician, metaphysician, physicist, physiologist, a student of music and a delicately accomplished draughtsman – a man who, in many ways, personified Renaissance humanism. 'If you would see his monuments, look round', reads his epitaph in St Paul's Cathedral.

In our own time we had poetic architects, Adolf Loos and Le Corbusier, pioneers of a new world to live in. Then there was Frank Lloyd Wright, whose influence as an architect ('Form should follow function') has been immense on three continents and whose writings and lectures have helped his crusades. Another crusader has been Lewis Mumford (1895–), literary and art critic, editor, lecturer, and social philosopher, who, without being a practising architect, brought much wisdom to city and community planning ('In the city, time becomes visible'), and to the sociological perplexities of twentieth-century urban life.

The Swiss dramatist and novelist Max Frisch started out as an architect and has ever since kept an even balance between the reality of buildings and the fictional rebuilding of man and his world. The title of one of his plays, *Don Juan or The Love of Geometry*, is typical of him. His ambivalent attitude toward women reminds me of the strange fact that versatility is rarer in women than in men – woman, the life-giver, is stronger, more earthbound and realistic than the dreamer in man – and seems to be essentially restricted to women as performing artists.

There are exceptions to the rule. Käthe Kollwitz, who wrote beautiful prose, was mentioned in the chapter on Barlach. The American sculptress Malvina Hoffman, who was awarded first prize in Paris (1911) for her *Russian Dancers*, wrote an autobiography, *Heads and Tales*, in 1930. Of course, there is Bettina von Arnim (1785–1859), whom Goethe called 'the strangest being in the world', who sang, composed, sculpted, drew, painted, and poetized. Rainer Maria Rilke wrote about her: 'How wonderful is Bettina Arnim . . . what a powerful personality, what transforming intensity, what a storm in the atmosphere of her time . . .' And Rilke thought he would have answered all her letters, and she was considered by many an obtrusive person, who loved to write letters in a letter-writing era.

There in front of me I can see the amazing figure of the Jewish poetess-paintress, Else Lasker-Schüler, (1876–1945), who lived outside reality in a beautiful dream world of Oriental splendour. She wrote poems as if in the manner of unknown hands weaving visionary images into carpets, she wrote prose and plays and letters full of colourful drawings. These and her lithographs reflected the sadness of life as much as the joy of living it. Nowhere was she at home, neither in Berlin nor later in Jerusalem, except in her heart, but her heart was always on a far away journey. A beggar all her life, she was the richest person I have ever known.

Lasker-Schüller, who called herself Princess of Baghdad, brings to mind two royal artists, both called Elizabeth. The Queen of Rumania wrote under the pseudonym of Carmen Sylva (1843–1916) extensively and with equal facility in German, French, English, and Rumanian. *Pensées d'une reine* and *The Bard of Dimbowitza*, an English collection of Rumanian folk tales, were her two outstanding books. She painted and was musical and would have loved to become a composer, she said. And what an artist would have become of the other Elizabeth (1558–1603), a poet, composer, and dancer, if she had been born in another era, or if she had not had to make an art of ruling and to play the architect, designing the blueprint for an empire destined to rule for more than three hundred years.

Coming back to the architects who became artists of renown, I must mention the world of musical wonder that Yanis Xenakis, an architectural disciple of Le Corbusier, has built out of the strange relationship of his mathematical and philosophical theories. Even though his 'stochastic' music, as he refers to his compositions, may compel the listener to tune in to a yet unusual wave length, he may learn to enjoy the beauty of Xenakis' string glissandi and sound concoctions. In the incessant flow of time has man not always succeeded in overcoming himself, in embracing the wonders of his own flights of fancy and in getting used to his own creations?

Having acted as an historian, critic, and, in a certain way, as an anthologist, I realize that none of the three can or should claim immunity from reproach, or pretend to have acted with the greatest objectivity. Although I tried to let my better judgment prevail, I have taken due advantage of the historian as a critic with hindsight, of the critic who knows how to mix the adventure of experience with the right doses of enthusiasm and scepticism, and of the joy of the anthologist, who has the chance of choice and can indulge in his likes and dislikes.

However many artists of multiple creativity have been gathered and dealt with in this book, and how many more the reader may miss, there is solace in knowing that there are many more artists who have shown no signs of versatility at all than those who have. Moreover, for all we know, there may have been quite a few artists who succeeded in keeping their versatile talents from the public eye. I could imagine that, in spite of the artist's Dionysian dynamism, of his proverbial vanity and publicly accepted narcissistic trend, one such artist or another may think of some of his talents as the 'hidden' ones and may try to keep them so. He may even practise them and still consider them as a part of his privacy – although I know of no such case.

## Some Inconclusive Conclusions

Now that we have seen a mosaic of magnitude formed of many shapes and colours, speaking to us through words and sounds, we can but stand in awe and gaze at the miracle of man's mind. Looking back for a moment to encompass the artistic image man has made in his name over the millennia, from the first caveman's creative signature on his wall, trying to find himself, to twentieth-century man's minimal art through which he has tried to escape himself, we can see a mysterious unity in the diversity of expression. There is an historic harmony in the constant flow of unlikeness, in the many manners and modes of artistic manifestations. It resembles the unfathomable will of Creation which has made a oneness out of the greatest diversity.

Whatever his rationalizations and motivations may be, man, the creator, has cast himself in the microcosmic role of God. Malraux pointed out that '. . . during the creative process, man's creation and God's follow the same rhythm'. There is a need in man, and to a heightened sense in the artist, to find himself, to confront himself with his own identity. Whether we see man lean over a thousand books trying to give so much diversified knowledge a sense of harmony; whether we see him ride his own Rosinante to challenge his illusions; or whether we see him fight his way through the wilderness of his solitude, the compelling force is always the same: to grow

337

within, to challenge his dream of tomorrow, to give meaning to his existence, to make good of the evil there is, to give direction to the senselessness of the outer and inner chaos, to fulfil life.

'The artist himself', Paul Goodman said, 'is ignorant of the divinity working in him, he makes the music by inspiration and lives his life a pathetic blunderer'. All human beings are unequal in spite of the fact that they all have the same basic needs in common, but the artist is more unequal because of his greater sensibilities and his endearing, though sometimes frightening, madness to insist on filching his private spark from the Creator. Since, in his strength and weakness, he is a bit more human than human, an emotional experience may easily force him to move into another direction. We all vacillate in the beginning of our life's career between wants, temptations, and the easy way out, we may turn away from one thing to another when we feel frustrated. Why should we not find an artist – searching as he is for his own identity – work at himself through the means of more than one medium and give himself time to decide on his preferences? After some years he may find out that he can live best with more than one medium. He may learn to realize that he can love his wife best and with greater passion when he can also play with the lightness of love in the arms of his mistress. Man's mind may be faithful, his senses rarely are – their adventurous tales are sometimes necessary to keep our mind true to its course.

Because of his heightened sensibility an artist sees, hears, feels, touches most intensely and often has the desire for direct involvement with an idea or experience. It may, as the subject matter from which this involvement finally crystallizes, demand a different medium of expression than the one in which the artist usually works. Thus the artist may be surprised by finding another facet of his personality in the new artistic environment, or it may surprise his public to find in both of his endeavours striking similarities of one and the same man.

In many cases, as exemplified in this book, there may be a fundamental need in an artist to reveal himself fully, to promote his ideas, a fact which invariably leads – and sometimes misleads – him to writing in the essayistic form of the teacher and theoretician; diaries and, in many cases, letters are the artist's monologues to clarify that, after all, the eternal question for him remains: how to be or not to be. The word has often been a lamp unto the artist's feet and a light unto his path. Sometimes it even helped in giving a new dimension to a different artistic form. On the other hand, the cheapness and handiness of this commodity has often tempted the compulsive talker or the amusing raconteur to take to writing in order to talk in print or to play the public's fool at its expense.

Thomas Mann said, 'A man lives not only his personal life, as an individual, but also, consciously or unconsciously, the life of his epoch and his contemporaries'. In an even more significant way, this holds true for the artist, who is nourished by his time in order to express it. Undoubtedly, there are periods in history in which the artist feels more challenged than in others and then translates the phenomena of his time into his own terms of experience. The defiance of his artistic mood will depend on the magnitude of the historic changes and sociological shifts. Transition periods, such as the Renaissance and our own century, must of necessity intensify the consolidation of the artistic will and, at the same time, compel the artist to strike out in as many directions as he can. His search reflects and anticipates the changes through which he lives.

Since, according to Montaigne, 'Everyman carries in himself the entire form of the human state', the artist only has to open up to the free-flowing interactions between the many forces and forms of life in order to recreate his experiences in as many ways as he feels compelled to. Versatility seems to be greatly induced by historic events and their cultural consequences, and on a superficial level even by the fashions and manners of an era. The occurrence of versatility, more strongly manifested in certain nations at certain periods than in others (as the nineteenth-century French writers who were painters) is as puzzling as the flourishing of one art form in a limited geographic area (as classical music in Austria or the opera in Italy). We can always trace the roots of, and reasons for, such occurrences, although we cannot always fully explain them.

Whatever the outside pressures, trends, and stimulations may be, in the final analysis artistic expression as much as multiple creativity remains very much an individual phenomenon. In essence, talent *per se* is only vaguely separated in different departmental activities, genius knows no limitations at all. The preference for, or preponderance of, expression in one, two, or more art forms is sometimes the result of environmental influences in early youth, but it is mainly a matter of temperament, of the philosophic and dynamic temperament, and chance events in later life. Education, the desire for knowledge, the hunger for experimentation, they all play their intricate and intriguing roles in the exercise of versatility.

Walter Sorell

339

All art is a rebellion against man's limitations and a triumph of his greatness. Riches exist everywhere for the strong, temptations for the weak. Only a dilettante, would-be artist, can suffer under the burden of an abundance of talent. The gifted artist will excel in one mode of expression and enjoy his secondary choice or choices as enrichment of his primary pursuit. The genius will feel, as Henry Miller intimated, that 'No one medium is sufficient to express the wealth of feeling which burdens the soul of an artist'. It may seem to us that the genius chooses his major form of expression, which, in fact, chooses him. Beethoven scribbled the words: 'Muss es sein: es muss sein' on the score of the last movement of his last quartet. Must it be: it must be!

# Footnotes

*Page 126*

[1]In a way Honoré Daumier ought to, but does not, belong to the artists who work in other art forms than the one they absolutely master, and this in spite of the fact that he lived in France and at a period conducive to versatility. But Daumier was close to the word through his daily political cartoons which spoke in unmistakable language, although through graphic images. Daumier, financially forced to feed the daily press, was a highly frustrated man. The world saw in him a witty humorist and political fighter, it did not take him seriously as a painter. But a painter was all he wanted to be, and even those paintings he found time to do show him as a social critic, paintings with 'rageful slashes', as Malraux described them. Daumier invented a kind of journalist painting in which his motto 'il faut être de son temps' found full expression, thus spiritually remaining close to the daily work of the cartoonist.

This book often calls attention to heredity as an important factor in a man's artistic inclinations. Hogarth's father was a schoolmaster and hack-writer. Hogarth says of him, 'My father's pen, like that of many other authors, did not enable him to do more than put me in a way of shifting for myself'. But it did not keep Hogarth from writing an autobiography and aesthetic treatise. Daumier's father, a glazier by profession, lived under the illusion of being a great poet, and his own son witnessed the tragedy of his father's desperate struggle for recognition. I realize it is a speculative thought – but one which may have psychological merit – to visualize his father's failure as a writer as having had a traumatic effect on Daumier, the frustrated painter.

*Page 211*

[2]In his novel, *Les Comedians sans le savoir*, Honoré de Balzac has the painter Dubourdin say: 'I wanted to ask Hiclar to compose a symphony for this picture; in looking at it, one should hear music in the style of Beethoven. The music would have to unfold the ideas of the painting and bring them closer to our understanding'.

*Page 251*

[3]A self-explanatory entry in the *Journals* of Edmond and Jules de Goncourt sheds light on some writers' intimate feeling for and visual dependence on colours. 'Sunday, March 17, 1861 – Flaubert said to us today: "The story or plot of a novel is of no interest to me. When I write a novel I have in mind rendering a colour, a shade. For example, in my Carthaginian novel I want to do something *purple*. In *Madame Bovary* all I was after was to render a special tone, that colour of the mouldiness of a wood louse's existence. The plot of the novel was so little a subject of concern to me that, a few days before beginning to write, I had still in mind a different character to the one I created. My first *Madame Bovary* was to have been set in the surroundings and painted in the tone I actually used, but she was to have been a chaste and devout old maid. And then I saw that this would be an impossible character." '

In the essay, 'Henry Miller, Iconoclast', I refer to the hallucinatory power of Arthur Rimbaud to see vowels and words as colour images.

*Page 291*

[4]William Morris was outstanding in his versatility. He wrote poetry, painted, engraved, and designed furniture, wall-paper and other household articles. He translated Icelandic sagas and wrote romances later in his life. His book *News From Nowhere* pictured a socialist Utopia. He was very influential in the arts and crafts movement as well as in the socialist movement of his time.

# BIBLIOGRAPHY

ALBERS, JOSEF, *Josef Albers. His work as contribution to visual articulation in the twentieth century*. New York: George Wittenborn Inc., 1967.

ARTAUD, ANTONIN, *Oeuvres complètes*. Paris: Gallimard, 1956.

AUDEN, W. H. 'The Icon and the Portrait', in *Nation*, New York, 13 January 1940.

BARBOU, ALFRED, *Victor Hugo and His Time*. Translated from the French by Ellen E. Frewer. New York: Harper & Bros., 1882; London: Sampson Low & Co., 1882.

BARLACH, ERNST, *Das Dichterische Werk*, 3 vols. Munich: R. Piper Verlag, 1956.

BAUDELAIRE, CHARLES, *The Mirror of Art*. Translated by Jonathan Mayne. New York: Phaidon Publishers, Inc., 1955; London: Phaidon Press, 1955.

BEMELMANS, LUDWIG, *The Best of Times*. New York: Simon & Schuster, 1948.

BLAKE, WILLIAM, *Complete Writings*. Edited by Geoffrey Keynes. New York: Random House, 1957; London: Nonesuch Press.

BREICHA, OTTO, AND FRITSCH, GERHARD, eds. *Finale und Auftakt Wien 1898–1914*. Salzburg: Otto Müller Verlag, 1964.

BUSCH, WILHELM, *Wilhelm Busch-Buch*. Berlin: Klemm, 1930.

CAGE, JOHN, *Silence. Lectures and Writings*. Middletown, Conn.: Wesleyan University Press, 1961.

CELLINI, BENVENUTO, *Memoirs of Benvenuto Cellini*. New York: E. P. Dutton & Co., 1952; London: J. M. Dent and Sons.

CHAGALL, MARC, *My Life*. New York: Orion Press, 1960; London: Peter Owen, 1965.

COCTEAU, JEAN, *Journals*. Edited and translated by Wallace Fowlie. New York: Criterion Books, 1956.

COOMARASWAMY, A. K., *The Dance of Shiva*. New York: The Sunrise Turn, Inc., 1918; London: Peter Owen, 1958.

DALI, SALVADOR, *The Secret Life of Salvador Dali*. Translated by Haakon M. Chevalier. New York: Dial Press, 1942; London: Vision, 1948.

DAVENPORT, MARCIA, *Mozart*. New York: Charles Scribner's Sons, 1932; London: Heinemann, 1933.

DELACROIX, EUGÈNE, *The Journals of Eugène Delacroix*. Translated by Lucy Norton. London: Phaidon Press, 1951.

DIRINGER, DAVID, *The Alphabet*. New York: Philosophical Library, 1948; London, Hutchinson, 1968

DÜRER, ALBRECHT, *Dürer: Schriftlicher Nachlass*. Herausgegeben von Hans Rupprich. Berlin: Deutscher Verein für Kunstwissenschaft, 1956.

ELLIOT, J. H. *Berlioz*. London: J. M. Dent and Sons Ltd, 1938.

EPSTEIN, SIR JACOB, *An Autobiography*. New York: E. P. Dutton & Co., 1963; London: Vista Books, 1963.

ERBEN, WALTER, *Marc Chagall*. New York: Frederick A. Praeger, 1957; London: Thames and Hudson, 1957.

ERNST, MAX, *Beyond Painting*. New York: Wittenborn, Schultz, 1948.

GALTON, SIR FRANCIS, *Hereditary Genius. An Inquiry into its Laws and Consequences*. London: Macmillan, 1928.

GAUGUIN, PAUL, *Noa Noa*. New York: The Noonday Press, 1957; Oxford: Bruno Cassirer, 1961.

GILOT, FRANÇOISE, AND LAKE, CARLTON, *Life With Picasso*. New York: McGraw-Hill, 1964; London: Nelson, 1965.

GONCOURT, EDMOND AND JULES DE, *Journals*. New York: Doubleday Co., 1937; London: Cassell, 1937.

GREENACRE, PHYLLIS, 'The Childhood of the Artist. Libidinal Phase Development and Giftedness'. *The Psychoanalytical Study of the Child*. New York: International University Press, Inc., 1957.

GROHMANN, WILL, *Wassily Kandinsky. Life and Work*. Translated by Norbert Guterman. New York: Harry N. Abrams, Inc., 1958; London: Thames and Hudson, 1958.

GROSZ, GEORGE, *A Little Yes and A Big No*. New York: Dial Press, 1946

GÜNTHER, HERBERT, *Künstlerische Doppelbegabungen*. Munich: Ernst Heimeran, 1938, 1960.

HAAG, ERNST VAN DEN, 'Creativity, Health and Art', in *Psycho-analysis and Contemporary American Culture*. Edited and introduced by Hendrik M. Ruitenbeck. New York: Dell Publishing Co., A Delta Book, 1946.

HANSON, LAWRENCE AND ELISABETH, *Passionate Pilgrim*. New York: Random House, 1955.

HESSE, HERMANN, *Siddartha*. Berlin: Suhrkamp, 1950.

HESSE, HERMANN, *Briefe*. Berlin: Suhrkamp, 1951.

HOFFMANN, E.T.A., *Gesammelte Schriften*. Berlin G. Reimer, 1844.

HOGARTH, WILLIAM, *The Analysis of Beauty*. Oxford: Clarendon Press, 1955.

KANDINSKY, WASSILY, *Concerning the Spiritual in Art*. New York: Wittenborn, Schultze, Inc., 1947.

KLEE, PAUL, *Tagebücher von Paul Klee, 1898–1918*. Edited and introduced by Felix Klee. Cologne: Verlag M. Dumont Schauberg, 1968.

KOKOSCHKA, OSKAR, *Schriften, 1907–1955*. Edited by Maria Wingler. Munich: A. Langen–G Müller, 1956

KUBIN, ALFRED, *The Other Side*. Translated by Denver Lindley. New York: Crown Publishers, 1967.

LEBEL, ROBERT, *Marcel Duchamp*. Paris: Trianon Press, 1959; Translated by George Heard Hamilton. London: Trianon Press, 1959.

LE CORBUSIER (JEANNERET-GRIS, CHARLES EDOUARD), *Oeuvres Complètes*. Zürich: Dr H. Grisberger, 1939.

LEONARDO DA VINCI, *The Literary Works of Leonardo da Vinci*. New York, London: Oxford University Press, 1939.

LEVY, MERVIN, ed. *D. H. Lawrence*. New York: Viking Press, A Studio Book. London: Cory, Adams & Mackay, 1964.

LIN YUTANG, *The Gay Genius*. New York: The John Day Co., 1947; London: Heinemann, 1948.

LOCKSPEISER, EDWARD, *Debussy*. London: J. M. Dent, 1936.

MacKINNON, DONALD W., 'What Makes A Person Creative?', in *Saturday Review*, 10 February 1962.

MANN, THOMAS, *Gesammelte Werke*. Frankfurt am Main: S. Fischer, 1960.

MENDELSSOHN, FELIX, *Letters*. Edited by Selden-Goth. New York: Pantheon, 1945; London: Paul Elek, 1946.

MICHELANGELO BUONARROTI, *Rime et Lettere*. Florence: G. Barbera, 1858.

MILLER, HENRY, *To Paint Is To Love Again*. Alhambra, California: Cambria Books, 1960.

MORSBERGER, ROBERT E., *James Thurber* New York: Twayne Publishers, 1946.

MOWAT, ROBERT B., *J. J. Rousseau*. London: Arrowsmith, 1938.

MOZART, WOLFGANG AMADEUS, *Briefe und Aufzeichnungen*, complete edn. Kassel: Bärenreiter Verlag, 1962.

*Museum of Modern Art Bulletin, The*, vol. XIII, nos 4–5, New York, 1946.

NOGUCHI, ISAMU, *A Sculptor's World*. New York: Harper & Row, 1968. London: Thames and Hudson, 1968.

PENROSE, ROLAND, *Picasso. His Life and Work*. London: Victor Gollancz Ltd., 1958.

PHILIPSON, MORRIS, ed. *Leonardo da Vinci.* New York: G. Braziller, 1966.

PICASSO, PABLO, *Le Désir Attrapé Par La Queue.* Coll. Metamorphoses XXIII, Paris: Gallimard, 1945.

PICASSO, PABLO, *1930–1935*, Editions 'Cahiers D'Art', Paris, 1949

QUENNELL, PETER, *Hogarth's Progress.* New York: Viking Press, 1955; London: Collins, 1955.

RAY, GORDON, *Thackeray. The Uses of Adversity.* New York: McGraw-Hill, 1955; London: Oxford University Press, 1955.

ROREM, NED, *The Paris Diary of Ned Rorem.* New York: George Braziller, 1966.

ROSSETTI, WILLIAM MICHAEL, *Dante Gabriel Rossetti as Designer and Writer.* London: Cassell, 1889.

SCHMALENBACH, WERNER, *Kurt Schwitters.* Cologne: Verlag M. Dumont Schauberg, 1968.

SCHÖNBERG, ARNOLD, *Briefe.* Selected and edited by Erwin Stein. Mainz: B. Schott's Söhne, 1958; translated by Eithne Wilkins and Ernst Kaiser, New York : St. Martin's Press, 1965.

SCHUMANN, ROBERT, *Der Dichter Spricht.* Selected and edited by Ludwig Kusche. Munich: Süddeutscher Verlag, 1956.

SEARLE, HUMPHREY, *Hector Berlioz. A Selection from His Letters.* New York: Harcourt, Brace and World, Inc., 1966; London: Gollancz, 1966.

SHAHN, BEN, *The Shape of Content.* New York: Vintage Books, 1957.

SHATTUCK, ROGER, *The Banquet Years.* New York: Harcourt, Brace and Co., 1955, 1957, 1958; London: Faber and Faber, 1959.

SICKMAN, LAWRENCE, AND SOPER, ALEXANDER, *The Art and Architecture of China.* Harmondsworth, England: Penguin Books, 1956.

STEINER, GEORGE, 'Schönberg's Moses and Aaron', in *Language and Silence.* New York: Atheneum, 1967; London, Faber and Faber, 1967.

STRINDBERG, AUGUST, *Skrifter*, Stockholm: Bonnier, 1945.

SUZUKI, D. T., *Zen Buddhism.* Edited by William Barrett. New York: Doubleday & Co., Anchor Books, 1956.

THURBER, JAMES, *The Thurber Carnival* Written and illustrated by James Thurber. New York and London: Harper & Bros., 1945.

*Treasury of The World's Great Letters.* Edited by M. Lincoln Schuster. New York: Simon and Schuster, 1940.

URZIDIL, JOHANNES, *There Goes Kafka.* Translated by Harold A. Basilius. Detroit: Wayne State Press, 1968.

VALÉRY, PAUL, *Oeuvres.* Edition selected and edited by Jean Hytier. Paris: Gallimard, 1957–1960.

VALLAS, LEON, *Claude Debussy. His Life and Works.* London: Oxford University Press, 1933.

VAN GOGH, VINCENT, *The Letters of Vincent Van Gogh.* London: Constable, 1927–1929.

VASARI, GIORGIO, *Lives of the Most Eminent Painters, Sculptors and Architects.* Edited by William Gaunt. New York: E. P. Dutton, 1963; London: J. M. Dent and Sons.

VERLAINE, PAUL MARIE, *Oeuvres Complètes.* Paris: Librairie de France, 1931.

WAGNER, RICHARD, *Sämtliche Schriften und Dichtungen.* Leipzig: Breitkopf & Härtel, 1911.

WALMSLEY, LEWIS CALVIN AND BRUSH, DOROTHY, *Wang Wei, The Painter-Poet.* Rutland, Vt.: Charles E. Tuttle, Inc., 1958.

WHISTLER, JAMES ABBOTT MCNEILL, *The Gentle Art of Making Enemies.* London: Heinemann, 1890.

WIGMAN, MARY, *The Language of Dance.* Translated by Walter Sorell. Middletown, Conn.: Wesleyan University Press, 1966.

WRIGHT, FRANK LLOYD, *An Autobiography.* New York and London: Longmans, Green and Comp., 1932.

# LIST OF ILLUSTRATIONS

55 Jacob Epstein. Head of George Bernard Shaw. Metropolitan Museum of Art, New York, Chapman Fund, 1948

56 Jean Arp. Chessman. Collection Mr and Mrs Charles B. Benenson, New York

57 Isamu Noguchi. Set for Martha Graham's ballet, *Herodiade*. Courtesy Isamu Noguchi

58 Isamu Noguchi. Man with Flute. Collection Ruth Schneidman, New York

59 Henrik Ibsen. Drawing. Nasjonalgalleriet, Oslo. Photo: O. Vaering

60 Gottfried Keller. Landscape. Zentralbibliothek, Zürich.

61 Franz Grillparzer. Manuscript page. Stadtbibliothek, Vienna

62 Friedrich Schiller. Drawing of the artist's hand made when he was a student. Courtesy Schiller-Nationalmuseum, Marbach

63 Georg Büchner. Manuscript page of *Wozzeck*. Geothe- und Schiller-Archiv, Weimar

64 Thomas Mann. Life. From Viktor Mann, *Wir waren fünf*, Südverlag Konstanz

65 Thomas Mann. Mother Nature. From Viktor Mann, *Wir waren fünf*, Südverlag Konstanz

66 Antoine de Saint Exupéry. Sketches. Artine Artinian Collection, Miami, Florida

67 Paul Valéry. Drawing of bed on ms. fragment. Artine Artinian Collection, Miami, Florida

68 Paul Verlaine. Child standing. Artine Artinian Collection, Miami Florida

69 Guillaume Apollinaire. La Cravate et la Montre. From *Calligrammes: Poèmes de la Paix et la Guerre*, 1913–1916. Paris, 1918. British Museum

70 Paul Verlaine. Arthur Rimbaud. From Verlaine's sketchbook. Inselverlag, Leipzig, 1912

71 Federico Garcia Lorca. Self-portrait in New York. Courtesy New Directions Publishing Co., New York

72 Johann Wolfgang Goethe. Drawing made at Bilin, 1810. Courtesy Johannes Urzidil, New York

73 George Sand. Landscape. Artine Artinian Collection, Miami, Florida

74 William Makepeace Thackeray. Manuscript page of *The Rose and the Ring*. Pierpont Morgan Library, New York

75 E. T. A. Hoffmann. Score of E flat major symphony. Deutsche Stadtsbibliothek, Berlin

76  Alexandre Dumas fils. Statue of a Bull. Artine Artinian Collection Miami, Florida

77  E. T. A. Hoffmann. Two Horseback Riders. Caricature. (The man in the three-cornered hat may be a self-portrait). Deutsche Staatsbibliothek, Berlin

78  Alfred de Vigny. Dante and Friend. Artine Artinian Collection, Miami, Florida

79  Victor Hugo. The Reverend Laquemin Herode. Artine Artinian Collection, Miami, Florida

80  August Strindberg. Sailing-mark. National Museum, Stockholm

81  Georg Trakl. Self-portrait. Leihgabe des Landes Salzburg, in the Salzburger Museum Carolinus Augusteum

82  Max Jacob. Mother and child walking. Artine Artinian Collection, Miami, Florida

83  Walter Mehring. An Italian Village. Courtesy Walter Mehring, Ascona, Switzerland

84  Max Jacob. Douarnenez, Finistère landscape. Artine Artinian Collection, Miami, Florida

85  Alfred de Musset. Male figure and angel with ms. verses. Artine Artinian Collection, Miami, Florida

86  Theophile Gautier. Portrait of Carlotta Grisi. Artine Artinian Collection, Miami, Florida

87  William Blake. Plutus. Tate Gallery, London

88  Dante Gabriel Rossetti. Dante's Amor. Tate Gallery, London

89  Jean Cocteau. Male figure. Artine Artinian Collection, Miami, Florida

90  Jean Cocteau. Portrait of Serge Lifar. Courtesy Wadsworth Atheneum, Hartford, Conn. Ella Gallup Sumner and Mary Catlin Sumner Collection. Photo: W. F. Miller and Co., Hartford, Conn.

91  Wilhelm Busch. The Broken Jug. Courtesy Wilhelm Busch-Gesellschaft, Hanover

92  Wilhelm Busch. Max and Moritz. Courtesy Wilhelm Busch-Museum, Hanover

93  Max Beerbohm. Rossetti's name is heard in America (Oscar Wilde lecturing). From *Rossetti and His Circle*, William Heinemann Ltd. London, 1922

94  Max Beerbohm. Mr Bernard Shaw (with self-portrait in background). From *Fifty Caricatures*, William Heinemann, London

95  Mark Twain. Leaving Heilbronn. Courtesy *Art in America* (March – April 1967)

LINE DRAWINGS IN THE TEXT

# NOTE ON TRANSLATORS

*The following extracts of poetry and prose were translated by the author: Bertolt Brecht:*In Memory of Marie A.,*p. 26; Wang Wei: poem, p. 35; Su Tung-po: The Tamed Bird, p. 35; W. A. Mozart: poem, p. 47; Richard Wagner: libretti for* Tristan *and* Parsifal, *p. 55/6; Robert Schumann: writings, p. 61/2; Heinrich Heine: The Romantic School, p. 84/5; Mary Wigman: The Language of Dance, p. 95; Michelangelo: sonnets, p. 115/7, 119; Giovanni Strozzi: poem, p. 118; Benvenuto Cellini: poem, p. 124; Edgar Degas: The Dance, p. 135; Paul Klee: poems, p. 161/2, 164/5; Pablo Picasso: poem, p. 175; Kurt Schwitters: So – So, p. 182; Wassily Kandinsky: Chalk and Soot, p. 187; Egon Schiele: prose and poems, p. 205, 207, 208/9; Paul Verlaine: Confessions, p. 230; Hermann Hesse: prose and poems, p. 256, 261/4; Walter Mehring: The White Man's Inn, p. 280; Georg Trakl: prose and poems, p. 286/8. Other extracts were translated by: Elizabeth Mayer (Adalbert Stifter, p. 226); Wallace Fowlie (Jean Cocteau, p. 303/4); Edward MacCurdy (Leonardo, p. 110/111); Ralph Manheim (Richard Huelsenbeck, p. 180); Ellen E. Frewer (Victor Hugo, p. 251/3); Lucy Norton (Eugene Delacroix, p. 134); Norbert Guterman (Wassily Kandinsky, p. 186/7); Eithne Wilkins and Ernst Kaiser (Arnold Schönberg, p. 57/9); Dorothea Tanning (Max Ernst, p. 183/4); Alfred H. Barr, Jr., ed. of* Picasso, Forty Years of His Art *(Picasso's prose poem:* Dreams and Lies of Franco, *p. 176/7); George Theiner (Miroslav Holub, p. 333).*

-7. DEC. 1977

1. ~~DEC. 1981~~

17. MAR. 1982

30. JUN. 1982

28. MAR. 1983

28. MAR. 1983

23. MAR. 1984

27. JUN. 1984

LIBREX—

27. JUN. 1984

-3. OCT. 1984

-3. OCT. 1984

20. MAR. 1985

-3. JUL. 1985

6. JUL. 1988

28. MAR. 1990

-4. JUL. 1990